MW00647782

To Utah
With the Dragoons

Volume eleven of the University of Utah Publications
in the American West, under the editorial direction of
the Center for Studies of the American West.
S. Lyman Tyler, Director
Brigham D. Madsen, General Editor

For
Robert A. Quigley
Friend, Historian, Philadelphian

PROCLAMATION
BY THE GOVERNOR.

CITIZENS OF UTAH---

WE are invaded by a hostile force who are evidently assailing us to accomplish our overthrow and destruction.

For the last twenty five years we have trusted officials of the Government, from Constables and Justices to Judges, Governors, and Presidents, only to be scorned, held in derision, insulted and betrayed. Our houses have been plundered and then burned, our fields laid waste, our principal men butchered while under the pledged faith of the government for their safety, and our families driven from their homes to find that shelter in the barren wilderness and that protection among hostile savages which were denied them in the boasted abodes of Christianity and civilization.

The Constitution of our common country guarantees unto us all that we do now or have ever claimed.

If the Constitutional rights which pertain unto us as American citizens were extended to Utah, according to the spirit and meaning thereof, and fairly and impartially administered, it is all that we could ask, all that we have ever asked.

Our opponents have availed themselves of prejudice existing against us because of our religious faith, to send out a formidable host to accomplish our destruction. We have had no privilege, no opportunity of defending ourselves from the false, foul, and unjust aspersions against us before the nation. The Government has not condescended to cause an investigating committee or other person to be sent to inquire into and ascertain the truth, as is customary in such cases.

We know those aspersions to be false, but that avails us nothing. We are condemned unheard and forced to an issue with an armed, mercenary mob, which has been sent against us at the instigation of anonymous letter writers ashamed to father the base slanderous falsehoods which they have given to the public; of corrupt officials who have brought false accusation against us to screen themselves in their own infamy; and of hireling priests and howling editors who prostitute the truth for filthy lucre's sake.

The issue which has been thus forced upon us compels us to resort to the great first law of self preservation and stand in our own defence, a right guaranteed unto us by the genius of the institutions of our country, and upon which the Government is based.

Our duty to ourselves, to our families, requires us not to tamely submit to be driven and slain, without an attempt to preserve ourselves. Our duty to our country, our holy religion, our God, to freedom and liberty, requires that we should not quietly stand still and see these fetters forging around, which are calculated to enslave and bring us in subjection to an unlawful military despotism such as can only emanate [in a country of Constitutional law] from usurpation, tyranny, and oppression.

This is, therefore,

1st:—To forbid, in the name of the People of the United States in the Territory of Utah, all armed forces, of every description, from coming into this Territory under any pretence whatever.

2d:—That all the forces in said Territory hold themselves in readiness to march, at a moment's notice, to repel any and all such threatened invasion.

3d:—Martial law is hereby declared to exist in this Territory, from and after the publication of this Proclamation; and no person shall be allowed to pass or repass into, or through, or from this Territory, without a permit from the proper officer.

{ L. S. }
          Given under my hand and seal at Great Salt Lake City, Territory of Utah, this fifth day of August, A. D. eighteen hundred and fifty seven and of the Independence of the United States of America the eighty second.

UU

BRIGHAM YOUNG.

To Utah
With the Dragoons
and
Glimpses of Life in
Arizona and California
1858-1859

Edited by
Harold D. Langley

University of Utah Press
Salt Lake City, Utah

Copyright © 1974 by Harold D. Langley
Library of Congress Card Catalog Number 73-80998
Standard Book Number 0-87480-087-0
Printed in the United States of America
All rights reserved

FRONTISPIECE: *The existence of this early version of Brigham
Young's* Proclamation *was not known until recently. Historians and
Brigham Young's* Diary *mention only the better known* Proclamation
*dated September 15, 1857. The content of both is the same, and why
this one dated August 5, 1857, was printed and not circulated remains a mystery.*

ILLUSTRATION CREDITS. Frontispiece: Western Americana Collection, University of Utah Library, Salt Lake City, Utah. Page 23: Kansas State Historical Society, Topeka, Kansas. Page 31: Philadelphia *Evening and Sunday Bulletin*, Philadelphia, Pennsylvania. Pages 33, 41, 47: Nebraska State Historical Society, Lincoln, Nebraska. Page 43: Ft. Laramie Historical Association, Ft. Laramie National Historic Site, Ft. Laramie, Wyoming. Page 58: Frederick Piercy, *Route from Liverpool to Great Salt Lake Valley* (Liverpool: F. D. Richards; London: L.D.S. Book Depot, 1855). Pages 70, 89, 98: Albert Tracy *Journal*, Manuscripts and Archives Division, The New York Public Library, Astor, Lenox and Tilden Foundations. Pages 92, 93, 206–9: National Archives, Washington, D.C. Page 103: Salt Lake Public Library Collection, Utah State Historical Society, Salt Lake City, Utah. Page 109: John D. Giles Collection, Utah State Historical Society, Salt Lake City, Utah. Pages 111, 122: Utah State Historical Society, Salt Lake City, Utah. Page 132: Clarence King, *U.S. Geological Exploration of the Fortieth Parallel*, vol. 1 (Washington, D.C.: U.S. Government Printing Office, 1878), Plate XXII. Page 144: La Riena Pamphlet 1903, Los Angeles, California. Page 158: J. Ross Browne, "A Tour Through Arizona," *Harper's New Monthly Magazine*, vol. 29, Oct. 1864, p. 556.

Contents

Illustrations

Maps

Preface

Information on the everyday life and adventures of those who visited parts of the western United States in advance or in the midst of the first American settlements are of constant interest to scholars and average readers. From the writings of persons long gone we catch glimpses of the West when it was new, fresh, and unspoiled. They help us to sense the feelings of those who lived through a frontier period and who beheld the awesome vistas of a great land. Our perspective in time helps us to appreciate many things that they did not. But their attempts to record their impressions speak to us across the years and continually give us new details and insights into a world we never knew. How well a man set down what he saw and felt depended on his talents, his personality, and his sensitivity. For that reason we can never have too many narratives of a region in various stages of transition. Each man's account is a unique prism reflecting some parts of reality as he saw it. By accumulating such bits of evidence we are better able to make generalizations about the past.

Most of the surviving letters and narratives by soldiers deal with warfare, for this is the ultimate justification for the existence of a military man. Active campaigning lends itself to more exciting letters than does routine garrison duty. But the day-to-day life of the soldier is also important. Because he did not think it very interesting to write about, we know less about many peacetime matters than we do of the details of wars. The value of the letters presented in this volume lies not only in the reactions of a man to the West, but also in the impressions he gives us of life in the Second United States Dragoons three years before the outbreak of the Civil War. He accepted the trials and hardships of the soldier's life without complaint, yet he gives us a feel of what it must have been like for others with a less adventurous, dedicated, or detached view. His letters also show us that while men might join the army to forget about domestic or political problems, there were many in the ranks who attempted to stay abreast of the news of their times. Through all of his letters there is an attempt to tell his readers about things as they really are. Experience has made him critical of politicians, newspaper reporters, and officers. His western travels made him sympathetic to the plight of the Mormons, the Indians, and the Mexicans. In politics he favored Whig and Republican candidates. He had an attitude of hero worship toward John C. Fremont. Since he was supposedly under twenty-one, his political activities prior to his enlistment consisted of participation in parades and rallies. Ordinarily he would cast his first vote in a presidential election in 1860, but his enlistment would not be up until 1863, and so might have to be deferred. Events conspired to get him out of the army before that date, but that is a story that appears elsewhere in this book.

These letters originally appeared in the Philadelphia *Daily Evening Bulletin* during 1858–59. For permission to edit and publish them in book form, the writer is grateful to Robert L. Taylor, president and publisher of the *Bulletin.* The work of copying and editing was made easier by the staffs of the Free Library of Philadelphia, the Library of Congress, the Smithsonian Institution, the National Archives, the Mullen Library of The Catholic University of America, by Mr. Ernest E. Doerschuk, the librarian of the Pennsylvania State Library; John Daly of the Philadelphia City Archives and by members of the staff of various county and local historical societies in Pennsylvania. Sara Jackson, formerly a member of the Old Army Branch of the National Archives, assembled for my use various records relating to the Second Dragoons and was helpful with advice and suggestions. Additional searches for specific items were carried out by Elmer Parker and Richard Meyers of the Old Army Branch and in the General Accounting Office records by Albert Blair. Their diligence brought to light items that enhanced this study. Professor Leonard J. Arrington of the University of Utah kindly checked Brigham Young's diary to see if the Mormon leader recorded his meeting with "Utah." Edgar Howell, Craddock Goins, and Donald Kloster of the Smithsonian Institution's Military History Division clarified xvi

various points relating to the uniforms and equipment of the pre-Civil War army. Todd I. Berens was responsible for researching and preparing the maps of "Utah's" travels.

Special thanks are also due to A. Russell Mortensen, Robert Utley, Francis P. Prucha, Harold Schindler, and Everett Cooley for their critical comments on earlier versions of this manuscript. I am indebted to Mrs. Norma Mikkelsen, director, Miss Peggy Pace, copy editor, and the staff of the University Press for their imaginative and comprehensive assistance in publishing this book. Preliminary typing of the manuscript was done by my wife, Patricia, and the final copy was typed to perfection by Mrs. Lillian Niffenegger.

Harold D. Langley
Arlington, Virginia
August 15, 1972

To Utah
With the Dragoons

Introduction

In 1857 and 1858 the president of the United States sent military forces into Utah to suppress an alleged rebellion by Mormons against federal authority. A disastrous winter overtook the first expedition before it reached Utah, and the resulting suffering of the troops rendered them ineffective for a campaign. A second and much stronger force was ordered to Utah in 1858. There was a certain amount of popular support for this punitive expedition including the young Pennsylvanian whose letters are published in this volume. As things turned out, the "rebellion" proved to be short lived, and some said that it never did exist. While actual fighting with the Mormons did not occur, the young volunteer found plenty of adventure. Seeing the vast stretches of the western territories with their majestic works of nature was compensation in itself. There was also the chance to see various Indian tribes, about which he had read and heard much. As a member of an army unit that went into garrison in Utah, there was the opportunity to observe the Mormons at firsthand. Within a few months the young volunteer found that many things were not as he had been led to believe — including the army, the Indians, and the Mormons. These revelations reinforced a latent tendency toward cynicism. He was no negative-minded individual, but he had a wry and detached view of life that showed wisdom far beyond his years.

Since the rationale for the young volunteer's enlistment was to put the Mormons in their place, vis-à-vis the federal government, some background information on that sect and their history seems appropriate. Also, from the point of view of the Mormons, the president's Utah expedition was one more wrong that they suffered in their first three decades of existence as a religious body — a period characterized by much dissension and violence.

2

Mormonism had its origin in Palmyra, New York, in a region so exposed to the emotional proselytizing of various religious groups that it was known as "the burnt-over district." [1] In 1820, the fifteen-year-old son of a poor and religious family reported that he had seen a vision of God the Father and Jesus, who told him that all existing religions were false and that he should not follow them. Joseph Smith, the fifteen-year-old boy, was to be the prophet of the new and true faith. Subsequently, he contended he was shown tablets on which an ancient tale was written in a strange language. With the aid of special glasses he was able to read the tablets. These revelations were published in 1830 as *The Book of Mormon*, and it became a bible of the new religion — the Church of Jesus Christ of Latter-day Saints. Many people in and near Palmyra knew the Smith family and had no respect for Joseph or his revelations. Local opposition and other factors caused Joseph Smith to move the young church to Kirtland, Ohio, in 1833. Here there were many converts. Joseph Smith said that angels had ordained him as the First Elder of the church and had given him the power to ordain others. He also claimed to be in frequent communication with God. Through various revelations, an elaborate hierarchy was built up under the presidency of Joseph Smith. Mormon doctrine was clarified. The settlement at Kirtland became the scene of a centralized and controlled economy.

Other Mormons settled in Missouri and built a tightly controlled religious and economic society. Mormons voted as a bloc according to Joseph Smith's wishes. Mormon beliefs, Mormon power, and Mormon attitudes worried their non-Mormon neighbors in Ohio and Missouri. Missourians were suspicious of Mormon missionary activity among the Indians. As citizens of a slave state they were hostile to the abolitionist views held by the Mormons. Nor were they reassured by Smith's promise to his followers that eventually the United States and the world would belong to them. Charges and countercharges of theft added to the tension. Then guerrilla warfare broke out between the Mormons and their neighbors. Meantime Smith's venture in banking in Ohio led to financial disaster and to deep dissension within his sect. He expelled a number of his critics from membership in the

[1] Whitney R. Cross, *The Burned-Over District* (1965), pp. 3–13.

church and fled to Missouri. Armed Missourians drove the Mormons from the state, captured Smith, but allowed him to escape to Illinois.

Near the village of Commerce, Illinois, Smith and the Mormons started to build again. Smith's ability to deliver a bloc of votes caused Illinois politicians to court him. In return he got a charter establishing the Mormon city of Nauvoo as a virtual state within a state. Almost unlimited powers were given to the mayor and aldermen, and the town maintained its own militia, the Nauvoo Legion. Large numbers of Mormon converts from England soon brought prosperity to the town. Once again the economic and political power of the Mormons antagonized the non-Mormons or "gentiles." But this time there were new factors to provoke emotional outbursts. Smith was now the mayor of Nauvoo, judge of the municipal court, hotelkeeper, official architect of the temple, a real-estate agent, a contractor, recorder of deeds, steamboat owner, lieutenant general of the Nauvoo Legion, and a merchant. In 1844 he ran for president of the United States on a platform calling for the reform of the penal system, abolition of imprisonment for debt, compensated emancipation for the Negro slave, the reduction by two-thirds of the size of Congress, and the annexation, if their inhabitants consented, of Oregon, Texas, California, and Mexico. Not all Mormons were happy about Smith's presidential bid. A few gentile newspapers began to voice misgivings about the growth of Mormon power. Reports that some Mormons were practicing polygamy brought forth strong expressions of moral outrage from their gentile neighbors. Polygamy was also creating disaffection among the Mormons. Although the doctrine was not formally announced until 1852, Smith had secretly revealed it to some of his trusted followers prior to 1843. The Prophet himself was married or "sealed" to nearly fifty women between 1836 and 1844, and at least twelve of these were married women with living husbands. Not all of these marriages were consummated, but the idea of plural marriage did not sit well with Smith's first wife or with a number of Mormons. A schism developed in the church. Apostate Mormons established an anti-Smith newspaper in Nauvoo, but they were only able to print one issue. Smith quickly suppressed it and brought the proprietors to trial. Other anti-Smith Mormons fled to nearby Carthage where their reports helped to mobilize the state militia for a march on Nauvoo. Joseph Smith and one of his brothers surrendered to the authorities at Carthage upon the promise of a fair trial, but were subsequently murdered by a mob. In less than two years following the death of their leader, the Mormons were forced to sell or abandon their property and leave Illinois.[2]

A small group followed the surviving members of the Smith family to a new home in Iowa. Another small group went to Wisconsin, and later to an island in Lake Michigan. The largest group acknowledged Brigham Young as Smith's successor and set out in search of a permanent home outside the jurisdiction of the United States. When the news of the outbreak of war between the United States and Mexico reached Brigham Young's followers, Mormon representatives persuaded the federal government to permit them to organize a battalion of volunteers to fight against the Mexicans. The Mormons hoped that the members of the battalion could earn money to help found the new Zion. The rest of the Mormons under Young sought for their promised land, and, after a long trek and much suffering, they settled in Utah near the Great Salt Lake. Here the Mormons established their new home in July 1847. In February 1848 the treaty ending the Mexican War was signed. Under the terms of the treaty vast areas of land were transferred to the United States and the Mormons found that they were now in a territory under the jurisdiction of the government in Washington. But Brigham Young was appointed the territorial governor, so in many respects things remained as they were before.

Nourished by the steady infusion of new converts from Europe and the states, the territory grew. Utah became a melting pot in miniature. It took a great deal of patience, understanding, and stamina to unite these strains into one people. Brigham Young was equal to the challenge. Danger helps to unite people, and once again the Mormons felt threatened.

[2] Fawn McKay Brodie, *No Man Knows My History: The Life of Joseph Smith, The Mormon Prophet* (1945), passim; Nels Anderson, *Desert Saints: The Mormon Frontier in Utah* (1942), pp. 7–29; Thomas F. O'Dea, *The Mormons* (1957), pp. 1–75; William Mulder and A. Russell Mortensen, eds., *Among the Mormons* (1958), pp. 9–201; Bernard De Voto, *The Year of Decision, 1846* (1943), pp. 72–98; and Alice F. Tyler, *Freedom's Ferment* (1944), pp. 86–107.

In 1854 President Franklin Pierce nominated Colonel Edward J. Steptoe to replace Young as the governor of Utah Territory. Pierce felt that the appointment of a non-Mormon governor would help to remove some of the prejudice of various Americans against the Mormons. The Mormons regarded it as another attempt to harass them. Steptoe had reason to wonder how effective he might be. In his military capacity he had captured Indians allegedly responsible for the murder of members of a railway survey party only to see them receive light sentences from a Mormon jury. Pierce finally withdrew Steptoe's name and reappointed Young as governor.

According to the reports reaching Washington, Brigham Young still ran things in Utah by virtue of his position as head of the Mormon church. Utah's Mormon controlled legislature passed an act stating that only those laws enacted by the governor and legislature were valid. A system of courts that paralleled the federal system was established. When Federal Judge W. W. Drummond resigned in March 1857, he charged that the only law and authority recognized in Utah was the Mormon church. Federal officials were insulted, frustrated, and even killed, he said. The Mormon majority thwarted attempts by federal officials to punish polygamy and murder or to protect gentiles who were victims of illegal actions. Charges similar to these were made by other federal officials. This was the atmosphere when James Buchanan became president in March 1857. Whose authority was to prevail there, that of the federal government or the Mormon church? The test was at hand.

President Buchanan appointed a group of new officials for Utah. Alfred Cumming of Georgia, an ex-Indian superintendent, was named as governor. The new governor set out for Utah accompanied by a strong military escort. Young's reaction to this news was to issue a proclamation forbidding the army to enter Utah. To enforce this prohibition he called out the militia and sent small groups of men out to watch for the federal soldiers. Remembrance of their past sufferings and threats of a new ordeal, coupled with the news of the assassination of one of their apostles, Parley Pratt, in Arkansas, brought some Mormons to a fever pitch of excitement. At this time a gentile wagon train from Arkansas was en route to California through southern Utah. Some of these emigrants were imprudent enough to abuse and berate the Mormons they met and to boast of complicity in the recent murder of Parley Pratt and even in the murder of Joseph Smith. For a variety of reasons still not clearly understood, the Mormons, joined by local Indians, attacked the wagon train. After a three-day siege, the emigrants were decoyed from their position and about 140 of them were killed. Seventeen small children were spared. Reports of this event, which became known as the Mountain Meadows Massacre, aroused the gentiles and produced some popular support for the president's plan to crush the Mormon uprising with a strong military force.[3]

From Fort Leavenworth, Kansas Territory, the Fifth and Tenth Infantry, plus two batteries of artillery, headed for Utah. On the march they were reinforced by the Second Dragoons, bringing the force up to about 2,500 men. Advance units of the army were between South Pass and the Green River when the Mormons struck. They burned the army's supply train and destroyed potential forage on the route of march. The raid put the army in a serious predicament. It would take time to replace the lost supplies and it was now early October. Hunger and cold assailed the troops as they marched through devastated regions. The Mormons refused to sell provisions to the army. The main force, reinforced by the Sixth and Second Infantry and the Mounted Rifles, pushed on to Fort Bridger only to find that it had been burned by the Mormons. The army, now under the command of Colonel Albert Sidney Johnston,[4] one of its best officers, was ordered into winter quarters in two locales in the Green

---

[3] Anderson, *Desert Saints*, pp. 28–165; Mulder and Mortensen, eds., *Among the Mormons*, pp. 293–98; O'Dea, *The Mormons*, pp. 76–104; Norman Furniss, *The Mormon Conflict* (1960), pp. 1–94; LeRoy R. and Ann W. Hafen, eds., *The Utah Expedition, 1857–1858* (1958), passim; Hubert H. Bancroft, *History of Utah, 1540–1886* (1889), pp. 512–43. The Mountain Meadows Massacre is treated in detail in Juanita Brooks, *The Mountain Meadows Massacre* (1950).

[4] Albert Sidney Johnston (1803–62) graduated from West Point in 1826 and saw service in the Black Hawk War and with the Army of the Republic of Texas. In 1855 he was appointed colonel of the Second Cavalry Regiment, United States Army, and he subsequently led the military force sent to subdue the Mormons. For his ability, zeal, energy, prudence, and meritorious conduct as the commander of the army in Utah, he was breveted brigadier general in 1857. During the Civil War he was a general in the Confederate Army commanding the Western Department. He was killed at the battle of Shiloh. See Charles P. Roland, *Albert Sidney Johnston, Soldier of Three Republics* (1964).

River valley in Wyoming. Johnston took an inventory of the available stores of food, clothing, horses, and other items and concluded that in the months ahead the army would be in very short supply. He therefore urged the War Department and the commander at Fort Laramie to rush supplies to him as soon as the spring thaw came. This was done, and the much needed supplies reached the army on June 10.

Johnston also needed animals for his command, and the nearest supply was at Fort Union, near Taos, New Mexico. He ordered Captain Randolph Marcy[5] to take a small force and go and get them. On November 24, Marcy set out with forty soldiers and twenty-four civilians. They endured cold, hunger, exhaustion, storms, and the threat of hostile Indians in the course of their long march. Two men finally reached Fort Massachusetts, New Mexico, and brought a relief column back to rescue the rest of the party. Marcy and his men reached Fort Massachusetts on January 18 and went on to Taos. Returning with horses, mules, and a few sheep, Marcy reached Johnston's army on June 11. Now well fed and reequipped, the army was ready to march to Utah.

Meanwhile Young's defiance of the federal government and the news of his hit-and-run tactics led to an outburst of anti-Mormon feeling, especially in the East. The citizenry cried out that the Mormons should be taught a lesson in obedience. Volunteer units in various states wrote to the War Department and offered their services. The department declined such offers with thanks. It had already decided that the subjugation of Utah was a job for the regular army. A plan was drawn up calling for the use of regulars in a summer offen-

[5] Randolph B. Marcy (1812–87) graduated from West Point in 1832 as a brevet second lieutenant in the Fifth Infantry. He rose steadily, was promoted to captain in 1846, and participated in the Mexican War. Between 1847 and 1859 he served in the Southwest in various capacities, especially in exploring and surveying expeditions and as a member of Colonel Albert S. Johnston's Utah expedition. Promoted to the rank of major and paymaster in 1859, he served in the Northwest until the Civil War. During that conflict he attained the temporary rank of brigadier general and postwar brevets to brigadier and major general. In 1878 he was promoted to inspector general of the army with the rank of brigadier general and retired two years later. Marcy was well known for his writing as well as for his exploits. In addition to the reports of his explorations, he wrote *The Prairie Traveler* (1859); *Thirty Years of Army Life on the Western Border* (1866); and *Border Reminiscences* (1872).

sive aimed at Salt Lake City. One difficulty was that most of the regular units were under strength. The first thing to do was to get additional men. Officers were detached from their units and sent to various large cities to look for men. The chances of finding the required numbers seemed good. The effects of the Panic of 1857 were still being felt, and unemployment added to the anti-Mormon sentiment might make the job of recruitment easier. For our purposes it is important to know that the Second Dragoons sent officers to Philadelphia where they found many men who were willing to serve.

For other persons, the coming of the winter months provided an opportunity to think the whole situation over. Such deliberation tended to make the idea of a military campaign against the Mormons less and less appealing. A Philadelphia clothing store used this division of opinion as the basis for the following advertisement:

> OFF TO UTAH. — Quite a number of individuals in this city have expressed anxiety to serve their country in Utah. These patriotic men will wear Uncle Sam's livery, while the more sensible people, who stay at home, will continue to array themselves in the elegant garments which are made at the Brown Stone Clothing Hall of Rockhill and Wilson, Nos. 603 and 605 Chestnut street, above Sixth.[6]

Members of the First Pennsylvania Regiment were among the most anxious of the militia units to get into the coming fight. These Philadelphians were fearful that volunteer units from states closer to Utah than Pennsylvania would be picked to bolster the regular army. To overcome this geographical disadvantage, the privates, noncommissioned officers, and musicians of the regiment offered to relinquish a month's pay toward the expenses of transporting them closer to the scene of operations. Their offer was transmitted by their officers to President Buchanan, a fellow Pennsylvanian, and was turned down.[7]

One of those who went to the Recruiting Officer and signed up to fight the Mormons was the author of the letters published in this book. He hid his identity behind the pen name "Utah." We know that he

[6] Philadelphia *Daily Evening Bulletin*, March 22, 1858, p. 3. Hereafter cited as *Bulletin*.

[7] Officers of the First Pennsylvania Regiment to President James Buchanan, May 10, 1858, "Letters Received by the Office of the Adjutant General" (Main Series) 1822–1860, microcopy 567, roll 586, Record Group 94, National Archives. Hereafter cited as "AG Letters."

enlisted for five years in the spring of 1858 and soon afterward was sent to Carlisle Barracks, Pennsylvania, for training.

The dragoons were a mounted branch of the army, created in 1833 to patrol and pacify the vast regions of the West. Sad experience had taught the army that infantry was of little use for chasing the mounted Indians of the Plains. The creation of mounted infantry and dragoon and cavalry units were attempts to give the soldier greater mobility. Mounted infantry rode to the scene of action and fought on foot. Dragoons and cavalry rode and fought on horseback or dismounted if necessary. When the Civil War broke out, dragoon units were redesignated as cavalry regiments. Since its organization, the Second Regiment of Dragoons had fought against the Seminole Indians in Florida and had served on the western frontier. It had a good reputation as a fighting unit. Given a choice, it was a far more appealing unit to a recruit in search of adventure than any infantry or artillery unit.[8]

The basic training of a dragoon recruit consisted of a good deal of drill and little else. A recruit who trained at Carlisle Barracks in 1840 remembered the daily schedule as being:

> Reville at day break, Stable Call 15 minutes after, which occupied 1 hour, Breakfast, Guard mounting at 9, drilling commenced immediately after. Carbine drill on foot until 11, Sabre exercises from 12 till 1. Dinner at 2, Saddles up for Mounted drill, which lasted until ½ an hour before sunsett. Stable call 1 hour. Supper, the evening being spent in cleaning accoutrements, amusements, &c. Tatoo at 9, signal to put out lights call Taps 15 minutes after.[9]

Guard duty was mainly for instructional purposes and fell about once every two weeks during the winter and probably more frequently in the warmer months. It is probable that the training schedule followed in 1858 was quite similar to that quoted above.

[8] For background on the origin and use of the dragoons see Francis P. Prucha, *The Sword of the Republic: The United States Army on the Frontier, 1783–1846* (1969), pp. 245–47, 264, 294, 309, 311, 330, 340, 360; Robert M. Utley, *Frontiersmen in Blue: The United States Army and the Indian, 1848–1865* (1967), pp. 22–27; and Theo. F. Rodenbough, *From Everglade to Cañon with the Second Dragoons* (1875).

[9] Anonymous, "Reminiscences of Some Incidents in the Career of an United States Dragoon Between the Years 1839 and 1844," *The Texas Quarterly* 9 (1966) : 7; Percival G. Lowe, *Five Years a Dragoon* (1965), pp. 5–11.

After about six weeks' training the dragoon recruits left for the war zone. First Lieutenant Dabney H. Maury,[10] the commanding officer of the post, reported their departure on May 4, 1858, as follows: "eight Buglars, Three hundred recruits and one Laundress left this Depot this morning for Fort Leavenworth, Kansas, intended for the 2nd Dragoons and a battery of Artillery now in Utah."[11] The route westward was probably by rail from Carlisle to Harrisburg, by canal boat or rail to Pittsburgh, and by steamboat from Pittsburgh, down the Ohio River and up the Mississippi and Missouri to Fort Leavenworth, Kansas Territory.[12] The recruits reached Fort Leavenworth on May 13.[13]

Fort Leavenworth, established in 1827, was one of the army's main posts on the way West. From here mounted troops went forth to remind the Indian tribes of the Plains of the presence and retaliatory power of the United States. The post also served as an important jumping-off place for army expeditions engaged in exploring and mapping the West. Beginning in 1855, tensions between the pro-slavery and antislavery settlers over the future status of the territory led to turmoil and bloodshed and made the presence of troops desirable to maintain order. Now, in the spring of 1858, the fort was the major point of concentration of supplies and men for the coming campaign against the Mormons.

[10] Dabney H. Maury graduated from West Point in 1846 and rose gradually in the army. Commissioned as a first lieutenant in 1853, he served as regimental adjutant from 1858 to 1860. His pro-Southern sympathies led to his dismissal from the army in 1861, and he became a major general in the Confederate Army. He died in 1900.

[11] Lieutenant Dabney Maury to the Adjutant General, May 4, 1858, "AG Letters," roll 587.

[12] The author of the anonymous "Reminiscences . . ." of a dragoon, cited in note 9, above, says the route followed in 1840 was by rail to Harrisburg, by canal to Pittsburgh, and by steamboat down the Ohio, up the Mississippi and the Missouri rivers. In 1850 a group of recruits took the train to Pittsburgh, the ferry to Toledo, then the train again from Toledo through Chicago to Alton, Illinois. From Alton they traveled by boat to St. Louis and up the Missouri to Fort Leavenworth. See Augustus Meyers, *Ten Years in the Ranks, U.S. Army* (1914), pp. 49–57.

[13] "Muster and Pay Roll of Lieut. Thomas J. Berry's Company A, Recruits of the Second Regiment of Dragoons, Army of the United States, Sixth Column, Utah Forces, from the thirtieth day of April 1858, when first mustered, to the thirtieth day of June 1858," R.G. 217, National Archives. Hereafter cited as Muster Roll, Company A Dragoon Recruits.

Brevet Brigadier General William S. Harney[14] was ordered by the War Department to command the troops designated for duty against the Mormons. At the headquarters of the Utah Forces in St. Louis, lessons had been drawn from the experiences of Colonel Johnston's command the previous fall. No longer would the army's supply trains be vulnerable to attack by the Mormons. The supply trains would be large and well organized. Twenty-six wagons constituted a train or section, and ten trains made up a supply division. Each supply division was given a military escort designated as a numbered column.

The First Column was given no escort duty. It consisted of the Sixth Infantry. On May 5, 1858, it had its marching orders and was on its way to Utah at the time our young dragoon recruit was leaving Carlisle Barracks.

The Second Column was made up of Company D, Second Dragoons, a section of the Second Artillery, and Headquarters and five companies of the Fourth Artillery. Its task was to protect the first supply division. On May 15, it set out for Utah from Fort Leavenworth.

Company K of the Second Dragoons, the four remaining companies of the Fourth Artillery, and a section of another battery were designated as the Third Column. Their job was to protect the second supply division, and they left Fort Leavenworth on May 20.

Responsibility for the third supply division was in the hands of the men of Headquarters and four companies of the Seventh Infantry, two companies of the Second Cavalry, and a section of a battery of the Second Artillery. This Fourth Column left Leavenworth on May 25.

The Fifth Column was made up of Headquarters and three companies of the First Cavalry at Fort Riley, Kansas, and Company C,

[14] William Selby Harney (1800–89) graduated from West Point in 1818 and served in the Seminole and Mexican Wars. He was promoted to brigadier general in 1858. He was first chosen to lead the Utah expedition, but later that task was given to Colonel Albert S. Johnston and Harney was assigned to Kansas. After the death of General Persifor F. Smith, he commanded the Department of Utah for a brief time. While in command of the Department of Oregon in 1859, he contributed to Anglo-American tensions by ordering the military occupation of San Juan Island in the Strait of Juan de Fuca. Later he was recalled and the matter was settled peacefully. The outbreak of the Civil War found him in command of the Department of the West, but he was suspected of Southern sympathies, removed, and did not get another active command during the war. See Logan U. Reavis, *The Life and Military Services of General William Selby Harney* (1878).

Third Artillery, three companies of the Seventh Infantry, and a section of another artillery battery at Fort Leavenworth. These units left Forts Riley and Leavenworth on May 28. They were the escort for the fourth supply division.

The Sixth Column was composed of three companies of the First Cavalry (two at Fort Riley and one at Leavenworth) and the remaining company of the Seventh Infantry. These were to march from the respective forts on June 4 to provide an escort for the fifth supply division.[15] Due to delays, it did not march until June 13. The young volunteer who joined the dragoons for adventure, and whose anonymous letters follow, arrived at Fort Leavenworth and found himself and his fellow recruits assigned to the Sixth Column. He began to write a regular series of letters under the pen name "Utah" which he sent off to the editor of the Philadelphia *Daily Evening Bulletin*. His contributions were usually printed on the first page of the newspaper and were obviously regarded by the editor as of interest to a wide readership. "Utah's" letters tell us a great deal about life in the regular army in 1858, about the attitude of the soldiers toward the Mormons and the Indians. They also provide us with a view of the West as experienced by an educated and sensitive young man.

By the time the six columns of the First Brigade, Utah Forces, were underway, the crisis that brought them into being was resolved. The Mormons, originally intent upon resistance, held a council of war on March 19 which resulted in a threat to evacuate their lands, move everything possible, and to burn the rest before the troops arrived. All of Mormondom was in motion and determined to destroy what had so recently been built. The possibility of relocating in northern Mexico or western Canada was investigated. Mormon elders in Europe were recalled; Mormon settlements in Nevada and California were abandoned. Military men and politicians among the gentiles began to appreciate that the subjugation of Utah might be a time-consuming, costly, and empty enterprise.

At this point a private individual resolved to try a last-ditch effort to settle the dispute. Thomas L. Kane, a Philadelphia lawyer, had

---

[15] Headquarters, Utah Forces, St. Louis, Missouri, General Orders No. 2, May 5, 1858, "AG Letters," roll 587.

visited the Mormons in 1846 and was popular with them. Following the publication of his pamphlet, *The Mormons*, in 1850, a deep and lasting friendship was established. His respect and love for them induced him to go to President Buchanan and offer to act as a mediator. Buchanan agreed, and Kane left for Utah to talk to Brigham Young. Kane was able to assure Young that the federal government would not interfere with the Mormon church, but that the supremacy of the government must be acknowledged in temporal affairs. Young gave his tentative assent to this formula. Next Kane sought out Alfred Cumming, the newly-appointed federal territorial governor, to get his views. He found him encamped with a part of the army at Black's Fork, a tributary of the Green River in southwestern Wyoming. Cumming welcomed the chance for a peaceful settlement, and he set out with Kane to see Brigham Young. They arrived in Salt Lake City on April 12. By now it was obvious that the Mormons acknowledged Cumming as their governor. Young dramatized this acceptance through a courtesy call and the delivery of the official seal of the Territory of Utah. Later, on April 25, at a public meeting in the Tabernacle, Young introduced Cumming to an audience of three or four thousand Mormons. In a firm, sympathetic, and tactful way Cumming explained that the Mormons must acknowledge the Constitution and the laws of the United States but that there would be no interference with religion. The soldiers en route to Utah would not be stationed near the Mormon settlements. Troops would be used only as a last resort to secure submission to the federal government. Cumming then asked members of the audience to express their views. Many took advantage of the opportunity to speak fervently about the wrongs they had suffered and the ingratitude of the government for their services in the Mexican War. Cumming told them that he knew that they had been wronged, and his patient attitude during this session added weight to his words. In the end the meeting served a most useful purpose by relieving the pent-up feelings of the Mormons. They realized that it would not be necessary to destroy their settlements and to seek a new land. Good sense and reason would prevail. Two federal peace commissioners worked out the final arrangements with the Mormon leaders in June. It was agreed that the army en route to Utah would march through Salt Lake City and construct a camp south of it. Led by Brigadier General Johnston, the first units of the army marched through the capital, still deserted because the Mormons feared the army might not keep its pledge. Thirty-six miles south of it, in Cedar Valley, they built Camp Floyd, named in honor of the secretary of war. With the Mormon crisis resolved, many of the troops that made up the Utah Forces were deployed elsewhere. The dragoon recruits that composed a part of the Sixth Column were among those who continued their march to Utah and took up quarters in Camp Floyd.[16]

Scarcely had the Mormon problem been resolved than the outbreak of Indian troubles in Oregon Territory made it necessary to send troops there. The sudden and sizeable increase of soldiers originally a part of the Utah Forces disturbed the Indians of the Plains and the Southwest. Later a cruel and undeserved attack by a unit of the Second Dragoons on an encampment of Utes helped to turn that tribe against the white men.

Further south a civil war was raging in Mexico. Some soldiers thought it might be necessary to station more troops near the border. Other more expansionist-minded Americans wondered if the unsettled affairs in Mexico might not provide an excuse for an intervention by the United States and the annexation of territory. An intrusion by the American William Walker and his armed followers into the affairs of Nicaragua showed that such things were possible.[17] With an administration in Washington that was sympathetic to Southerners, who could say that a new Mexican venture might not result in new slave territories south of the border?[18] Above and beyond these

[16] The most recent treatment of the Mormon difficulties is Furniss, *The Mormon Conflict*. Also helpful are the works of Anderson, Bancroft, Brooks, and Hafen. See notes 2 and 3 above. Life in Utah immediately after the conflict is depicted in Richard F. Burton's, *The City of the Saints* (1861). President Buchanan's role is treated in Philip S. Klein, *President James Buchanan: A Biography* (1962). Government documents relating to the affair are in the *Senate* and *House Executive Documents*. The Senate documents are 35th Congress, 1st session, vol. 3, doc. 11; 2nd session, vol. 2, doc. 1; 36th Congress, 1st session, vol. 2, doc. 2; vol. 3, doc. 2; and in James D. Richardson, ed., *A Compilation of the Messages and Papers of the Presidents, 1789–1897* (1897), vol. 7.

[17] For a full treatment of Walker and his activities, see William O. Scroggs, *Filibusters and Financiers* (1916), and Laurence Greene, *The Filibuster: The Career of William Walker* (1937).

[18] In December 1859 Buchanan proposed to Congress that the United States send a military force into Mexico to obtain an indemnity for the violations of the

problems and speculations, the growing strength of the antislavery forces in the political life of the nation were increasing domestic tensions. The Republican party, organized in 1854, was committed to a policy of forbidding the extension of slavery to new territories. It had increased its strength with each election. Given this state of affairs, men looked ahead to the presidential election of 1860 with varying degrees of fear, hope, and anticipation. Although far removed from the scenes of political debate, the young dragoon volunteer was not unaware of the problems that faced the nation in the settled areas as well as on the frontier. There was much for an intelligent young man to speculate about as he moved with his unit toward Utah.

rights of Americans during the civil war and disorder there. See *Senate Executive Documents*, 35th Congress, 2nd session, vol. 1, doc. 1, pp. 16–18; *Senate Journal*, 35th Congress, 2nd session, p. 343; and Richardson, ed., *Papers of the Presidents*, 7: 538–40.

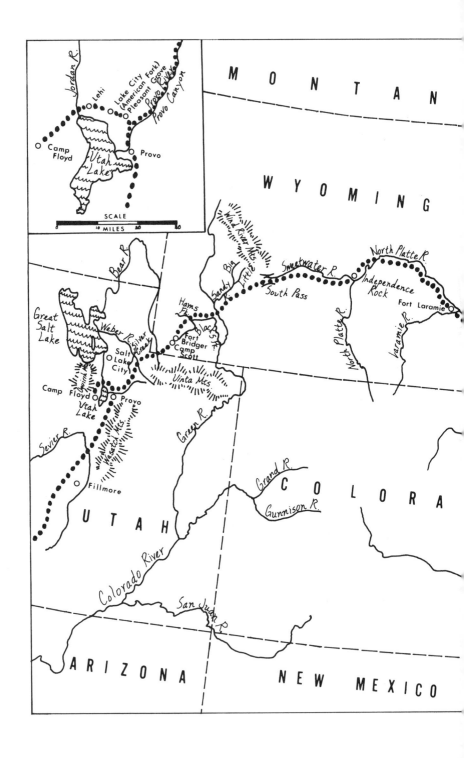

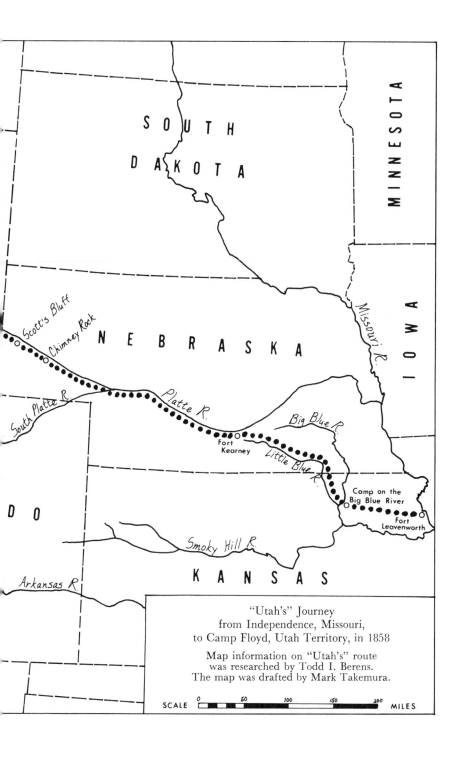

SOUTH DAKOTA

MINNESOTA

IOWA

Missouri R.

NEBRASKA

Scott's Bluff

Chimney Rock

South Platte R.

Platte R.

Big Blue R.

Fort Kearney

Little Blue R.

Camp on the Big Blue River

Fort Leavenworth

DO

Smoky Hill R.

Arkansas R.

KANSAS

"Utah's" Journey
from Independence, Missouri,
to Camp Floyd, Utah Territory, in 1858

Map information on "Utah's" route
was researched by Todd I. Berens.
The map was drafted by Mark Takemura.

SCALE | 0 | 50 | 100 | 150 | 200 | MILES

Fort Leavenworth, K.T.

May 28, 1858

[1]

The troops continue moving from this fort towards Salt Lake City, and it is very evident that the Government has resolved to crush out the "relic of barbarism" that pollutes the fair soil and clime of Utah. To-day, the fifth column, consisting of two companies of dragoons, one company of artillery, and three companies of infantry, under the command of Col. Chas. A. May,[1] left here for the seat of war, and an order from Gen. Harney,[2] who has succeeded Gen. Persifor F. Smith,[3] as commander of the expedition, directs the sixth column, composed of two companies of dragoons, two companies of cavalry, and some infantry, to start on the 4th of June. Fresh troops are arriving at the Fort almost every day, and they are being equipped for the march as speedily as possible, though the number leaving here are much less than the arrivals.

It is thought by many that the movement in Utah is a mere feint to attract public attention, while the administration is preparing for a blow at Mexico, under the guise of protection as laid down in Sam Houston's revolution.[4] This may be correct, and will account for the

---

[1] Charles Augustus May graduated from West Point in 1836 and served with distinction during the Mexican War. In March 1855 he was promoted to major and the following October transferred to the Second Dragoons. He was ordered to take command of Fort Kearney, Nebraska Territory, in July 1858 with a force of three companies of artillery and one of dragoons. May resigned from the army in 1861 and died in 1864.

[2] See note 14 in the Introduction.

[3] Persifor Frazier Smith (1798–1858) graduated from the College of New Jersey (later Princeton) in 1815 and served in the Seminole and Mexican Wars. Commissioned a brigadier general in 1856, he was given jurisdiction over the Department of Utah in 1858. While organizing his forces to put down the Mormon "rebellion" he died in Fort Leavenworth on May 17, 1858.

[4] Under the terms of the Gadsden Treaty of 1853, the United States purchased from Mexico a tract of land south of the Gila River for use as a railroad route from

President's anxiety to raise regular troops instead of volunteers to carry out the Mormon war. I think, however, that if such were the case, they would not send such a man as Col. May away to Salt Lake, while his services were needed in a more important locality. The Col. may not go far, however, before orders to proceed to Mexico overtake him. Be this as it may, it is evident that Old Buck[5] is "spoiling for a fight," and intends to try his hand somewhere. Some are contemptible enough to insinuate that the old man, having lived so long without getting a wife, is envious of Brother Brigham's success among the ladies, and takes this mode of venting his rage.

That Young's career in Utah should be arrested, no one will deny: none will attempt to apologise for his crimes and those of his fanatical followers. The cause of morality demands the extermination of this nest of adulterers, and no further time should be wasted in attempts at compromise or windy discussion. It were useless to attempt their reformation — the only missionaries that can make headway with them are such as wield the sabre and bear the musket. But this question arises in my mind: Are the men the United States are sending there, fit champions of order and morality; and will the presence of a body of such men as compose the American army, be likely to bring about a healthier moral state of society than exists under the present Mormon rulers? To both parts of this question, I answer no,

Texas to California. The United States also got the right of transit across the Isthmus of Tehuantepec with the authorization to protect this grant. The treaty did not secure enough of the Mexican state of Sonora to provide a suitable connection with the Gulf of California. It also did not settle the question of American claims against Mexico or the question of raids across the border. Complicating the situation was the belief of some American settlers that all of Sonora had been purchased, and who were arrested by the Mexicans in 1854 and charged with entering the country without passports. Likewise, early in 1854, William Walker, the American filibuster, proclaimed himself the president of Sonora (an area embracing Sonora and lower California) but was arrested by American authorities and tried for a neutrality violation. Other groups also had plans for detaching a portion of Mexico. Many Northerners, apparently including "Utah," believed that the generally pro-Southern attitude of the Buchanan administration made it sympathetic to the plans of Walker and others like him. Border problems and the inability to get money from Mexico for claims led Buchanan in December 1858 to ask Congress to authorize the establishment of a temporary protectorate over the northern parts of Chihuahua and Sonora. Congress refused. See James M. Callahan, *American Foreign Policy in Mexican Relations* (1932), pp. 214–59; Hubert H. Bancroft, *History of Texas and the North Mexican States, 1801–1889* (1890), 2: 695–96; and Allan Nevins, *The Emergence of Lincoln* (1950), 2: 481–87.

[5] A nickname for James Buchanan.

unless, indeed the old saw that "an old rogue makes the best jailor," will be verified. Company A, second dragoon recruits is a fair specimen of the missionaries that are to reform the Mormons, and the following extract from their morning report of May 26, will show what they are:

"Privates in confin[e]ment 49; charges — stealing 11; drunkenness and disorderly conduct 23; gambling 7; attempt to rob 4; attempt to desert 3; attempt to murder 1. . . . . Total strength of this company 53." [6] Are not these pretty creatures to send out on an errant connected with the moral state of our community? It is a melancholy fact that few, except the lowest dregs of society will enlist in the American army; while on the contrary it might be rendered the most respectable and polished body of soldiers on the globe, without one cent additional expense to the Government. I do not believe there is one private out of every hundred who is not an habitual drunkard, and in this, they have the countenance of Gen. Harney, who "goes in" for Free Whiskey, and admits many violations of military law to go unpunished, where the offender should feel the entire weight of the penalty, from circumstances peculiarly aggravating. My idea is this: Gen. Harney wants to be President. He thinks, by allowing his men to act rowdy with impunity, to obtain the reputation of being a kind-hearted officer — a character very popular with the masses — and thus increase his prospects for election. But I hope that this ambition of his will be as effectually checked as his efforts to injure Col. Sumner,[7] since he stoops to such low means to cajole and humor the mob. Though I say this, I disclaim any ill-feeling towards Gen. Harney, who has, no doubt, rendered some service of a secondary importance to the nation during his military career.

Rumors prevailed here a few days since that a collision had occurred between the Free State men and the Border Ruffians, but I have since heard it contradicted on good authority, and hope I may

---

[6] The original of this report has not been located by the editor in the War Department records in the National Archives.

[7] Edwin V. Sumner (1797–1863) had a military career dating back to 1819, including service in the Mexican War. In the summer of 1857, as a colonel, he led two companies of cavalry and two of dragoons in a campaign against the Cheyenne Indians. While en route to Fort Laramie he received orders to detach his dragoons for a campaign against the Mormons. He left them at Fort Laramie. Later he became commander of the Department of the West with headquarters at St. Louis.

Ft. Leavenworth, Kansas Territory, in 1858.

say it is untrue. On the strength of the report, however, a company of the Second Dragoons were ordered under arms to be ready to march at a moment's warning. Thank Heaven they were not called out, as I cannot see how such men could do otherwise than affiliate with their brother ruffians of the Missouri border. May heaven save Kansas from ever needing the protection of Federal bayonets; and may the nation never be reduced to the necessity of having to rely on her regular soldiers for defence. I would rather, were fighting to be done, take five hundred volunteers (such men, for instance, as the Scott Legion[8] of Philadelphia) into the field, than five times the number of regular soldiers. Were you in Fort Leavenworth one week, you would form the same opinion in the case that I have.

Yours, etc.,

UTAH

[8] After the Mexican War several volunteer units took the name "Scott Legion" honoring General Winfield Scott, the commander of the army that marched and fought its way to Mexico City. In Pennsylvania there were three units bearing the name "Scott Legion." It was one of these to which "Utah" refers.

On the *March* for Utah
June 25, 1858
[2]

The sixth column of the forces for Utah left Fort Leavenworth on the 13th inst., after being several times under arms and ready for the march, and when about to move being ordered into camp again. The causes for these delays I do not know, but presume they were prompted by the wisdom of our great military commander, Major Emory,[1] whose *forte* appears to be a "masterly inactivity." It consists of three companies of Cavalry, three companies of Infantry, and a company of the Second Dragoons, of which latter your correspondent is a member. We have been marching along at the rate of about twelve miles a day, and when it rains we lie idle in camp. You may imagine the great danger that threatens Salt Lake City, when I tell you, that though we are now fourteen days out, we are not yet ninety miles from Fort Leavenworth. I think, if we persevere, that we will arrive in Utah about the time my term of service expires, and that the young Philadelphians who enlisted to have a bout with the Mormons, will have to re-enlist to have their desires gratified. But to us this slow motion is glorious. We breathe the pure, fresh air of Kansas, that braces and invigorates the puny frames of city bred youths, and on fine nights we sleep with the clear canopy of heaven for our covering, and awake in the morning to shake off the dew and feel a heartiness and strength we never could experience in the cooped up streets of a city. 'Tis true we have none of the comforts of civilized life, but then

[1] William H. Emory (1811–87) graduated from West Point in 1831 and had experience in the artillery, topographical engineers, and infantry. He was promoted to the rank of major in the Second Cavalry in March 1855, but served with that unit less than three months before transferring to the First Cavalry. Emory's contributions as a topographical engineer are described in William H. Goetzmann, *Army Exploration in the American West, 1803–1863* (1959).

we have few of its evils. I do not deny that we possess what the
majority of those who enlist prize as the greatest boon of civilization — plenty of intoxicating drink — and it were useless to attempt
to do so. Nearly every house that we have passed since we commenced
the march, has had painted over the door in uncouth, straggling
letters, that look as though the artist had been paid for his work in the
beverage they announce, and received his recompence before the job
was completed, the word *Whiskey*. Whether all the inhabitants of
Kansas are dealers in "liquified strychnine" or not, I cannot say, but
certainly I have encountered none who were not. As I see no cus-
tomers, I presume the soldiers, teamsters, &c., who pass through the
country, are the principal dependence of the dealers. Shak[e]speare
says that "all the world's a stage," and a writer on Kansas might say
that all the inhabitants of the Territory are rumsellers.

We have not yet met with anything of particular interest, and the
only thing that enlivens the monotony of our life is the occasional
flogging of a poor devil for some offence against military law, and the
pursuit, generally fruitless, of a deserter who has grown tired of "the
pomp and circumstance of glorious war" — three buscuits and a
piece of fat pork a day. I saw two poor fellows flogged a few days
since. A stout bugler laid the lashes on, and at every blow the blood
spurted until their backs were mangled masses of blood and lacerated
flesh. The victims writhed beneath the infliction but the others looked
on in calm, stoical indifference, though a very slight offence would
render them liable to the same punishment.[2] Yesterday, one of our
company deserted, in a manner, the cool baldness of which was ad-
mirable. Orders had been given to allow no one to leave the camp;
yet, in open day, he put on his sabre, shouldered his rifle, strapped his
great coat and blanket on his back, and walked away in the presence
of the Commander of our company, who was too much astonished at
his daring to stop him, or give the necessary orders to his subordinates.
He was pursued, but a few minutes walk from the camp was a woods

[2] Congress passed a law in May 1812 forbidding flogging in the army, but it
was still inflicted, especially in frontier areas. In 1833 the army induced Congress
to pass a law allowing it to flog men convicted of desertion by a general court-
martial. The tendency to punish men for other infractions by flogging persisted,
and the Congress was obliged to reassert the prohibition in 1861 and 1872.

in which he concealed himself, and thus escaped.[3] Desertions are quite frequent. Of seventy-seven men who left Carlisle Barracks in our company on the 4th of May, only fifty-nine remain; and of these, three are captured deserters.[4] Many of these deserters were ruthless rowdies, but some of them were the best men in the company. The cause of this I cannot satisfactorily explain, as our company Commander is a good man and kind to his soldiers. You cannot imagine how uncomfortable a soldier is when it rains, and he cannot lie out upon the prairie. Fifteen men, with their saddles, valises, great-coats, blankets, sabres, rifles, horse accoutrements, &c., are huddled together into a small tent, into which you could not introduce a good sized double bed, and there they lie, disposed the best manner they can invent. Our saddles serve us as seats during the day, and pillows at night, and I am using mine now for a writing table, while a party of wild, reckless Dragoons are playing cards, smoking, swearing, and drinking whiskey on all sides of me. How would you like to write a leader for the BULLETIN under such circumstances? But you must not suppose we have no fun, or are destitute of men who can appreciate humor. We have a theatre in our company, and last night we had "an original drama," of which the following will give you some idea. An American soldier is met by a cadaverous looking individual, surrounded by a band of dirty white men and dirtier Indians. The latter exclaims:

> "These are the Mormons, brave and strong;
> And, Yankee, I am Brigham Young."

Pointing triumphantly to his motl[e]y followers, the Yankee replies:

> "Come on, ye dogs, and don't be shy,
> For I'll be darned if e'er I fly
> As Fitz James did to Roderick Dhu,[5]

---

[3] This must have been Andrew Regan, who enlisted at Boston on April 10, 1858, and deserted from the camp on the Nemaha River [Creek?], K.T., June 23, 1858.

[4] A muster roll for the period April 30 through June 30, 1858, shows one officer, three sergeants, four corporals, two buglers, and fifty privates. One enlisted man was discharged in Harrisburg while the company was en route to the West, and by the end of June eighteen men had deserted. See Muster Roll, Company A Dragoon Recruits.

[5] Fitz James and Roderigh Vich Alpine Dhu are characters in Sir Walter Scott's narrative poem, *The Lady of the Lake*, published in 1810.

> So Brigham, I reply to you:
> Although in all this prairie land
> There is no rock 'gainst which to stand,
> Come one, come all, this rock shall fly
> From its firm base as soon as I."

And thus the play goes on, until Brigham is brought to the ground, and the Yankee stalks triumphantly to his tent. The bill announcing this play attached the character of Brigham to John H. Gould,[6] and that of the Yankee to Frank Clinton,[7] both members of our company, and they "sustained the characters admirably," of course, (I was a "dead head") and were greated with applause that would have cheered the heart of an actor, who was not rich enough to buy the support of your Sunday papers and its crowd of backers.

Gen. Harney passed us three days ago en route for the seat of war, and, I presume, is making rapid progress. He was accompanied by a pretty strong escort, and is said to have declared that he had orders to bring old Brigham to terms, or knock the city about his ears. For my part, I continue in the belief that the United States do not want to punish Young at all.

UTAH.

[6] The reference is undoubtedly to Private John S. Gould, age twenty-one, a printer who enlisted at Buffalo, New York, on March 22, 1858. He had blue eyes, brown hair, a fair complexion, and stood 5 feet 6½ inches tall. Subsequently he was assigned to Company E, Second Dragoons, in September 1858 and was given a disability discharge in May 1859. See chap. 26.

[7] Private Francis G. Clinton, age twenty-one, was a printer who enlisted at Philadelphia on April 19, 1858. He was described as being 5 feet 6¼ inches tall, with hazel eyes, brown hair, and a fair complexion. Later assigned to Company G, Second Dragoons, at Camp Floyd, Utah, he deserted on January 21, 1859. See chap. 26.

In Camp on the Big Blue, N.T.
July 2, 1858
[3]

Slow as the sixth column has marched, since it left Fort Leavenworth, it came up to the fifth column, day before yesterday, encamped
at this place, and here both columns lie, awaiting further orders, I
believe. We are satisfied, however, to remain here some time, as the
country is the most glorious one can wish for. We are encamped on a
level spot, amid tall grass, that makes a most excellent resting place;
near us runs the Big Blue, the banks of which are covered with trees,
and clear, sparkling water bubbles from the solid rock at every few
hundred yards. The prairie is not one dull, level plain, but hundreds
of acres of tall grass, and stony patches of nearly the some [same]
extent, deep ravines and strips of woodland are interspersed, so that
the New Hampshire man is reminded of his own granite State, where
they shoot the corn between the stones with a gun, and the Pennsylvanian of the tall pines and sturdy oaks and pure air and water of his
native Alleghenies, all amidst the roses and luxurious herbage of the
Western plains. A soldier's life is far from being a pleasant one, taken
in the whole, but then the joys of an encampment on a spot like this
repays months of toil and privation.

Since we came here we have had plenty of food for excitement.
The first night of our encampment Lieutenant Magruder,[1] a young
officer attached to our company, was shot and instantly killed by a
resident of Palmetto, a little village about one mile from our camp.
There are two different stories afloat in regard to this affair. One is
that a settler had cheated a drunken soldier out of his blanket, and

---

[1] John T. Magruder was appointed to West Point from Virginia in 1853.
Upon graduation in 1857 he was breveted a second lieutenant in the Second Cav-
alry, and in April 1858 he was transferred to the First Cavalry. He was killed on
June 28, 1858.

28

that Lieut. Magruder had made an effort to take it from the swindler. This so exasperated the man that he way-laid the officer on his return home, and shot him. This is the story of Magruder's friends. The other and by far the most likely one, is not nearly so creditable to the officer. If it be correct, as is generally believed among men in the camp, the man that killed him would have been justified even by a Philadelphia jury.

The day after his death his remains were interred with the military honors due to his rank. We dug him a grave upon the prairie, a rough board coffin was constructed, and he was carried to his grave in a commissary wagon drawn by four mules, the entire column joining in the procession. A pile of stones amid the tall grass marks his resting place, and soon that pile will be all that will remind us of a man who might have been of service to his country, but would not.[2]

But death did not stop here. Scarcely had we buried him, when a wagon master belonging to our column shot a teamster, for some trivial offence. Major Emory issued an order for his arrest, but as that worthy is noted for his aversion to rapid movements, the wagon master was far beyond his reach when the authority to apprehend him was given. There are stories of other murders in circulation, but these are the only two that have taken place.

There is a rumor in camp to-day that the cavalry and infantry belonging to our command are to be ordered back to Fort Leaven-

---

[2] The Washington, D.C., *Evening Star* of July 14, 1858, printed this report of Magruder's death: "The Late Lieut. John S. Magruder. — The War Department have received the following official explanation of the death of this esteemed gentleman, information of which very recently reached this city: 'Headquarters Sixth Column Utah Forces, Camp near the Blue, June 29, 1858. Colonel: It is my painful duty to report to you the death of Brevet John S. Magruder, 1st cavalry. He was killed in Marysville, near the camp of the 5th column, last night at about ten o'clock, in an unfortunate personal encounter with a citizen of Marysville named Poor.

"Lieut. Magruder had been on a visit to the camp of the 5th column, and when about a mile from that camp, on his way to the camp of the 6th column, the encounter took place, which ended in his immediate death. Lieut. Plummer, of the 7th infantry, and Lieut. Wildrick, of the artillery, both belonging to the 5th column, were present when the unforeseen and deplorable event took place.

"The news of the occurrence reached the camp about 12 o'clock, and Lieut. Berry, with two officers and ten men, were immediately dispatched to bring in the body of Lieut. Magruder, and the civil authorities to bring the murderer to justice.'" This report was addressed to Colonel Samuel Cooper, the Adjutant General. The original is in "AG Letters,'" roll 584.

worth, and that the company of dragoons will proceed to Utah, where their regiment is stationed. How much truth there is in this report, or whether there is any at all, I cannot say, but I should not be surprised if it were correct. The circumstances of the Fifth Column lying here so long, looks as though nothing serious was intended against Utah, and that the whole affair was a sham, got up to cover some other purpose.

May not this concentration of forces here be for the purpose of having them near at hand in case they should be needed to crush out "abolitionism" in Kansas, without subjecting the government to the accusation of keeping a large armed force in that territory?[3] To me it is inexplicable. The Mormons were in April last declared to be in open rebellion against the government of the United States by the Proclamation of the President; troops have been sent from the States to punish them, and the two largest columns have as yet got no further than the Big Blue, one hundred and twenty miles from Fort Leavenworth. This is certainly a very singular mode of enforcing the laws, and reminds one of the Chinese astonishment when the British did not fly at the sound of their gongs. If the President wishes to crush out rebellion in Utah, why does he not do it? If he wishes to let Brigham and his saints continue in their course, let him be a man and say so. One thing is quite certain, if the young men who compose our column are led by energetic officers and employed to enforce the laws, the rebellion in Utah, that sore upon our nation, will soon be removed, and Brigham and his men will serve as warnings to those who may hereafter feel disposed to resist our national authority.

Utah.

---

[3] Governor James W. Denver of Kansas Territory protested the removal of the troops at Fort Scott and requested that the matter be referred to the secretary of war and to the president. See Denver to Brevet Major F. W. Sherman, June 29, 1858, "AG Letters," roll 590. Robert M. Stewart, the governor of Missouri, wrote to President Buchanan on August 9, 1858, asking for troops to protect citizens from marauding bands. See "AG Letters," roll 584.

Daily Evening Bulletin.

ALEXANDER CUMMINGS, SIMON PEACOCK, Proprietors.

OUR WHOLE COUNTRY.

BULLETIN BUILDING, 112 SOUTH THIRD ST.

VOLUME XII—NO 113.

PRICE TWO CENTS.

PHILADELPHIA, MONDAY, AUGUST 23, 1858.

AUCTION SALES.

M. THOMAS & SONS, Auctioneers.

FOR SALE.—A splendid short tail bay Horse, very handsome, perfectly sound and kind in all harness. To be sold very low.

4162 BAGS Prime RIO COFFEE, from sales pier, now landing, for sale by...

FARINA CRACKERS.—FOX'S celebrated...

OIL AND CLARET.—150 boxes...

TO SOUTHERN AND WESTERN MERCHANTS...

THE CABLE.—The Grand Telegraph...

MARKING WITH INDELIBLE INK...

REMOVAL.—Bishop Simons & Co. have removed from the NORTH WEST corner of ARCH Street, above FRONT...

MERCHANTS AND FARMERS...

MATTRESSES.—The largest and best assortment of...

MACNICHOL & HARPER.

EVENING BULLETIN.

MONDAY, AUGUST 23, 1858.

From Utah—Letter from a Dragoon.

[Correspondence of the Phila. Evening Bulletin.]

FORT KEARNEY, July 21st, 1858.—The Sixth Column arrived here to-day, at two o'clock, having accomplished the journey from Fort Leavenworth to this place, a distance of about two hundred and ninety miles, in thirty nine days. This is an evidence of what Uncle Sam can do when he tries, and is a performance of which our military men may well be proud...

Fort Kearney is situated on a gentle rise on the prairie, about two miles from the Platte River...

Four Days Later From Europe.

THE ANGLO-SAXON AT QUEBEC.

THE REJOICING IN ENGLAND.

IMPORTANT FROM CHINA—CAPTURE OF AN AMERICAN SLAVER, &C.

COMMERCIAL NEWS.

[From the St. Joseph Journal, 19th.]

POLITICAL.

The Illinois Fight—Lincoln on the Demoins and Toom-be Controversy...

The front page of the Philadelphia Daily Evening Bulletin for August 23, 1858, with "Utah's" article.

Fort Kearney
July 21st, 1858
[4]

The Sixth Column arrived here to-day, at two o'clock, having accomplished the journey from Fort Leavenworth to this place, a distance of about two hundred and ninety miles, in thirty-nine days. This is an evidence of what Uncle Sam can do when he tries, and is a performance of which our military men may well be proud. For the purpose of crushing a rebellion, we actually marched, with good roads and fair weather, something more than seven miles a day! and beaten the fifth column at that. The latter are camped in the rear of the Fort, and we are on the outside of it. To-morrow they march on, and we remain here until they are thirty-miles ahead, when we will follow.

Fort Kearney is situated on a gentle rise on the prairies, about two miles from the Platte River. It is an insignificant post, there being but two respectable buildings, and they would not accomodate three hundred men. These, with some tumble-down shanties, and a few such huts, constitute the "Fort." The country around is very pleasant, and the elevation on which the Fort is built, permits the fresh air of the prairie to fan unobstructed the sun-embrowned cheeks of the soldiers. Did I wish to be stationed at a post, I would choose Fort Kearney in preference to any I have seen yet.

There are four or five thousand Indians about the Fort, Pawnees and Cheyennes, awaiting the arrival of the Indian Agent, to give them the goods, &c., allowed to them by the Government.[1] We passed through the Pawnee camp this morning, and had a fair opportunity of seeing the "Poor Indian." They are now returning the compliment, and about a hundred and fifty of them are running through our camp, exhibiting their skill at archery "for a consideration," begging, sell-

---

[1] In treaties whereby Indian lands were ceded provision was made for yearly annuities.

An early view of Ft. Kearney, Nebraska Territory.

ing moccasins, &c., &c. The Pawnees are not calculated to give a very elevated idea of the Indian character. They are naked, except a cloth about the loins, and are most disgustingly dirty. They are inveterate beggars, continually asking for bread, meat, money, whiskey and old clothes. Of the first two we have scarcely enough for ourselves; of the third none at all; the majority of our men would part with their soul's salvation rather than their whiskey; and as for clothes, were we to part with those that are ragged, we would be in a worse condition than the Pawnees themselves are. So, you will perceive that they do not make much of us. If these naked, half-starved wretches are specimens of the race who once owned this great continent, I see no cause to grieve, that they were dispossessed of it. They are, with all their filthiness, very vain, and as I write, some six or seven of them are looking on. Could they but read my remarks, would there not be dark frowns and angry mutterings?[2]

[2] For a similar critical view of the Pawnees see Burton, *City of the Saints*, pp. 44–46. The history of the tribe has been written by George E. Hyde, *Pawnee Indians* (1951).

On Saturday last, the three companies of cavalry that left Fort
Leavenworth with the sixth column, marched in the direction of Fort
Riley, the Indians in the neighborhood of that post having become
somewhat troublesome. This, with some other changes, reduced the
forces composing the column to two companies of infantry and a company of the second dragoons. With the cavalry went Major Emory,
the distinguished and energetic officer of whom I have heretofore
spoken, and we are now commanded by Brevet Major Gabriel H.
Paul,[3] Captain of Company I, Seventh Infantry, under whom, I
hope, we will make somewhat more rapid progress towards Salt Lake.
I was not in the least anxious to reach that place until we received
intelligence of the restoration of tranquility, but now that there is no
danger threatening us, I wish our marching was over. And I believe
that, had Major Emory been aware of Brigham's intention to "knock
under," he would have pushed on boldly towards the "seat of war."
I do not, by any means, impeach the Major's bravery, but then, you
know, "discretion is the better part of valor," and, as somebody says,

> "He who *bobs* the bullets sent
> May live to run for President."

Since Emory left us we have done better marching than formerly.
On Monday we marched sixteen miles, twenty yesterday, and twelve
to-day. This is light marching for mounted men, but I pitied the poor
Infantry men as they toiled on through the sun over the hard ground,
foot sore and dusty, carrying their heavy muskets on their shoulders.
We walk some ourselves, but it is not more than enough to straighten
our limbs after riding an hour or two. Our officers have to walk with
us, and they will not do that more than absolutely necessary, as many
a day we, too, would wish ourselves anything else than soldiers, as I
often hear the Infantry express themselves on coming into camp.
While their men trudge along on foot, the infantry officers ride in
front of them and seem to expect them to keep pace with the horses.
This they would have to do were it not for one honorable exception —
Lieutenant Bootes — who always walks with his men, saying that it

[3] Gabriel R. Paul graduated from West Point in 1834 and rose steadily in the
army, becoming a captain in 1846. During the Mexican War he won a major's
brevet for gallant and meritorious conduct at the battle of Chapultepec.

gives the men better spirits to see their officers marching with them.[4] Lieutenant Bootes served as a private soldier in the Mexican war, and was commissioned for his bravery and good conduct.

Last night we camped on the Platte river, where it runs through a low level prairie. It is a wide, shallow stream, and the banks are very low, scarcely two feet high at the place where we camped. Although over half a mile wide, we did not see the river until we were within thirty yards of it, the land around being lower than the banks. A rise of two feet in the river would deluge the country for miles around. I enjoyed a bath in its waters. Although a mountain stream it is not cold, — in fact, it is tepid, and you have no chilling sensations on plunging into it, even though you be drenched with sweat. I wish some of the poor devils who are employed in the task of "getting up" a daily paper could take a tour to Fort Kearney at this season of the year. It would cause them to dream of Paradise for months after their return to the dungeon walls of a newspaper office. You may imagine yourself "better off" than we are, but I would not exchange with you — notwithstanding all the "glory" and "honor" of speaking to and for the people — if you were to offer me the BULLETIN office "to boot."

Imagine, if you can in your dismal "sanctum," how glorious it is to be a

"Warrior taking his rest
With his martial cloak around him." [5]

with no other covering save the star-spangled canopy of Heaven. And then how happy we are when we spring up at the first note of the reveille — which sounds at three o'clock, A.M. — put on our arms and fall in for roll call. Whew! the very thought must be exhilirating.

[4] Levi C. Bootes enlisted in the army as a private in 1846 and within two months he became a sergeant. By the fall of 1848 he had won both a brevet and a regular appointment as a second lieutenant in the Sixth Infantry. He was promoted to first lieutenant in 1853 and to captain in 1860. After meritorious service in the Civil War, he retired in 1874 with the regular rank of lieutenant colonel. He died in 1896.

[5] An excerpt from Charles Wolfe's poem, "The Burial of Sir John Moore at Corunna," published in 1817. The poem commemorates the death of an English general in the Peninsular War in Spain against the forces of Napoleon in 1809. The complete stanza is as follows: "No useless coffin enclosed his breast,/ Not in a sheet nor in a shroud we wound him,/ But he lay like a warrior taking his rest/ With his martial cloak around him."

Now that the "war" is over[6] our company is to march on to Salt Lake City, where we will be quartered for the winter, the remainder of our regiment being there now. I presume we will have a "good time" in Mormondom — good quarters, plenty to eat, and nothing to do except to attend to our horses and make love to the maidens of that far famed land. The latter, you know, is part of a soldier's duty.

As we are about entering the Indian country, I hope to be able to pick up some interesting items, and if we happen to have a skirmish with the redskins on the route, you may expect full particulars by the first express that leaves camp, unless an arrow or a bullet should bring to a sudden close the career of one of the many who went out to fight the Mormons (but didn't get a chance) in

UTAH.

P.S. — 22d ult. — While my letter was waiting for an express, an opportunity of seeing an Indian fight presented itself. The Pawnees were moving their camp to-day, and the Cheyennes taking advantage of the confusion attempted to stampede the ponies of the former. In so doing they killed two Pawnees' squaws, one of whom uttered a "death yell" that aroused here [her] entire tribes, and soon the cry of vengeance resounded all around. I was in the Pawnee camp at the time, and the rapidity with which the warriors rushed in, seized their arms, and "dashed to the flag" was astonishing. In a few moments the whole tribe were upon the cowardly Cheyennes who yelled difiance and prepared for battle. I mounted my horse and rode to the battle field, just as the Pawnees darted upon their foes. The struggle lasted but a few moments when the Cheyennes broke and fled towards the Fort for protection. The exasperated Pawnees pursued them, and would have wrought summary vengeance upon the cowardly butchers of their women had not the troops interfered and put an end to the fight. The Cheyennes lost some eight or ten killed, and nearly an hundred wounded. Only one of the Pawnees was slain — a brave young warrior, a son of the chief of the tribe. Our company were paraded in "order of battle," but we were not required to take a

---

[6] In June 1858 the final arrangements had been worked out between the federal peace commissioners and the Mormons. On June 26, troops under the command of Brevet Brigadier General Albert S. Johnston marched through Salt Lake City. Thirty-six miles to the south of the city they began building Camp Floyd.

part in the proceedings. I had no idea that the miserable looking Pawnees were possessed of so much bravery and skill as they displayed on this occasion, and am inclined to pardon their vanity which appears so ridiculous when we see their every day appearance. The parties have ag[r]eed to remain neutral until they have returned to their own hunting grounds.[7]

Gen. Harney arrived here to-day on his way back to civilization.

UTAH.

[7] While en route to St. Louis, General Harney wrote from Fort Leavenworth to the assistant adjutant general that he had spoken to four Cheyenne chiefs who were anxious to be at peace with the white men. Harney said that he could not make a treaty with them but that next summer the president might do so. "I told them also that it was necessary they should discontinue their hostilities toward other tribes with which we were at peace. This they were willing to assent to, but said that a war party from their tribe was then out which they could not get word to before it would have made an attack on the Pawnees in retaliation for robberies which the latter had committed upon them; and in fact on my arrival at Fort Kearney I found that an attempt had just been made with some success probably by this party to drive off the animals of a large band of Pawnees encamped a few miles below the post, resulting in a skirmish in which one Pawnee was killed and two or three were wounded. These collisions, with which depredations upon the Whites are almost constantly connected, will continue inevitably until they are interdicted by a combined treaty of the various tribes with the government. The Pawnees with whom I had a talk at Fort Kearney after the affair alluded to, expressed their willingness to enter into such an agreement; and I take occasion to repeat the recommendation made in my previous communication that authority be given to effect it next Summar." General W. S. Harney to the Assistant Adjutant General, August 3, 1858, "AG Letters," roll 593.

Ash Hollow, Nebraska Territory
Aug. 5
[5]

Since we have received definite news of the settlement of the Mormon difficulty, the Sixth column has moved at a greatly accelerated pace. We left Fort Kearney on the 24th ult., and since then have "made" from sixteen to twenty miles per day. On the second day out we met the Peace Commissioners returning, and they gave us the joyful intelligence that there was no fighting to be done.[1] They were escorted by half a dozen dragoons, and had made the journey so far without meeting with any difficulty, the Indians being at this season of the year in the buffalo country, preparing for the necessities of Winter. I was near Major Paul when he received the news, and saw his eye kindle and his cheek glow with pleasure at the information; and I feel confident that there was not a single epauletted coat that did not at that moment cover a lighter heart than it had since the march commenced. I have always disclaimed making any charge of poltroon[er]y against our officers, and still do, — attributing their actions entirely to that "rascally virtue" excessive prudence. But their joy was of short duration, for, like thunder from a cloudless sky, came the doleful news of Col. Steptoe's defeat by the Snake River Indians,[2]

[1] The federal peace commissioners were Lazarus W. Powell, ex-governor and then a Democratic senator from Kentucky, and Major Ben. MacCulloch of Texas, a famous Indian fighter.

[2] Colonel Edward J. Steptoe left Fort Walla Walla, Washington, on May 13, 1858, with 152 men from the First Dragoons and Ninth Infantry for the settlement at Colville, near the Canadian border. He hoped to talk to the whites and Indians in the region and to work out a more harmonious relationship between them. When he crossed the Spokane River he found a large party of armed Indians demanding to know if he came to attack them. Steptoe denied this. He camped and began to retrace his route the next day. The Indians attacked the rear of the column and a running battle began. After some casualties Steptoe took up a defensive position. By nightfall his losses in killed and wounded and the limited supply of ammunition induced him to lead a forced march back across the Snake River

38

and the semi-official statement of the New York *Herald* that "a large portion of the troops originally intended for Utah would be marched to the new scene of war." [3] I am inclined to think that our present rapid marching is to get far enough ahead to prevent the express from overtaking us before it is too late to commence the campaign this Winter, and then "Peace Commissioners," money, blankets, trinkets, etc., may settle the matter before Summer sets in. Verily, Barnum's Museum[4] and the White House at Washington were great humbugs in their day, but West Point and the Army Headquarters overshadow their glory entirely.

For the last few days we have been travelling through the country of the Sioux Indians. They are much superior to the stunted Pawnees, upon whom they look with sovereign contempt. The men are tall, erect, and well formed; the women are generally good looking, and they are all pretty flashily dressed. Soldier's clothes and feathers appear to command a premium, and many of our men disposed of old jackets and "tar-bucket" hats — the old uniform pattern[5] — for buffalo robes, moccasins, and other articles of Indian manufacture, to their own benefit, and the pleasure of our copper-colored cousins. I visited a camp composed of about two hundred wigwams, and had quite a "talk" with some of the men who could speak English. They were cordial and friendly, and expressed great respect for Uncle Sam,

and to safety. His losses were reported to be two officers, five enlisted men, and three friendly Indians killed, fifteen wounded, and one missing. The Indians were identified as probably the Cayuses, Walla Wallas, several tribes of the Yakima nation including the Palouses, and a few young men from the Spokane, Coeur d'Alene, and Colville tribes. News of the disaster reached Washington by July 17. Preliminary reports appeared in the St. Louis *Daily Missouri Republican* on July 19 and 20. Steptoe's own letter on the fight appeared on July 24.

[3] *New York Herald*, July 1, 1858. The *Daily Missouri Republican* of July 20, 1858, after relating the news of Steptoe's defeat, added: "Recent news from Utah seems to indicate that the Mormons have given way, and are fast evacuating their homes; if so, there will be an adequate force conveniently at hand, indeed, to move on these insensate Indians and administer prompt punishment."

[4] Phineas T. Barnum (1810–91), the great American showman, opened the American Museum in New York City in 1842. It combined stage performances, freak shows, educational exhibits, lectures, brass bands, and baby beauty contests.

[5] The "old jackets" were the 1833 pattern retrimmed with orange to meet the 1851 regulations. The "tar bucket hats" refer to the high, cylindrical, shako type of uniform cap worn by the infantry between 1832 and 1851 or the more tapered version worn by dragoons from 1833 to 1851.

and kindly feelings towards his soldiery. While in the midst of a social conversation, during which the red pipe passed freely around, I whiffing with the redskins, we were startled by a sudden uproar in another part of the camp. I recognized the voices of some of our company, and ran to see the cause of the disturbance. On reaching the scene of confusion, I found four dragoons beating an Indian, and about fifty of the Sioux endeavoring to pull them away. Calling up some of our men, who was [were] sober enough to do what was fair, we separated the combatants, and then let the soldiers fight the Indian one at a time, and that night there were four as well thumped men in our camp as ever were met with after a bruising match in the prize-ring. The fair play showed to the red skin in this matter, so pleased our Indian brethren than we could scarce get away from them in time to answer our names at retreat or roll-call. The wigwams of the Sioux are well furnished, and everything is kept scrupulously neat and clean — the accommodations and comforts being far superior to those Uncle Sam allows his soldiers, who labor so hard to protect his youthful Territories and unfledged States. Were they at the present time, to become troublesome, the United States would have a hard foe to handle, as they are all well armed, and skilled in the use of weapons, and their black eyes and firm lips tell of courage and determination. But they are peaceable, and if fairly treated will long remain so, though I think any attempt to infringe upon their rights would cause the war cry to ring from the Platte River to the Canada lines.[6]

We have encamped upon the Platte river every night since we left Fort Kearney, and have generally met with good grass, so that our horses have fared very well. Wood, however, is very scarce, and we have been compelled to use "Buffalo chips" [7] to cook our food. When we get into camp and pitch our tents, the order "Every man for Buffalo chips" is given, and away we go to collect that, to many of us, novel fuel. Some carry it in by armfuls, others take their blankets and fill them with it, while others again take a wagon, man it and drag it over the prairie till it is loaded, and then with cheers and yells, run it

---

[6] For a sympathetic picture of the Sioux and a pessimistic view of the future of their relations with the United States government see Burton, *City of the Saints,* pp. 120–23.

[7] The sun-dried excrement of buffalo.

into camp. These "Buffalo chips" make excellent "fire-wood," and when we can obtain a little cedar or cottonwood to mix with them, they make a much warmer fire than the best hickory or oak of Pennsylvania. To be sure we cannot make "ash-cakes" of our flour, when we use this prairie firewood, but then we find it far superior to any other fuel for the purpose of baking "flap-jacks," so we put the best face on the matter we can, and declare that the former are "nowhere" when the latter are on hand. But when we can neither obtain wood [n]or buffalo chips, you will think we are hard put to, and there you would be right. For two days we were thus situated, and had to subsist on hard bread, raw pork and river water, the latter the best of the three, and the only article of which we had as much as we wanted. But we must "get used" to hard times, and I presume before many of us are free again we will often have to follow this semi-starvation mode of living, or starve outright. However, we have taken our chance, and must await the revolution of the wheel, and though we may starve the glory remains — to be reaped by lazy cadets and epauletted cowards.

A word for "Ash Hollow." Ash Hollow is one of the meanest, most contemptible pieces of work that Nature has attempted in this part of creation. If ugliness be picturesque, then Ash Hollow is picturesque, and *vice versa*. The hills of fine sand rise on the South bank of the Platte, and between them Ash Hollow lies. It is destitute of herbage or shrubbery, and as far as the eye can reach there is nothing

Looking north across Ash Hollow.

but sand and water. The sand rises here and there in little hills, and
when the wind blows it drives the light sand in every direction. There
is nothing interesting in it — everything is dull and lifeless.[8] Yet here
we must pass the night — must spread our blankets upon the sand
and take whatever comes. Uninteresting as it is, there is a shanty
away up towards its western extremity where an enterprising individual sells tobacco, cigars and whiskey at astonishing prices, and
by the way our boys rush up to his establishment, I judge he is doing
a brisk business. But we have marched twenty-five miles to-day, and
I am tired and sleepy, so, I think, I will close my letter, and leave it at
the aforementioned shanty, as long before he wakes to-morrow morning, we will have started again for

UTAH.

[8] Ash Hollow lies in the valley of the Platte River about 150 miles below Fort
Laramie. Here, in 1854, Colonel W. S. Harney attacked a Sioux village and killed
eighty-six (mostly women and children) and took seventy hostages in a misdirected
retaliation for the killing of an officer and thirty-two men. For an insight into
other travelers' reactions to Ash Hollow, see Robert L. Munkres, "Ash Hollow:
Gateway to the High Plains," *Annals of Wyoming* 42 (1970): 5–43.

Ft. Laramie, Nebraska Territory.

Fort Laramie
August 13, 1858
[6]

The sixth column arrived here to-day, having made the journey from Fort Kearney — a distance of about three hundred and fifty miles — in twenty days. This is rather an improvement on the Alexandrian movements of our column when under the command of Major Emory. Then we averaged about seven miles a day, and since Major Paul heard of peace, we have averaged over seventeen miles a day, and I think our men are in much better condition now, than they were when we moved at Emory's favorite snail-like pace. We will lie here two or three days and then again strike our tents and off again for Utah. It is thought that we can make the journey, from here to Salt Lake City, in about thirty-five days, so that our travelling will be over before the winter sets in, though I anticipate many cold fingers and blue noses ere we reach the Mormon Jerusalem. And we are illy prepared to encounter such, for more than one half of the command is bare-footed, and but few of us can boast a whole pair of trousers or a jacket complete. We had hoped to obtain fresh clothing at Laramie, but I am sorry to say that the Quarter Master's store is entirely empty.[1] Many of our men have spent their money for whiskey and now find themselves lacking necessary articles to make a chilly night comfortable. Though your correspondent, when a free man, was never accused of excessive prudence, he is now better prepared to meet old winter than any man in the company, having a whole pair of boots, a blanket and a buffalo robe. By this you can see what constitutes a soldier's luxuries. You would not deem such articles any

---

[1] E. B. Babbitt, the assistant quartermaster officer at Fort Laramie, complained to Colonel D. D. Tompkins, the assistant quartermaster general, that it was impracticable to get clothing for troops from the supply trains en route to Utah. See Babbitt to Tompkins, July 26, 1858, "A.G. Letters," roll 584.

thing extr[a]ordinary, I presume, but then you are not a soldier on a four month's march across the western plains — with the rough winds and biting frosts of the Rocky Mountains staring you in the face — with no other mode of carrying your wardrobe, etc., than upon your horse.

Fort Laramie is quite a respectable post, the barracks are neatly constructed, clean, and apparently recently white-washed. It has all the necessary appurtenances for an artillery post, and is in every way far superior to the trifling affair known as Fort Kearney. It is garrisoned by two companies of artillery, commanded by Brevet Colonel Monroe.[2] It is situated on the Laramie river, a small stream that joins the Platte a short distance below, and is surrounded by beautiful scenery. Around it rise high hills, covered with herbage and shrubbery, each hill rising in an almost circular form to a peak, and between them tumble streams of clear, pure water. The Fort itself is built in a prairie flat, that extends for several miles, through which rolls Laramie river. On the whole it is as pleasant a spot as I have met with in the march, and am surprised that Uncle Sam did not think it too good to put soldiers in.

Encamped a short distance above the Fort are several companies of volunteers, who have been through the entire Utah campaign, and are now returning to their homes, perfectly satisfied with frontier soldiering. They give a very poor account of the condition of the Mormons, declaring that many of them are almost in a state of nudity, and that notwithstanding all the fertility of Salt Lake Valley, the prospect of starvation during the coming winter, stares its inhabitants in the face. The Mormons were too intent upon the incendiary movements of their prophets and high priests, to give the proper attention to their crops, and the result is what might be expected, a barren harvest. That their report is true, I am inclined to believe, from the statements of a party of Mormons we passed about a week since. They were returning to the States, and declared that had they known what they would have to endure in Utah, Brigham Young and ten thousand angels could not have induced them to go there. "But being

[2] Brevet Lieutenant Colonel John Munroe, with companies A, C, and I, Fourth Artillery, and the headquarters band, took command of Fort Laramie on August 2, relieving Brevet Major Isaac Lynde of Company F, Seventh Infantry. See Munroe to the Adjutant General, August 6, 1858, "AG Letters," roll 584.

there," said they, "we did the best we could, until the prospect of next winter appalled us." "I have left all behind," said an old man. "I went there wealthy — I return a beggar. I took two sons with me, but the Lord of Hosts gathered them to Him. My lot is hard, but as Job saith, 'The Lord giveth, and the Lord taketh away, blessed be the name of the Lord.' " "My faith failed to sustain me," said another. "Life among the Gentiles is preferable to death among the Saints." I asked about Brigham, and why he did not return if they truly represented affairs in their territory. "God is great," they replied, "and will sustain his chosen ones. The ravens fed the ancient prophet — the widow's slender store became a mighty store in famine time — multitudes fed upon a few loaves and fishes, and yet many fragments remained." I could not but admire their obstinacy in proclaiming Brigham the chosen one of Heaven, but I think that when we read of him and the ravens the matter will be somewhat different from that of the ancient prophet to which they referred. But when I get there I can tell you better.

For about a week past, our journey has been through an interesting part of the country. Five days ago, we forded the Platte river where it was about a mile and a half wide, and deep enough to reach our knees as we sat upon our horses. The Infantry crossed first — stripped to the skin, and carrying their knapsacks slung on their muskets. At their head marched Lieut. Bootes, of whom I have heretofore spoken, cheering on the men as they splashed through the water. (By the way, speaking of Bootes, reminds me of a conundrum current in camp: Why should company B, (of which he is commander), never be barefooted? Because they always have Bootes (boots) with them.) When the Infantry were about half way across the stream, we entered, and for a while the entire Sixth column were wading the river, presenting an excellent opportunity for a party of hostile Indians to give us "Hail Columbia." We got across the river without anything unpleasant occurring, except some of our men being thrown into the water by their horses; yet a ducking in the Platte can scarce be called unpleasant, for the water is warm, and though muddy, is the most charming bathing place I ever had the good fortune to meet with. For three days we traveled in sight of the "Chimney Rock," [3]

[3] Chimney Rock, made of yellowish friable marl, was a thin, perpendicular, and quasi-conical shaft which stood about 2½ miles from the south bank of the

A sketch of Chimney Rock as it appeared in 1857.

and one night encamped within eight miles of it. Next day I paid it a visit. It is a column of hard clay, I should say, though the materials of which it is composed resemble Bath brick, and rises for one hundred and twenty-two feet perpendicular. It is about twenty feet in diameter at the base, and across the top it measures sixteen feet and a half. It is situated on a circular mound, the top of which is nearly two hundred feet above the level of the prairie — making the top of the spire over three hundred feet from the ground. By the aid of my spurs, which I strapped on my toes, and the pin of my Lariat rope, I reached the summit and viewed the country for miles around. It requires a great deal of perseverance to ascend Chimney Rock, but the fine prospect it affords amply repays the trouble. After enjoying the landscape for some time, I commenced the descent, but that proved the most difficult task, for I suddenly found myself making towards the ground rather faster than was convenient — leaving my picket pin sticking about half way up the column. I struck the mound and then rolled down to the plain, tearing my shirt to tatters but receiving no serious injury. Satisfied with the adventure, I mounted my horse and rode off after our command. Day before yesterday we passed through

Platte River. Burton wrote that it had originally towered 150 to 200 feet above the apex of its foundation, but in 1858 was only 35 feet high. See Burton, *City of the Saints*, pp. 92–93.

Scott's Bluffs, a wild, romantic spot, where a man named Scott was left to die some years ago, and from whom it takes its name.[4] The Bluffs rise on each side of the road — which is rather serpentine in its windings — for about a mile, stern, bold and perpendicular. They are composed of hard baked clay — the same material as the Chimney Rock — and are covered with stunted trees and sun-burnt grass. I looked in vain for a stone along the road between the Bluffs, and could see nothing but the hard clay, cut in square blocks as regular as though it were the work of human art and ingenuity. Yesterday we passed a spot where an Indian Chief, a United States officer, and twenty-nine soldiers are buried. Eight years ago the Sioux and other tribes had a great feast there, and thirty soldiers and an officer participated therein. The soldiers brought liquor with them, and the officer became drunk. For some fancied insult, he drew his sword and killed Alabama Bear, a greatly respected war chief. This act so enraged the Indians that they set upon their white guests and slew all but one, who escaped to Laramie, to tell the tale. The Sioux buried their chief according to the customs of their tribe, and in one hole they buried his murderer and the murderer's followers. This tale the Sioux tell of the bloody affair, and when their war-council gathers, the spirit of the Alabama Bear, they say, arises and tells them to beware of the white man, for through too much trust in them he fell.[5]

[4] Named for a member of a westbound party who was taken ill or wounded and abandoned by his companions. The next summer one of the party suddenly came across Scott's skeleton. Supposedly he had crawled sixty miles from where they left him.

[5] This is a rather distorted version of the Grattan massacre. Brevet Second Lieutenant John L. Grattan had boasted that he could crush the Sioux with a small body of infantry and a howitzer. In August 1854 a Mormon emigrant came to Fort Laramie with the report that a straying cow had been butchered by an Indian from one of the Sioux camps on the Platte River. Conquering Bear, the head chief of the Indian involved, asked Lieutenant Fleming, the commander of the fort, to postpone action until the Indian Agent arrived and restitution could be made. But Fleming yielded to Grattan's request to arrest the offending Indian. The next day Grattan arrived in Conquering Bear's camp followed by twenty-seven privates, two noncommissioned officers, and an interpreter. The soldiers trained a twelve-pounder mountain gun and a twelve-pounder howitzer on the encampment while negotiations for the surrender of the cattle-killing Indian proceeded. When Conquering Bear refused to give up the man, Grattan ordered his men to fire. The chief was killed, but the artillery was aimed too high to damage the encampment. The Indians then attacked the soldiers, routed them, and wiped them out. See Utley, *Frontiersmen in Blue*, pp. 113–14.

We are still in the Sioux country, and many of them daily visit our camp. They continue friendly, and though we are at least two hundred miles from the place where the Indian whipped the four dragoons, in fair fight, they all know the story, and say approvingly, "Good white man; show fair play." One of them today presented me with a beautiful pair of mocassins, which I would send to you if I could do so. They do work of this kind so neatly, and I have seen some beaded buffalo robes, that had work upon them that would astonish the most active civilized worker in embroidery. Soon we shall leave the Sioux, and pass into the land of the Pawnees, and Crows, and Blackfeet, where I presume, our relations with our red skinned breathren, will be of an entirely different nature. For my part, I much prefer having them friendly than be constantly on the watch for a mocassin track, or a plumed head-dress — being somewhat officer-like in that matter.

This afternoon a stampede was got up among our horses, and about forty of them scattered pell-mell over the prairie. Whether it was an Indian trick to obtain a fresh stock of horse-flesh or not, I cannot say, but if it was, I fear it has proved only too successful, for only about ten have as yet been re-captured. My horse — a noble, high spirited animal — is yet among the missing, and night is fast approaching. If he is not caught before dark, by the time morning comes the Indians will have him, and your correspondent will probably have to foot it from here to Salt Lake City. This will be rather unpleasant, but "what maun be maun be," and I presume I will have to "grin and bear it."

I presume our Democratic friends are taking great credit from the peaceful settlement of the Mormon affair, to be set down to the account of James Buchanan and the people, but if what some returning soldiers declare — that Brigham could not muster a thousand fighting men at any time to oppose the United States, you will perceive that, like many other humbugs of the day, there is a "great cry and very little wool" about this tremendous "rebellion," "high treason," &c., in

UTAH.

On the March
Aug. 21, 1858

[7]

Gold mines have been discovered about a hundred and fifty miles southwest of Fort Laramie, and teamsters are "quitting" and soldiers deserting to seek their fortunes in this new El Dorado.[1] California and Australia, and all the other gold-producing localities, are thrown entirely in the shade, by this newly discovered "land of promise." When I left, on Tuesday morning, the entire world of Fort Laramie was in a state of feverish excitement, and nothing was spoken of but "heaps of gold," "rich diggings," "fortunes in a month," &c. It is said that the miners there are making from fifteen to fifty dollars per day, each, and that there is "lots of room" for others. This rich prospect is very tempting, when compared with the eleven and twelve dollars per month paid to the soldier, and, as is quite natural, many of them have, within the past few days, taken "French leave" and are, as the Articles of War say, "liable to arrest as deserters." Three men deserted from our company, last night, taking with them their arms, accoutrements, horses, etc., and by this time, are, no doubt, far on their way to fortune's new-found clime. If they succeed, very well; but if Uncle Sam ever gets his hands upon them, fifty lashes, well laid on with a "raw hide," is the least they can expect, provided, of course, that they are not wealthy enough to give each member of the Court Martial a keg of whiskey. What truth there is in these reports of the great wealth of this new Eldorado, I do not know, but I presume there is some foundation for them, as the stories told of their wealth, and of the rich crops gathered by the miners, are very straight forward and uncontradictory. When I first heard of them, I thought the rumor too trifling to notice, but at every ranch we pass, the gold mania is raging, and the talk is about "selling out and going to the mines." So you may

---

[1] This started the Pikes Peak gold rush.

50

tell the adventurous young men of your city that away in the far West they can reap a golden harvest, if they show industry and enterprise. Were I not a soldier, I would visit them, but our route lies in a different direction, and I am bound to "follow the leader."

For the past four days we have been travelling through a portion of creation entirely different from that met with in the first part of our journey. Instead of the flat, level prairie we have, or are in a country of hills and hollows; in fact, since we left Fort Laramie, the road has been a mere succession of up and down hill, not one quarter of a mile of level have we as yet encountered. On all sides round, tower high hills covered with shrubbery and stunted pines, and hemlocks. The cool breezes of the mountains fan our cheeks while the sun pours its stream of bronzing heat upon us and the dry dust rises from our horses' feet, almost blinding us in its intensity. Thus, you see we have our comfort and discomfort combined. To the latter we have become long since accustomed, and on the whole, we are the gainers by the acquisition of the former. The nights are considerably colder than they were at the first part of our journey; though the sun blazes fiercer during the day. But myself and my "bunky," Fred Smith,[2] "a noble specimen of the American soldier,["] join our blankets and laugh the cold air to scorn, and shake defiance at its power.

The scenery that we have been viewing since we left Laramie amply repays the sacrifice a man makes when he sells his liberty to become a soldier. On the second day out, we encamped on an island formed by the division and junction of a mountain stream. Above us towered the hills, their tops covered with clouds, while we lay among the tall grass, our white tents forming a beautiful contrast with the dark, waving green. Over our heads hung huge rocks, that seemed every moment to threaten to roll down upon us and annihilate our tiny force. But, Dame nature had chained them fast, and though rugged and frowning, we were safe and secure beneath their ruffled brows. The banks of the creek were covered with small cherry trees,

[2] First Sergeant Frederick H. Smith, age 26, was born in Prussia. He was five feet nine inches tall, had hazel eyes, black hair, and a dark complexion. There is no record of his Florida service (see p. 55) — perhaps it was done under another name. A machinist as a civilian, he enlisted at Boston on April 10, 1858. Subsequently he was assigned to Company I, Second Dragoons, and deserted on September 29, 1859. See "Register of Enlistments in the U.S. Army, 1798–1914," microcopy 233, roll 25, R.G. 94, National Archives, and chap. 26.

that were literally covered with fruit. Upon these cherries our men feasted unsparingly, and many of them laid in a stock for further service, a precaution entirely unnecessary, as we have ever since encamped among the same fruit, in greater abundance, if possible, than where we first met with them. The march that day was for about twenty miles, through a country entirely destitute of water, the sun at a boiling heat, and the dry dust filling our eyes at every step. When we had marched about the distance mentioned, we reached a couple of springs of clear cold water, that bubbled through the sand in sparkling globules, reminding one in that parched region of Byron's

"Though a desert should surround me,
It hath springs that may be won." [3]

Here we halted, opened our haversacks, and eat a few biscuits with the clear water, and then off again, and marched sixteen miles further, making a march of thirty-six miles that day before we reached a fitting camping place for mounted men.

That we are in earnest now in our endeavors to reach Utah, you may suppose from the marching we have done for the last three days. Wednesday, thirty-six miles; Thursday, twenty-nine miles; and Friday, thirty-two miles — making ninety seven miles in three days. Our officers do not much relish the thought of passing through the Rocky Mountains in the winter, and so push on at a rapid rate. To us this is very agreeable, as our horses have to bear the brunt; but as weeks' marching, at the rate we are now going, will, I fear, exhaust the energies of the infantry corps, I pity the poor fellows as they trudge along after their officers, each doing his best to keep good spirits in circulation. They start two hours before us in the morning, and as we pass by them on the road, they look at us with envious eyes that say as plain as words: "Who would be a foot-soldier?" Not I, for one. When them come into camp they are the most forlorn objects I ever saw — limping, dejected and dusty. Their officers are mounted, and do not feel the fatigue of the march, and the comfort of a soldier is too trifling for an epauletted coat to be troubled with.[4]

[3] From Lord Byron's poem, "My Boat is on the Shore," lines 11–12, published in 1817.

[4] For a brief account of the march of the Sixth Column as experienced by an infantryman, see the letter of Hiram W. Studley, Company D, Seventh Infantry,

To-night we are encamped in a little grassy spot between the hills, through which rolls a small stream, teeming with fish that gambol sprightly over the sandy bottom. Our camp is encompassed with cherry trees and goose berry bushes laden with fruit, and here and there a wild currant bush raises itself and invites us to come and take. And as I write, the entire column is making a foray upon them that would shock the nerves of those delicate individuals who consider "fruit unhealthy at this season of the year." The bushes resound with shouts of triumph, and the merry laugh rings all around, for anything good is so great a rarity that our soldiery consider a jollification demanded by the bountiful liberality with which nature has bestowed the luscious fruit.

Our camp was the scene of a tremendous excitement the other night. About half-past eleven we were suddenly aroused by the infantry drums beating the "long roll," and our bugles sounding "To Arms." In an instant the whole camp was in an uproar. Men, half-dressed, tumbled out of their tents with their arms in their hands; officers rushed hither and thither with their sabres drawn; and Major Paul sprang forward in his night-dress demanding the cause of the disturbance. But no one knew; no one could give the least information on the subject. After considerable inquiry it was discovered that one of the drummers was drunk, and had commenced to practice the "long roll" on his own responsibility. This quieted the nerves of our officers, and some of them declared they were "d—— glad it was nothing serious." The drummer being a mere boy — eleven years old — was pardoned. As this was his first offence, the Major gave him a lecture about sobriety, etc. But the boy is a keen chap, and seeing that Major P. was in a kindly humor, he said: "If I had had reason to beat the "long roll,["] (the approach of the enemy) I fear that it would not have been as agreeable to you, sir, as the discovery that it was a mere drunken freak." The lad was impudent, but he spoke the truth, and the remark applies to many other officers now *en route* for

UTAH.

dated Camp Floyd, U.T., October 16, 1859, "Letter Describing a March to Utah in 1859," *Annals of Iowa*, 3rd series, 13 (1923): 611–18.

Camp on Sweetwater Creek
August 27th, 1858
[8]

The sixth column arrived here to-day. Sweetwater is a rapid-running stream, about forty yards wide where we struck it. It is quite cool and pleasant in its taste. Where it got the name I do not know, as there is nothing peculiar in its flavor. I have come to the conclusion that it was named by an Englishman or a Frenchman, as the former always calls England *Great* Britain, while it is notoriously diminutive, and the latter calls his native country *la belle France*, while, to my notion, it is superlatively ugly. But Sweetwater is beyond question, a pleasant stream, and we are told that its banks are well covered with grass as far as we follow its course. It is about one hundred and sixty miles from Fort Laramie, which distance we have marched in eleven days, averaging a little less than fifteen miles per day. It is about one hundred and fifty miles from here to Fort Bridger, where our troops lay last winter, and where a portion of the infantry corps of our column is to remain. The rest of us are to go to Cedar Valley, about one hundred and eighty miles further, and fifty miles the other side of Salt Lake City, where we will rest the ensuing winter. Thus, though we are now seventy-six days' march from Fort Leavenworth, we have yet three hundred and thirty miles to march, and that, too, over the hardest part of the route — the roughest road, the least grass, wood and water.

Since I last wrote to you we have passed through a country much similar to that I then spoke of. The only difference is that grass is still scarcer and the roads dustier than ever. The length of our marches has dwindled down considerably, and has almost reached the Emory standard. Our commander has ascertained that we are not going to Oregon, and that the Utah Indians have become troublesome; and, consequently, the hurry that prompted the "General" to sound at five o'clock A.M., is over,[1] and we are taking the matter as easy as possible. Besides, our infantry brethren are become footsore, and cannot keep up with us at the rate we moved when Major Paul first took command. But I do not object to this, as the country is quite picturesque, and I can find time for many a run over the hills and through the valleys, gathering curious stones and plants and indulging in many pleasures not altogether soldierly, as their chief pleasure is supposed to consist of getting dinner and playing poker. But, withal, I do not like the idea of travelling through the Rocky Mountain country in the winter time, and we already feel the hoary-headed fellow's breath when we turn out at "reveille." Ugh! but we shiver, when we throw off our blankets and rush out into the cold air to respond "here," as our names are called. Fred Smith, my "bunky," is inured to this by a five years' campaign in the swamps of Florida, and he laughs at us green hands as we draw our great coats closely around us, and thrust our hands into our pockets to escape the biting chill. And this is in August; how it will be in October, I cannot say, but I expect that experience will render me fitted to give you an idea of it. But we will ere long become hardened to these hardships, and then in turn can laugh at the young hands, as Fred now does at us. It all comes in five years, you know, and then we hope to sit once more by the hearthfire of home and add tales of our own adventures to those of our grandfathers, as the little ones cluster around his knee to catch the sounds he breathes when he warms upon the subject of the days when he left his plough to fight the Britishers, who strove to shackle the young spirit of freedom that throbbed in the breast of every young American; and, as his story lengthens, his cheeks glow and his eyes sparkle with all the energy of youth, and he forgets that his hair is grizzled, and his limbs trembling beneath the weight of years. He lives once more in the scenes of his boyhood, and once more he rallies his fading energies, as he rises from his chair to —

"Shoulder his crutch, and show how fields were won." [2]

But I am rambling off the track I ought to follow, and it is time to draw the curb and bring my pen to its proper task. On the 23d inst.

[1] A drum beat or bugle signal for troops to prepare for a movement.

[2] From Oliver Goldsmith's poem, "The Deserted Village," line 158, published in 1770.

we met the famous Captain Marcy on his way to civilization, to rest himself after his long and tiresome march from New Mexico to Utah, with horses and mules for the army.[3] Capt. M. is a fine looking man, and seemed to bear well the fatigue of his late fatiguing journey. He was accompanied by two men only, and was making rapid strides Statesward. As he was not known to any of our officers, he did not halt, and so I had not the pleasure of hearing him speak. The same day we met with three infantry officers, going home on furlough, and they told us that the grass was very poor west of the Rocky Mountains; in fact, for one hundred and fifty miles not a blade of grass would be met with. They were in a glorious condition "deeply, darkly, beautifully blue," and before they left us, our officers, from the effects of frequent draughts of a suspicious-looking liquid that they carried in a demijohn, were rendered quite good-humored, and for the rest of the march that day, made the hills re-echo with promises to "bet their money on the bob-tail nag — du-da, du-da-day." [4] I do not say our officers were intoxicated, but they acted very eccentric for sober men, and the contents of afore-mentioned demijohn smelled somewhat like old Monongehala.[5] Be that as it may, I know that were a soldier to act as they did, he would have got in the guard house for being *drunk*.

On the 24th we met a party of sappers and miners returning from Utah. They were a fine looking body of men, sturdy and well-built. They seemed the embodiment of hardihood, and, although they had been almost constantly marching for over four months, they stepped along in a manner that would have charmed the heart of any of our prize pedestrians. They corroberated the stories of the officers we had met the day before, concerning the prospects for grass, &c., on the way before us. That day we camped away from the infantry part of our column, and being "ration day" another man and myself went for the provisions, with a wagon. On our way we got off the road, darkness having overtaken us, and rambled over the desert for over three hours, without the least substantial hope of finding our camp. About one o'clock A.M., we accidentally stumbled upon our tents, and found that

[3] See note 5 in the Introduction.

[4] Lines from Stephen Foster's song, "De Camptown Races," published in 1850.

[5] Old Monongahela was a favorite beverage of President Buchanan. See Klein, *President James Buchanan: A Biography*, p. 332.

the greatest excitement was prevalent there, it being feared that we had fallen into the hands of the red-skins, and that a party of men had been sent in search of us. We were overjoyed when we found ourselves safe, and you may well suppose that the boys were glad to see us back, as the prospect of travelling next day on an empty stomach stared them in the face, in case we did not return. To cap-sheaf[6] the affair, the men who went in search of us lost their way also, and did not overtake us until late the next evening. This afforded a great deal of fun to our infantry companies, but I think before we part with them the dragoons will make them "laugh on the other side of their face."

On the 25th we crossed the Platte for the second time and then bid it farewell striking off in a direction nearly opposite to its course. From the majestic river it was when we first met it, it has dwindled down to a petty stream, that scarce deserves the name of "creek" — many larger waters having that designation. But it is still muddy, and dashes along at a rapid rate, seething and foaming as it pours over its rocky bed. That night we encamped in a shady place, and had as pleasant an encampment as we have had since we passed Kearney. The next day nothing of interest occurred. We had a good camping place again, with plenty of grass, wood and water — all we require.

To-day, we encamped in a nice grassy spot, at the foot of an immense rocky hill that rises abruptly from the plain to the height of about three thousand feet. Fred Smith and myself scrambled up to the highest point, and had a good view of the country for many miles around. When we first set out, we deemed it but a trifling ascent, but when we reached the first ledges, from which, to those below we seemed to have almost reached the clouds.

> "Hills peeped o'er hills,
> And Alps o'er Alps arose."[7]

But we had set out with the determination of reaching the summit, and, though the hard rock presented a rather threatening front, we continued our journey. On we went, clambering from rock to rock,

---

[6] According to Eric Partridge, *A Dictionary of Slang and Unconventional English*, 5th ed. (1961), 1: 752, sheaf is incorrect for sheath. The expression dates from the late seventeenth century but was rare in the nineteenth century.

[7] From Alexander Pope's poem, "An Essay on Criticism," part 2, line 232, published in 1711.

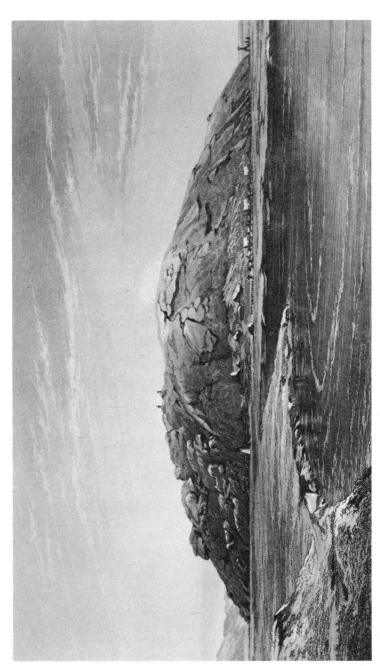

Independence Rock, from Frederick Piercy's Route from Liverpool to Great Salt Lake Valley.

jumping over yawning crevices; now creeping along the slippery face of the rock, and now sliding down the hill to gain the opposite side of a gulf that was too wide to leap. At one point we were almost baffled. For about twelve feet the rock was perpendicular; and, so far as we could see there was no crevice up which we could creep. But Smith, who is a strong, athletic man, was not going "to give it up so." Taking me — you know I am quite a light man — in his arms, he threw me up to the top of the rock. I then took off my belt and let the end of it down to him. Bracing myself, I held on to the belt like vengence, and in a trice Fred was by my side. This done, we trudged on, and when we reached the top we were nearly exhausted, and did not in the least envy John C. Fremont his famous ascent of what is known as Fremont Peak.[8] This ascending of steep hills and lofty peaks is well enough to read about, very pleasant to talk over after it is done, but not at all a matter of pleasure to do, especially when you have to do it within a stated time, or "be liable to arrest as a deserter," (vide the "Regulations"). 'Tis true that the glorious opportunity of viewing creation amply repays the toil, but when this is prefixed by a day's march through the dust of Nebraska Deserts, a man is much more likely to give up the pleasure to be gained in view of the obstacles to be conquered, than one who rests a day before he undertakes the task and goes to work fresh and unfatigued. But where "there's a will there's a way," you know, and when Fred and myself pull together, it is a tough tug that breaks us down. On the top of the rock we built a huge fire, which sent great bodies of smoke up into the air, forming clouds as it rose, and then floating away off to the westward. Our ascent was difficult enough for all practical purposes, but when we attempted the descent, the "tug of war" came. The great part of the way we were compelled to slide down upon our haunches, to the utter destruction of a pair of uniform pants, besides some scrathes that will keep me out of the saddle for some days to come. Shreds of sky blue were to be seen upon every sharp point that we slid over, and in some places the part of the body that comes next to the trowsers left its outside natural covering with the cloth. When we had nearly reached the foot of the

[8] Fremont Peak in the Wind River Mountains was named by Lieutenant John C. Fremont, of the United States Topographical Engineers, who led the first official expedition to the Rocky Mountains in 1842. See note 2, chap. 9 for more information on Fremont.

hill one of my feet caught between two rocks, and I was suspended by
the heel. Fred caught me by the shoulders and "jerked me out of my
boots," which went tumbling to the bottom of the crevice, entirely
beyond our reach. The worst of the matter is, that I had but one pair
of boots, and now I am compelled to go bobbing round with one boot
and one shoe — the latter being picked up by us on our way down.
On the whole we might alter the negro melody "Jim along Josey,"
and say "Such a getting down stairs I never did see." [9] The rock we
ascended is a scion of the mighty Rocky Mountain chain, and is
known in this locality as "Independence Rock." [10] It is composed of
immense boulders, heaped one upon the other. Someplaces it is strewn
with the remains of immense trees whose roots still show themselves
among the rocks, though from whence they drew their subsistence I
cannot see. There is, at the present time, not sufficient soil to grow a
corn stalk upon, where we met with huge trunks of trees, ten feet in
diameter. That it was at one time covered with vegetation is very
evident, but now it is hard, stern rock, without a single blade of grass,
or shrub, or flower upon its towering sides. Around it stand many
smaller rocks, like the satellites that dance in the train of the great
planets that bespangle the blue firmament. The hoary old monarch
stands high above the others, his head almost reaching the clouds, and
the smaller ones look towards him with veneration and respect. Grim,
stern and hard-featured he is, but there is a charm about him that
tempts one to make his acquaintance; he is very difficult of access, as
I found out, but once in his clutches you find it much harder to get
out — witness my torn trowsers and lacerated flesh. I have thus made
the acquaintance of one of old Rocky's children, and I hope soon to
know the old fellow himself. I promise myself some hearty runs over

9 "Jim Along Josey" as sung by Mr. John N. Smith. Arranged for the Piano
Forte, by an Eminent Professor, New York. Published by Firth & Hall, 1840. The
first verse and chorus goes as follows: "I's from Luci-an na as you all know,/ Dar
whare Jim along Josey's all de go,/ Dem niggers all rise when de bell does ring,/
And dis is de song dat they do sing./ Hey get a-long, get a-long Josey/ Hey get
a-long Jim a-long Joe!/ Hey get a-long, get a-long Josey/ Hey get a-long, Jim
a-long Joe!" See Hans Nathan, *Dan Emmett and the Rise of Early Negro Minstrelsy* (1962), pp. 435–38.

10 Independence Rock was a reddish gray turtleback stone that rose 155 feet
above the Sweetwater River. Located 171 miles beyond Fort Laramie, it was the
most famous landmark east of South Pass. Many travelers on the Oregon Trail
carved their names on the rock.

his ledges and through his rocky paths. By the next time I write to you, I shall probably be satisfied, as we are likely to be there in a few days. I have been told that we will have about four marches in the South Pass, so that I will have a fair opportunity of examining one of the greatest works of nature, as well as one of the most famous, from its connection with the name of Fremont, to be met on the route to

UTAH.

Camp of the Sixth Column
Near the South Pass
September 5th, 1858
[9]

Slowly and snail-like, the Sixth column drags its weary length along. To day we march six or seven-miles, and to-morrow we lay over, is the routine of our doings since my last letter. Lazy officers, weary men, and dusty roads are the cause of this; but think you if the officers were not lazy that the weariness of the men, or the almost insufferable dust of the roads, from which the officers are well protected, would prevent us from marching rapid marches? I think not. But there is another consideration. Major Paul, who is but a Major by brevet, receives full pay while in command. We are commanded by a Lieutenant, as are also the two other companies composing the column, and all three receive ten dollars per month extra, while acting as captains. When we arrive at our destination all this will be ended, and ten dollars is not to be "sneezed at." This latter view may account for the milk in the cocoa-nut. Yesterday, however, we, the dragoons, made a heavy march to find grass for our horses, and will lie here to-day and to-morrow, to allow the Infantry to come up to us again, and it is probable that they will have a "rest day," the day after. Our camp is in a nice little spot, hemmed in by hills covered with sage bushes. Where we are the grass is luxuriant, but outside of the one spot, about six acres in size, there is not a blade to be seen. I have not yet had time to stroll over the hills, and the mail is in sight, so I shall give you what I have up to date.

On the 27th of August I last wrote to you, after a delightful scramble over some of the mountain peaks of the Great West, interspersed with "ground and lofty tumbling" that left me aching bones for a week after. As I then anticipated, I was kept out of the saddle for two days, and even then it was almost torture to keep my seat. Fortunately, I am now fit for duty of any kind and am prepared to scale even Fremont's peak itself, if I can get an opportunity to do so.[1] I fear, however, it is useless to hope so, as the peak is too far distant from our route to expect to get a chance to visit it. But this I am resolved upon, to clamber up its sides and see if I cannot, as the great John Charles did, get my toe nails froze off and catch a humble-bee on the summit before I again set foot upon the soil of good old Pennsylvania. By the way, it appears to me, that if our worthy explorer was to be elected President of this great country, it would not be more than an adequate reward for the sufferings he must have endured when he made his winter trip through the South Pass — labor and suffering alone considered. But, when we view him as a benefactor of his country, and as a man of science and practical utility, does he not soar far above the pigmies who so violently traduced him during the last Presidential campaign? As usual, I am off the track I ought to follow. But who can avoid thinking and speaking of Fremont when you are marching over the route he did, when he gave us that much-travelled causeway — the South Pass. In fact, I sometimes find myself singing the campaign song of 1856, and invoking the people to let our watchword be "Free Speech, Free Press, Free Soil, Free Men, Fremont and victory." Nor am I alone, as every one is discussing the merits and demerits of the "Pathfinder." [2]

Our journey for some days past has been a constantly ascending inclined plane, and every night we have encamped on more elevated ground than we did the night previous. As we ascend, it grows still colder, and now we have ice water to drink every morning — in fact, it is so cold that whiskey froze in our canteens on the night of the first of September. But the days are still warm, my thermometer standing on the 2d instant at ninety degrees. The roads continue dusty, and goggles command a premium. Having been so unfortunate as to have

---

[1] See note 8, chap. 8.

[2] John C. Fremont (1813–90) won fame for his explorations and surveys of the West while a member of the army's Topographical Engineers. During the Mexican War he played a prominent role in the conquest of California, but was subsequently court-martialed, pardoned, and resigned from the army. After the war he made two additional crossings of the continent, served briefly as a senator from California, and in 1856 was the first presidential candidate of the newly organized Republican party. He lost to Buchanan by 500,000 votes, and some persons such as "Utah" fully expected that he would again be the candidate in 1860. Instead Lincoln was nominated and elected.

mine broken when I tumbled down Independence Rock, I am now completely at the mercy of the dust. But as my place is near the head of the column, I do not suffer much, though the poor devils in the rear "catch Jessy." [3] I have seen some almost completely blind, on our coming into camp, while their hair and whiskers were covered with the fine dust, as the wigs of our forefathers used to be with powder. This dust causes many laughable incidents. Our Lieutenant's name is Berry,[4] and we have a Berry in the ranks. One day the Lieutenant rode to the rear and told one of the men to get him a canteen of water, "Who are you?" demanded the man, not recognizing the voice. "Berry," replied the officer. "Well, I think," retorted the man, thinking it was private B., "that you were a goose-berry to ask me to carry water for you." Again, Major Paul called upon one of our men to lend him his horse, the Major's having given out on the way and the soldier demanded who he was. "Paul" replied the Major. "Paul to be blowed," was the reply, "I would not lend him to *Peter* were he to ask for it." The officers were indignant at first, but of hearing the matter explained, let the poor blind fellow off with a lecture.

We have met with no grass for three days, the ground being entirely covered with a species of sage, that grows to the height of about four feet, and interweaves its branches so that it is impossible to pass through it. It is most excellent firewood, and gives a clear bright flame that rises and curls in fantastic shapes through the air, as the wood crackles like the distant echo of musketry. It emits no smoke and its ashes are as white and fine as those of the most delicate cigar. It emits a pleasant odor as it burns, and I ground some of it fine and smoked it in my pipe as an experiment. Its flavor thus used is somewhat like that of scented tobacco, though it has the same effect on the mouth that smoking paper has. The proper name of this shrub I do not know, but we call it "wild sage."

Our lot often falls in romantic looking spots. Three nights ago we encamped near an overhanging rock, that seemed to threaten every

[3] To give a person jessy was to thrash him. See Partridge, *A Dictionary of Slang*, 5th ed., 1: 437.

[4] Thomas J. Berry graduated from West Point in 1857 and was made a brevet second lieutenant in the First Dragoons. A year later he was commissioned as second lieutenant in the Second Dragoons. During the Civil War he was a lieutenant colonel in the Confederate Army.

instant to tumble from its position and overwhelm everything on the plain beneath. My tent, which is on the extreme right of the camp, was immediately under the rock, and sometimes I fancied I saw the monster tremble as though he were about to spring from his elevation, and crush my canvas castle to the earth. I was too busy that day to make an ascension, and Fred was on guard, so that I cannot give you an account of the appearance of its summit.

On the 30th I was detached to watch for the mail from America, as our boys say when they speak of the States, and while waiting in the roadside for it, a Mormon train, *en route* for Salt Lake, came up. There were about forty men, and nearly three times as many women in the train. The head of the party, who rode a splendid horse and carried a German rifle before him on the saddle, halted and bid me "good day." I entered into a conversation with him about his journey, etc., and he told me that it was a train of Danish Mormons sent over to see the country, and that if they reported favorably, one half of the Kingdom of Denmark would soon be in the land of the "Latter Day Saints." He contended that the United States misunderstood the Mormons, and he thought the Mormons misunderstood the United States. He said that his brethren wanted nothing but freedom of conscience, and the privilege of worshipping God in their own manner. Some black sheep in the flock might wish rebellion, rapine and murder, but the vast majority carried in their bosoms an inherent respect for the land of Washington, that could never be extinguished though Brigham himself should head the anarchists. "In our native country," he said, "we were taught to revere the Mighty Republic of the Western Hemisphere — the young giant, that trampled despotism almost to death — and when we reach her shores it is with the resolve to obey her laws, to love her people and to defend her constitution.["] The Mormons were afar off from our people of different persuasions, and he thought they would remain isolated until their intentions were properly understood and appreciated. They admitted polygamy, but very few practiced it, and he thought it would soon be abandoned altogether, except as a matter of belief and a portion of their creed. "We are not libertines or debauchees," he said, "and have no wish to indulge in anything not essential to our happiness. One wife is enough for any man, and this is the view of many of our brethren." He said that if the General Government properly understood the Mormon character, there would be no need of sending the soldiers to preserve peace at the point of the bayonet and the edge of the sabre. "I, for one," he said, "would rather die by the hands of my own brother than raise my voice in opposition to the laws and constitution of this glorious constellation of liberty." He spoke considerably in this strain, and did not leave me till his train was some miles ahead. The train consisted of thirty ox-teams, and were well supplied with everything necessary to a journey across the Plains. They had also articles of household furniture sufficient for the outfit of several dwellings, and were in the best spirits imaginable. Some of the children tarried awhile with their leader, and were greatly pleased with my sabre, which I loaned them to examine, little thinking that I was one of the "bold soldier boys" who enlisted for the purpose of "playing thunder" with their brethren in Utah. I was much pleased with the conversation of the leader, and have formed a much higher estimate of the Mormon character than I formerly had. Their women, however, did not strike me favorably, coming as I do from the good old Keystone State, where a homely woman would make the fortune of Barnum. Of nearly a hundred and fifty, there was not one among them who would not come under the head of — well, ugly is an unpleasant term to apply to the fair sex, but I must tell the truth. At home I know at least a dozen fair damsels whom I would have no objection to bring under the Mormon doctrine; but if these I met are a specimen of Mormon beauty, one is more than I want. The men, on the contrary, were fine looking fellows, tall, erect and well-formed; their handsome faces adorned with neatly trimmed black whiskers and moustaches — there was not a bare-faced man in the crowd.

The same day a Yankee Mormon passed me. He had a horse hitched to a light cart, and said he was going to Utah according to American ideas of travelling. He had come from Leavenworth in twenty days, and was going to make "the city" in eight more. His horse drew the provisions and he trudged alongside, whistling Yankee Doodle, or chanting a Mormon hymn. He said that in a few years Uncle Sam would recognize Utah as one of his most promising children, and that polygamy would soon be as great a power in our National Government as slavery now is, and that he would not be surprised if Brigham Young or Doctor Bernhisel[5] was the next candidate of the Democracy for President. He said that he was a Mormon, heart and soul, and that he expected, ere he was a year in Utah, to be either a high priest or a delegate to Congress. I said I did not think our bachelor President was ever likely to countenance Mormonism, as he did not appear to be favorable even to our moderate custom of taking one wife, consequently he could not be expected to go as far as the Saints do. "Bah," said he "your logic is not worth a straw." He views matrimony as Pope did education:

'A little learning is a dangerous thing,
Drink deep or taste not the Pierrian spring.' [6]

"More than that," he continued, "it is a domestic institution, and Buck don't meddle with matters of that sort." "What would you do," I asked, "if we were to attempt to put down your practice of polygamy and other peculiar doctrines?" "Well, I do not know," he replied, "but I think I would side with the soldiers and get appointed Chief Justice, and then declare polygamy legal." He was evidently a cute one, and, unlike the Danish emigrants, prompted by other considerations than those of liberty of conscience and loyalty to the government of this country. But we find such people everywhere, and it is not at all to the discredit of our Mormon cousins to say that there are villains, hypocrites, tricksters, agitators, and demagogues among the good and honest people of

UTAH.

[5] John M. Bernhisel (1799–1881) was trained and practiced as a physician before his conversion to Mormonism. He was ordained a bishop in 1841 and rose high in the councils of the church. After the Mormons settled in Utah he became their agent to Congress and later the first territorial delegate. In 1852 he tried unsuccessfully to get President Millard Fillmore to send a commission to Utah to investigate conditions there. For a recent account of his career see Gwynn W. Barrett, "Dr. John M. Bernhisel: Mormon Elder in Congress," *Utah Historical Quarterly* 36 (1968): 143–67.

[6] From Alexander Pope's "Essay on Criticism," part 2, line 15.

Fort Bridger, Utah Territory
September 11, 1858
[10]

The Sixth column arrived here to-day, having made the journey from Fort Leavenworth in ninety-one days. The distance is thought to be about one thousand miles, and according to this calculation we have made a little over ten miles a day — tremendous marching that, eh? Bridger is well situated, in a pleasant valley between the clay hills of Utah. The Fort proper is only large enough to contain two companies, but quarters for eight companies are in progress.[1] Immediately around the Fort grass is very scarce, but good pasturage can be found at the distance of five miles. Our horses are "on herd" about six miles from camp, and I understand that the grass is very good there, although I have not yet been out to see. At the Fort there are three companies of Infantry, under the command of Col. Cranby,[2] and two companies of the Second Dragoons, under the command of

---

[1] Fort Bridger was established in 1842 or 1843 by Jim Bridger, the famous mountain man and fur trapper, and Louis Vasquez, his partner, as a trading post for emigrant trains. It was purchased in 1853 by a Mormon named Lewis Robison (also known as Lewis Robinson or Jack Robinson) who was presumably acting as an agent for Brigham Young. When the Mormons began to settle in the area of the Green River and its tributaries, the fort served as an important center of their activities. In 1857, amid the rising tensions between Brigham Young and the federal government, the Mormons burned Fort Bridger. Colonel Albert Sidney Johnston established his headquarters there in 1857 in anticipation of military operations in Utah. The fort was rebuilt and used as a military post until 1878 and again in 1880–90.

[2] The reference is to Edward R. S. Canby (1815–73) who graduated from West Point in 1839 and who served in the Second Seminole and the Mexican Wars. In 1855 he was promoted to the regular rank of major and took command of the Tenth Infantry at Carlisle Barracks, Pennsylvania. Two years later he led his regiment to Utah as a part of Johnston's punitive force. When the Mormon difficulties ended, Canby was ordered to assume command of Fort Bridger.

68

Major Sibley,[3] the patentee of "Sibley's tent," [4] which is now coming into general use in the army — the former being commanding officer of the post. I understand that company "I" of the Seventh Infantry, which has accompanied us here, is to be stationed at this post. This will reduce our column to two companies — one Dragoons and one Infantry. With this slender force we are to proceed to Cedar Valley — one hundred and eighty miles further — and go into winter quarters.

The soldiers stationed at Fort Bridger have a perfect little paradise of their own in the midst of a howling wilderness. Several streams of clear, cold water roll through the valley in which it is built, and everything necessary to a soldier's comfort, with what the government gives him, is to be found. The Mormons in the neighborhood bring daily into the Fort, and sell, at pretty fair prices, all kinds of vegetables and fruit to be found at this season of the year. Unlike last year, provisions are abundant, and the soldier, obtaining his full ration, can, by savings thereon, provide himself with many "extras" not furnished by the government. The hills around are covered with wild sage, much greener than any I have before met with, which looks glorious in the sunshine. The air is clear and pure, and to-day is quite pleasant for September; the sun is shining brightly, and away in the distance can be seen the Green River Mountains, their tops covered with snow. A more pleasant spot than this for a soldier's home could not well be found, at least at this season of the year; but the settlers tell me that when the winter comes in its might, the North wind sweeps the valley with terrific fury, and that the snow comes driving down with the Ice King's breath, striking cold death to every breathing creature. It is pleasant now, however, and no doubt will continue so for a day or two, when I will have left it, perhaps never again to set foot upon its soil.

[3] Henry H. Sibley graduated from West Point in 1838 and was appointed a second lieutenant in the Second Dragoons. He rose steadily to the rank of captain in 1847 and was breveted a major in the Mexican War. The regular rank of major was attained in 1861, but he resigned his commission to enter the Confederate Army, where he became a brigadier general.

[4] A circular tent, patented by brevet Major H. H. Sibley, was being developed by the army since 1855. Some 250 of them were acquired for the use of the troops in the Mormon War. This campaign was the first field test of the tent.

Ft. Bridger, June 5, 1858, from a drawing by Albert Tracy in his Journal.

Mt. Eart — with Camp beyond —
June 5th 1858

About five miles from here is Camp Scott, where General Johnston[5] and his brave band passed the terrible ordeal of cold and hunger during the last winter. Very little remains to mark the spot save a breastwork of sods thrown up when the Mormons had grown rather too daring to be considered harmless, and here and there a mud structure used as a bake oven or cooking place. The soldiers tell many tales of the hard times experienced last winter. For five months they were compelled to live upon ten ounces of flour and four ounces of fat pork per day; coffee was a luxury, and once a week it was dealt out to the men. When wood was wanted, the men had to take hold of a wagon — the mules having died from cold and hunger — and act the part of draught animals. Twenty men formed a team, and they trudged along through the snow, pulling with one hand, and carrying their rifles in the other. Here would be seen an infantry wagon, there an artillery wagon; here came a dragoon wagon, and there one belonging to the mounted rifles; the men dressed in full uniform and armed to the teeth. And this was the routine of soldier's life at Camp Scott. The poor fellows bore it bravely, and put the best face possible on the matter, laughing at their toil, and cheering one another on. It was a hard life, but such things must be expected when we leave our homes and set out on a journey through the American wilderness. I may have to endure such hardships myself, but come what will, I will endeavor to do my duty and fulfil my vow to serve the country faithfully. This winter, matters will go much better, as the troops have their winter stock of wood gathered, and quarters are in progress of erection wherever troops are to be stationed. But for all this, we must anticipate rough usage, which will be especially severe on green lads like myself. It is soldering, however, and we must "grin and bear it."

On the fifth inst., we did not march, and I shouldered my rifle and started on a hunting expedition. A dragoon carries a Sharp's rifle,[6] as well as a sabre and a revolver. I am not an unerring marksman, but by dint of perseverance I succeeded in bagging several "sage chickens," which are very abundant among these western hills. Game

[5] See note 4 in the Introduction.

[6] Rifles and carbines were made with a mechanism patented by Christian Sharps in 1848. "Utah" undoubtedly means a carbine; by 1858 the First and Second Dragoons and some First and Second Cavalry companies carried the Sharps carbine. See Utley, *Frontiersmen in Blue*, p. 26.

is very plenty among the sage, and I saw at least an hundred antelopes and nearly five times that number of chickens and rabbits, within two miles of our camp. The first spring up at every few steps and bound away with the speed of the wind, and the two last named are found crouching under almost every sage bush on the hill sides. I fired at several of the antelopes, but did not succeed in wounding any severely enough to render him *hors du combat*. The rabbits dart through between the bushes, which are too closely interwoven to admit of any probability of capturing one if you did put a bullet through him. The chickens rise when you approach them, and you have to pop them on the wing. This is an easy matter for a good marksman, as they fly slowly and never rise to any great height — seldom over ten feet above the bushes. But to an inexperienced hand, like myself, it is somewhat of an undertaking. Perhaps you think that I should be pretty well "up to" the use of firearms by this time. If so, you are mistaken; for though now nearly five months wearing Uncle Sam's livery, I have but twice been at target practice, and we are not allowed to use our rifles on any other occasion — except when on guard — a duty from which I am exempt — without special permission. Tis true, I have no difficulty in obtaining leave; but I do not care for asking favors of any man, if he does wear an epaulette and carry a commission in his pocket. The majority of our company and the entire Infantry corps of the column were "out hunting" on the 5th. You must not be shocked at our desecration of the Sabbath, for a man soon forgets the holiness of that day when he is out here in the Western wilds, and has to do the regular routine of the soldier's duty on that as well as other days — and such a banging of guns and cracking of pistols was, I dare say, never before heard by the inhabitants of this region. Very few of the hunters returned without game, and many of them had enough to spare. Egad, but there was fat living among the soldiery for a day or two. "What will you have, hare, chicken, or antelope?" took the place of, "let's see, do we get three or four biscuit (hard bread) to-day?" the ration being alternately three or four crackers per day. Fat pork, our usual fare, was at a discount, and even beef, heretofore a delicacy, stood below par. When we will have another such a day, I do not know, but would have no objection to frequent returns.

The hills around our camping place are composed of slaty stones and hard clay except along the verge of the stream that runs through the valley, there is no vegetation save the sage bushes, and whence they draw their nourishment I do not know, as I dug down to the depth of twelve feet where the bushes were green and flourishing, without finding any moisture, or meeting with anything but hard, dry clay. During the afternoon we had a heavy shower of rain, and the stony parts of the hills were reduced to the consistency of stiff dough, the slaty material of which they are formed could be moulded like putty, and one ball that I rolled up, and dried by the cook-fire, became as hard as granite in a few seconds, yet on dipping it into water, it immediately became soft again. I am not sufficiently acquainted with the science of geology to explain the philosophy of the matter, but give you what I know of this, to me, singular material. Though the stones softened this [thus] before the rain, the clay gave scarcely any evidence of its effects. The surface was dampened, that was all. The moisture did not penetrate to the depth of a quarter of an inch, as I ascertained by scraping the surface in several places. Yet on the clay the sage grows most luxuriantly.

About six miles from our camp was a high rock, which I visited, and though I walked entirely round its base, I found no places where it was possible to make an ascent. It is about two thousand feet high — when I speak thus I mean higher than the plains around — and presented naught but a solid rocky face to the visitor. I should have risked my neck in making an attempt to ascend it, but my time was nearly up, and I had to hasten back to camp; for if I were once to abuse my privilege, I could never expect to have it renewed — I would never ask it. All around the base, as high as a man could reach, names were cut and painted. Following the example of those who were before me, I raised myself by means of a heap of stones, and cut my name in large letters, about twelve feet from the plain. Though I may never have a monument raised to my memory in any of our great cities; though my name may never be met with on history's pages; though my statue may never stand in public places, or on the top of pedestals; though no stone may deck my last resting place; though I may fall on the battle field, fighting for my country's honor, and my bones be left to whiten on the Western Plains, without even a sod to cover them;

so long as that rock stands he who visits it will know that such a man as "Utah" lived, and that he placed his name where it would be almost immortal, high above all others who preceded him. What a glorious idea that is! He who reads my letters may soon forget me, he who heard my name may pass it by unnoticed, but away on the Western Plain I have a mighty monument that keeps my name undying, until the rock shall melt or tumble to the plain. Among the names, I saw that of Christopher (Kit) Carson;[7] but his does not come within five feet of being as high as mine. Ah, Kit, old hunter and traveller though you be, a boy, scarce three months from civilization, overtops you. But so it should be. He who reaches highest should succeed, and he who is content with lowliness, should shine there.

As I expected, we did not march on the sixth. The Infantry marched, however, and a happy time they had of it, for scarcely had the command "Forward — route step — march," been given, when it commenced to snow at a rate that would astonish a Laplander. Down came the heavy flakes thick and fast, covering the face of nature with a white shroud as far around as the eye could reach. Being unprepared for winter, this struck us all with terrible fierceness, and many a soldier wished, between his chattering teeth, that he was once more at home by the fireside, instead of lying with naught to keep out the cold but the canvas of our tents, and the folds of our blankets; but how much more severely must the Infantry have felt it, having packed their coats in the wagons, and nothing to shield their shoulders save their woolen shirts which were rendered worse than useless by the fast falling snow. Their officers, mounted and wrapped warmly in their great coats, felt not the cold air, and would not allow the men to take out their coats, and the poor shivering fellows had to keep up the "route step" through the snow for four long hours, and then pitch their tents on the wet, cold ground. You never lay in a tent with the snow falling around you? I never did before, and, though I thanked my stars that I did not have to march that day, I have no wish to face

[7] Christopher (Kit) Carson (1809–68) was the famous trapper, Indian fighter, and guide for Lieutenant John C. Fremont's first two exploring expeditions. In 1853 he was appointed a United States Indian Agent in charge of two tribes of the Utes.

the Winter King another day, without something more substantial than a French Bell Tent[8] between his breath and my blanket.

On the 7th we marched forty-seven miles, and passed the Infantry, who had marched thirty-two miles in the two days. We entered the Territory of Utah that day, and encamped about sunset on Green river. By a singular mistake, as I take it, on the part of the man who named the stream in this portion of creation, there is a foundation in the stream for the name it bears. The *Big* Sandy river is a petty stream with muddy banks and bottom; the *Little* Sandy is also muddy, but is nearly twice the size of the one dubbed *Big*; but Green river has a positively green color, varying, as the stream is deep or shallow, from a dark green to a light blue. Its bottom is composed of round stones of an almost uniform size, and the current flows quite rapidly for a stream of its dimensions. Its water is cool and quite pleasant to the taste, and whence it derives the green color very much puzzles our Surgeon[9] — the only scientific man in the command. For my part, I venture no suppositions in regard to the matter. The vegetation along the stream is much the same as that of the country we have for some time been marching through — wild sage and cactus. We travelled along the banks for nearly twelve miles, without finding grass, and at last found about three acres of pretty fair pasturage, where we encamped..

On the 8th, we waited for the Infantry to come up. It was ration day, and the commissary train was behind us, so that the company had to fast until 3 o'clock P.M. when it reached our camp. Deeming it better to "put in my time" in making a trip through the sage, than in lying in my tent, and hearing my hungry comrades curse their lot, I shouldered my rifle and set out. About two miles from camp I came upon a couple of Indian wigwams — they contained the first Indians I have met with since I left Laramie — and purchased some sliced buffalo meat, with which I returned to camp. On my way back, I shot two fine rabbits and a sage chicken, and felt that come what would, I would not starve that day. On coming into camp, I found

[8] The French Bell Tent was a circular tent designed to hold twelve men and their equipment. The United States Army experimented with it in the hope of replacing the six man "common tent," but some quartermaster officers considered it too expensive.

[9] Bennett A. Clements, appointed assistant surgeon in 1856.

that Fred had caught some fine large fish in the river, and by uniting our stores, he and I lived well that day in the midst of hunger. I met with nothing interesting about the river, no mountains nor rocks to scale, nor any Indian legend to listen to. On the 9th and 10th we made short marches, camping on the 9th, at Ham's Fork, and on the 10th, at the second crossing of Black's Ford, Green River.

I forgot to mention that on the 7th, we passed by where a party of emigrants had been attacked by a number of Indians, and all butchered. The remains of the wagons are still there; tires and boxes, and other iron parts are scattered around, and the ashes of the wooden parts are still there, in spite of the effects of wind and rain for several seasons. I found some human bones lying among the ashes, and our guides told me that none of the unfortunate beings had been buried, but that they had been left for food for the wolves and ravens of the plains. It is hard to think that this is the last of a man, and that when he falls beneath the tomahawk of an Indian, his fellows pay no respect to his remains, and that his bones are thus left to whiten and moulder in the elements. But we must expect to meet these things when away from civilization, and within the limits of that term we cannot yet include

UTAH.

Camp on Silver Creek, U.T.
September 20th, 1858
[11]

We left Fort Bridger on the 13th inst., having laid over there one day. Here twelve of our company were transferred into other companies of our regiment, among whom was my friend and fellow soldier, Fred. Smith. I had become acquainted with Fred. on the first day of my arrival at Carlisle Barracks, and ever since he had been my companion and bed-fellow. He was at that time corporal, and on the march became first sergeant of the company; after serving a few weeks as sergeant, and through the different grades of non-commissioned officers, he was the same with me, unlike many who, in their elevation, forget those whom they affiliated with before. On assuming the office of first sergeant, he added to those of a friend the duties of tutor, and in-structed me in all the details of company and regimental business and military duty, in all of which he had, by five years' experience, become *au fait*. To part with him was, of course, a separation far from pleasant, for he stuck to me as a brother and a guiding star. In vain I tried to be transferred with him; in vain he tried to continue with me. My captain would not consent to my going, nor would he allow any to be substituted for him. This was my first disagreeable experience in the army; and, as I know of none to whom I would concede his place, I do not expect anything as unpleasant to again occur. You must pardon me for intruding my own affairs upon you, for this man was all in all to me, and worthy of the highest praise and honor.

We left Fort Bridger at half-past three o'clock, P.M., with the intention of marching seven miles — taking a route different from that heretofore travelled. The Infantry corps belonging to the column

78

had left during the forenoon, and we were to march after them. Our Captain remained at the Fort, and owing to a mistake of the Lieutenant in command we got off the road, and after marching about fifteen miles, darkness came upon us. Another man and myself were sent ahead to search for water and grass, or the place where the infantry were encamped. We galloped ahead about seven miles, when we found, in a pleasant little valley, plenty of the articles required, but no signs of the rest of the column. To this point we conducted the company, and the wagons failing to come up, we were compelled to lie all that night in the cold, frosty air, with nothing to shield us but our saddle blankets, having deemed it unnecessary to bring our bed blankets or great coats with us. Wood, however, was quite plentiful, and we soon built ourselves great camp fires, that drove the cold from our bones and added greatly to our comfort. But, towards morning, the fires died out and such a set of shivering mortals as were at *reveille*, I never saw before, or wish to see again. As soon as we had rebuilt our fires and warmed ourselves, "boots and saddles" sounded, and we again took up the march. After marching about ten miles, we came to excellent grass, with plenty of wood and water convenient, and halted. At one o'clock, P.M., the Infantry came up to us, bringing our wagons with them, and the column encamped, we having been twenty-four hours without food, meanwhile marching about thirty-two miles.

The fires that we left at our camping place on the morning of the 14th caught among the sage and brush-wood, and soon the hills around were covered with flames and dense columns of smoke rolled up towards the heavens, darkening the sunlight and filling the air with the peculiar odor of the sage. We did not march on the 15th, and the fire steadily moved towards us, until within half a mile of our camp, when we turned out *en masse*, and checked its progress in our direction. I went up on a hill near our camp, and East, North and South, as far as the eye could reach, the fire was spreading, and sending up its dense and darkening smoke. Our efforts had effectually checked its career Westward. On the evening of the 15th we saw for the first time, though some insist that they saw it a week before, a comet almost directly North of us. It has caused considerable excitement in our camp, many of our soldiers being believers in the doctrine of

Cumming,[1] that a comet is to knock us all to smash, some of these fine mornings. Being at such a great distance from civilization, and very seldom being so fortunate as to meet a newspaper, I have not yet seen any thing concerning this comet, but presume that it has the same effect with certain classes of your people, that it has with the ignorant and superstitious soldiery.

On the 16th we again took up the march, and reached Bear River, a little stream that rolls through among the hills of Utah, supplying clear, pure, cold water to the thirsty traveller, who to reach it has to march about twenty miles through a country entirely destitute of water. On both sides of the stream, for the distance of about nine feet, forming a fine forest row, all along the river majestic trees throw their branches to the air. The trees are principally pine, and rise to a height that would astonish a backwoods Pennsylvanian — I call myself one of these and pride myself upon it, and I never saw such majesty in my native forests. We found no grass near the place where the Infantry encamped, and I was sent out to search for that desirable article. About two miles from the river I found five hundred acres of excellent grass, but no water. Deeming this too good a place to pass by without strict examination, I dug down about a foot with my sabre and in a few seconds the hole was full of water. I conducted our company to the spot, and our horses had the best pasturage they have had since we left the plains of Kansas. We had to take them to the river for water, but this was but a trifling trouble, compared to the advantages of good grazing ground. The country is dotted with fertile spots like this, ranging from an hundred to five thousand acres in extent, and in none of them have I failed to find water at the depth of two feet. The soil is soft and free from stones; though I have generally found a stony formation at the depth of from six to ten feet. In some places these oases are perfectly square, some are circular, and others are narrow strips ranging from twenty to fifty feet wide. I followed one of them for nearly two miles that did not, at the widest part, exceed twenty-two feet. On the edge of these spots the sage is very thick for

[1] John Cumming (1807–81) was an English divine who was widely known for his writings on the interpretation of prophecy which stated that the Apocalypse would take place between 1848 and 1867.

the distance of about five feet, forming a complete hedge, impenetrable to anything larger than a rabbit. Thus, all that any one, who wishes to "squat" in this part of creation has to do, is to "go in and win."

On the 17th we marched along a well worn trail that led through a pleasant valley, on both sides of which arose high hills, covered with sage. The valley ranged from ten to two hundred yards wide, and was covered with most excellent grass and well watered. We reached a narrow pass that extended for nearly two miles, and in passing through this the hills rolled far apart, and at some distance closed again, forming a handsome nook in the mountains. Here we encamped, and our horses had the full range of the prairie, being herded instead of picketed.

On the 18th we started at 5 o'clock, A.M., and marched eight miles. The road passed over that day, if not the veritable "Jordan," famous as "a hard road to travel," must have been its twin-brother. It was a constant succession of "chuck holes," steep ascents and terrific descents. You may imagine the condition of the road from the fact that our wagons were fourteen hours in marching the eight miles. Scarcely had we reached the camping place when we discovered that the grass, about three miles below us, was on fire, and that the flames, assisted by the wind which was blowing towards us, were rapidly approaching. The entire column turned out to check its progress, but our labors were in vain. Remembering having read many tales concerning fire on the prairies, I took the plan ascribed by story-writers to the heroes of such conflagrations, and fired a strip a hundred yards wide near the edge of our pasturage, and by the time the fire reached the "jumping place" we had the barrier completed. This plan succeeded effectually, and the fire came to a dead stop. Having succeeded in arresting its progress, I was sent out, with twenty dragoons, to ascertain, if possible, the origin of the fire; curiosity taking the place of alarm and anxiety. About five miles from camp, we discovered three Indians, mounted on ponies, not two hundred yards from us. Halting my men near a thicket that effectually concealed them, I rode towards the red rascals. When within fifty yards of them, they uttered a yell of triumph, and galloped towards me. I grasped my revolver nervously, and inwardly resolved never again to leave my companions behind me when I was near the Indians. As they dashed past me, one of them made a fierce thrust at me with his spear. It fell short, however, and I discharged my revolver at the rascal. I missed him, but [a]s I cocked my pistol a second time the entire sq[u]ad that accompanied me fired and he fell from his horse dead. The others fled, and though we gave chase, their ponies were too fast for our jaded horses, and we gave up the pursuit in a short time. These must have been the miscreants that fired the prairie, probably with the intention of stampeding our horses and destroying our camp. On returning, we picked up the dead body of the Indian and buried it. He had nineteen balls in his body, only one shot failing to hit him.

On the 19th we made another short march, but the road was very good, except about half a mile, where the only space between the hills was the bed of the stream that waters this long valley. Through this we marched, the infantry pulling off their unmentionables and throwing them on the points of their bayonets. This was a pretty hard tug for the teams, but they succeeded in getting through without much trouble. When the guard, which rides in the rear of the train, came into camp, our captain discovered that one of the men was drunk. Not wishing to have the men subjected to a court-martial, the captain ordered him to be tied up for an hour. The miserable ingrate, instead of thanking the officer for his leniency, commenced a terrible tirade of abuse, coupled with most opprobrious epithets, insulting language and unhallowed blasphemy and profanity it has ever been my lot to listen to. Captain Anderson[2] bore the fellow's abuse patiently, simply ordering the process of tying him up to go on, until the fellow burst from the hands of those who were endeavoring to bind him, and rushed upon the officer. I threw myself in his way, but with a blow that would have felled an ox, he sent me to the ground. He had counted without his host, however, for the Captain sprang nimbly towards him, and with a well directed blow, laid him by my side. When I arose, he (the officer) merely said, "Sergeant, silence that man, and prevent him from doing further mischief." In vain I strove

[2] Richard H. Anderson was a graduate of West Point who was commissioned as a second lieutenant in the Second Dragoons in 1844. He served with distinction in the Mexican War and by 1855 he was a captain in the Second Dragoons. In the Civil War he joined the South and attained the rank of lieutenant general in the Confederate Army.

to reason the fellow into submission; he would resist, he would curse the officer, then [than] whom a better man does not carry an epaulette. Finding all gentler means inefficient, I "bucked and gagged" him, and thus rendered him perfectly quiet and harmless. This was the first man severely dealt with since Captain Anderson joined us, and some of the disorderly spirits of the company commenced talking about it being shameful, and a few even threatened to release him. But a "barking dog seldom bites" says the old saw, and the sight of revolvers in the hands of a few resolute men, known to be loyal and trusty, soon silenced all murmuring and hushed all threats. We kept the miscreant bucked and gagged for an hour, and then ironed him, and he now awaits trial on three distinct charges, for either one of which says the "Articles of War," he shall be punished by death or such other corporal punishment as a Court Martial may deem proper. If he escapes hanging he will be fortunate, and justice will be cheated out of her rights. He is an Irishman, named Patrick Kallagher,[3] and those who threatened to release him were his countrymen.

In the foregoing, I have made use of the term "bucked and gagged," which perhaps will need explanation to some of your readers. It is a punishment never resorted to except in aggravated cases, and this is, I understand the first case that has occurred in Captain Anderson's company since he entered the army. To "buck" a man, his wrists are first firmly bound together as close as possible. He is then placed in a sitting posture, and his knees are forced between his arms. A stick is then introduced between the bend of his legs and the

---

[3] Patrick Callaghan was tried by a court-martial on October 12, 1858, for two offenses committed while a member of Company A, Dragoon Recruits. The first was for drunkenness on guard. The second was for conduct "to the prejudice of good order and discipline." The specification of the second charge states that Callaghan "did make use of insolent, abusive and mutinous language to Lieut. [R. H.] Anderson, the commander of the recruit company to which the said Callaghan belonged. This at the Camp of Company 'A' Dragoon recruits on White Clay Creek en route from Fort Bridger U.T. to Camp Floyd U.T. on or about the 19 day of Sept. 1858." Callaghan pleaded guilty to both charges and to the specification of the first charge. Private Charles King, a witness for the defense, testified that Anderson and Callaghan were arguing. Callaghan called the lieutenant a s.o.b. and Anderson struck him about three times with a saber. The court found Callaghan guilty and sentenced him to be confined at hard labor for eight months while wearing a twenty-five pound iron attached to his left leg, and to forfeit nine dollars a month for the duration of his sentence. See "Judge Advocate General's Office, Court Martial Records," HH–976, box 166, R.G. 153, National Archives. See chap. 14 for "Utah's" comments on Callaghan's court-martial.

bend of his arms; and he is unable to move without tumbling over on his back, which, from his helpless condition, is no pleasant feat to perform. "Gagging" is simply introducing a stick between his teeth and fastening it with strings behind his head. I have seen Infantry men "gagged" with a bayonet that was drawn so tight as to cut the corners of their mouths, and cause the blood to flow down on their coat collars. But this is too severe, and few officers resort to it except to silence a man who cannot otherwise be induced to keep quiet.

To-day, we reached Silver Creek; (having made a short march yesterday, without meeting with anything of interest,) a clear, sparkling stream, that rolls along through the hills, every now and then burying itself in the ground, running under a hill and bursting out on the other side, then rolling on until it reaches another hill and again disappearing. During our march we passed through a "canon" about three miles in length, that had they been anxious to prevent the progress of the United States troops, would have afforded the Mormons an opportunity to annihilate almost any force that could be sent against them. The bottom was just wide enough for the wagons to pass, and the sides rose almost perpendicularly to the height of from a thousand to three thousand feet. In some places, the sides of the "canon" was so high and steep, that we could scarce see the second man from us, so dark was the passage. But the Mormons had no wish to measure swords with the United States, nor to refuse obedience to their laws and requirements, notwithstanding the blustering of those who maintained that treason, blasphemy and crime, walked hand in hand in

UTAH.

Camp Floyd, U.T.
"The Other Sides of Jordan"
September 25th, 1858
[12]

The Sixth Column arrived here — the end of its journey — to-day, after marching one hundred and five days, having left Leavenworth on the 13th of June last. The entire column is in excellent health and spirits, there being but one sick man in the entire command. None show any signs of fatigue or hardship, and I find that I have gained nearly twelve pounds in weight since we set out. Immediately after our arrival here, the different corps were transferred to their own regiments, and the column disbanded. Our company has been broken up, and the men belonging to it attached to other companies of our regiment, and we, who by our "good conduct, loyalty and soldiery behavior," earned promotion to the different grades of non-commissioned offices, have to pull off our cherries, and go to work again as privates.[1] To many of our boys this is a hard tumble, as they loved dearly the authority and extra pay of their rank. However, there are ups and downs in the army, as well as out of it, and we may soon reach the top notch again.

Camp Floyd is one of the most miserable, disagreeable and uninteresting places that ever disgraced the earth.[2] It is built upon a dry plain, entirely destitute of grass, or, indeed, any vegetation, except the

[1] This is the only known reference to the use of these symbols for temporary or acting ranks in the pre-Civil War army.

[2] Richard F. Burton described Camp Floyd as follows: "It lies in a circular basin, surrounded by irregular hills of various height, still wooded with black cedar, where not easily felled, and clustering upon the banks of Cedar Creek, a rivulet which presently sinks in a black puddly mud. For a more thoroughly detestable spot one must repair to Gharra, or some other purgatorial place in Lower Sindh." See Burton, *City of the Saints*, p. 405. The history of the post can be found in Thomas G. Alexander and Leonard J. Arrington, "Camp in the Sagebrush: Camp Floyd, Utah, 1858–1861," *Utah Historical Quarterly* 34 (1966): 3–21.

sage, that flourishes where nothing else will grow. The dry clay, pulverized by the numerous wagons passing in and about the camp, forms a fine dust, that drifts with blinding fury for miles around. When the wind blows, the dust drives through the camp so fierce and thick, that you can scarce see three yards ahead, and sore eyes, red and inflamed, are everywhere met with. The troops here are as yet in tents, but quarters built of "dobied" sun dried brick — are in rapid progress.[3] In about two weeks I presume Uncle Sam will have a mud village reared in Cedar valley. There is no water near here except a little dirty stream that runs near the west end of the camp, scarcely large enough to drown a mouse. To obtain wood we have to send nearly twelve miles, and there they have nothing but light cedar. And yet this place is the head quarters of the department of Utah, and of four regiments of the army — 2d Dragoons, and the 5th, 7th, and 10th Infantry. Besides these regiments there are four companies of Artillery here,[4] so that we have a pretty strong corps: and not at all liable to attack from either Mormon or Indian. General Johnston[5] is here, but as he has command of the Department, the post is under the command of Col. Morrison[6] of the 7th Infantry. Col. Cooke,[7] the commander of our regiment is absent, and Lieutenant Colonel Howe[8] has command pro-tem. He is an energetic, enterprising officer, and under his direction the "doby" houses are getting along

[3] Burton described the process as follows: "The material is clay, or silt, from the creek, puddled with water, and if saltish it is better than sweet soil; unity of colour and formation are the tests of goodness. Each brick weighs, when dry, 16 lbs., and the mould is mostly double. On the day after making they are stacked, and allowed to stand for two months; the season is June, July, and August, after which it becomes too cold." See Burton, *City of the Saints,* p. 419.

[4] The four companies were a part of the Third Artillery.

[5] See note 4 in the Introduction.

[6] Pitcairn Morrison was commissioned as a second lieutenant in the Corps of Artillery in 1820. In the Mexican War he won a brevet as major for gallant and meritorious conduct and in 1847 was given a regular major's commission and transferred to the infantry. By mid-1853 he was a lieutenant colonel of the Seventh Infantry.

[7] Philip St. George Cooke graduated from West Point in 1827 and was originally assigned to the infantry. He was promoted to first lieutenant in the First Dragoons in 1833 and to captain two years later. By 1858 he had reached the rank of colonel. He led the Mormon Battalion during the Mexican War.

[8] Marshall Saxe Howe graduated from West Point in 1827, became a first lieutenant in the Second Dragoons in 1836, and by 1858 was a lieutenant colonel.

Camp Floyd, U.
March 3ᵈ 18..

Albert Tracy's sketch of Camp Floyd done on March 3, 1860, from his Journal.

Camp Floyd from H. C. Taylor
Sunday March 3¹, 1860

with marvelous rapidity. We have four fine regimental bands here, that at different times during the day discourse most excellent music for the benefit of the soldiers. Were it not for the dust and barrenness of the soil Camp Floyd would be quite a pleasant place, but as it is now, it is almost intolerable, and though Gen. Johnston may be a man of energy, tact, and bravery, he is by no means a man of taste, at least Camp Floyd is evidence that such is the case.

About fifteen miles from here we crossed the river Jordan, a stream that runs from Utah Lake, a small body of water that lies near the City of Provo, to Great Salt Lake. It is a deep stream, about one hundred yards wide, and rolls very lazily through the "valley of Jordan." Though, named Jordan, the wilderness of Utah, so far as I have seen, is met with after crossing it. According to the usual custom practiced in this far west region, this is exactly right, everything being called by an inappropriate name.

Before coming to the Jordan we passed through three villages, Pleasant Grove, Lent City, and a town not yet named, built on a creek known as American Fork. These towns were composed of houses built of "dobies," the principal building material of the country. The streets were beaten hard and solid and the side walks were paved with some dried brick. Around each of the towns mud walls were built, with port holes so arranged as to sweep the entire country round. These towns were built and fortified thus, as a means of defence against the Indians, but now, since the troops are here, in sufficient numbers to overawe the red skins, the walls are permitted to tumble down and soon but little will remain of them. They were, no doubt, pretty strong places in their day, and when the Indians assailed them, were effective shelters for the inhabitants, but they would amount to very little in a war against the United States, as a single cannon shot would send the walls tumbling about the ears of the defenders. Every thing around was neat and clean, and the men were as well dressed and tidy as any well to-do farmer in our own State. The women were much superior to those I have heretofore seen, many of them being quite handsome, and but few of them coming under the head of ugly as I once was compelled to class them. Around the villages fine fields of corn were growing, and the stubbles in others showed that a good crop of other grain had been already gathered. The people told me that there [they] were compelled to irrigate the soil, or it would be impossible to raise any crop without so doing. "But when we do it," said they, "we defy any other part of the United States or their Territories to produce the equal of these valleys so dry and sterile by nature."

On the 23d we passed through "Provo Canon," a pass thirteen miles in length. At the entrance we took a road built by the Mormons, which is without exception, the best piece of road between here and Fort Leavenworth. The builders had great difficulties to overcome, but notwithstanding the narrowness of the passage, the hardness of the rock and the almost perpendicularity of the mountainsides, they succeeded in making a road fit at any time for a railroad track. This canon is the place from whence the city of Provo, a town of some five thousand inhabitants, that lies eight miles west of our route, obtains its firewood, and we met quite a number of Mormons, with their teams, preparing for the cold blast of winter, which will soon be upon us in full fury. They were all very friendly, and furnished us with considerable information concerning the route to Camp Floyd, which we found to be correct in every particular. Like all the Mormons I have met with, they disclaimed having ever entertained a single thought hostile to the government of the United States, and protested that all the ill feeling manifested by them towards Judge Drummond[9] was but the natural consequences of his own evil conduct. They denounce him as a slanderer, a libertine, and a debauchee; and I believe they are right in so doing, as I have heard from "Gentiles," whose veracity is unimpeachable, stories that sat harder against His Honor than any told by the "Saints."

"Provo Canon" is one of the most interesting and picturesque places I have met with on the march. Provo river, a fast running stream, about fifty feet wide, rolls in all the majesty of a mountain torrent through the entire canon. Away up the steep sides of the mountain tall cedars raise their tops towards the sky and fling their broad branches to the air. Adown the sides roll streams of water issuing from the rocks, in many places five hundred feet from the bottom, and making the descent by a few jumps that resemble minia-

9 W. W. Drummond was one of the associate justices for Utah Territory appointed by President Franklin Pierce. When he resigned in 1857 he wrote to the Attorney General that federal authority was powerless in the face of the dictatorship of Brigham Young. Bancroft says that Drummond's charges were one of the principal causes of the Mormon War. See Bancroft, *History of Utah*, p. 490.

Waterfall in Provo Canyon from a sketch by H. V. A. von Beckh who traveled with Captain James H. Simpson's expedition of U.S. Engineers in 1859.

ture Niagaras, and come foaming and seething to the river. I clambered up one of the highest points, and away in the distance I could see the white tents of Camp Floyd and the roof tops of the houses of Salt Lake City. I could see the country for many miles around dotted with little settlements, fields of waving corn, tall cedars and broad placid lakes. The many colored hills of Utah arose every where and there, adding to the beauty and attractiveness of the scene. Outside of this dusty hole, where Uncle Sam has stuck his "bold soger boys," Utah Territory is one of the most beautiful pieces of work Dame Nature ever gave to man. The hills are not only decked with every color, but with every shade, and he who would grow weary of viewing this glorious scenery, "is only fit for treason, strategy and spoils." I do not wonder that Brigham selected this fine Territory for the home of his followers; nor should I be surprised to see it soon become one

The Simpson expedition approaching the mouth of Provo Canyon sketched by H. V. A. von Beckh in 1859.

of the most populace and flourishing States of our Union. Every inducement is offered to the industrious and enterprising settler to come here and build himself a home, where, as Pat says, "Potatoes can be got for the digging, and the barley grows of its own accord" — provided you irrigate the soil. Had any one stood there with me, who was in search of a home, he would have descended into the valley with the firm resolve to go no further. It is a great sacrifice for a young man to "throw himself away" by becoming a soldier, but so long as we can roam through such glorious regions as Utah and Kansas, to obtain opportunities to scale the peaks of the rocky mountains, and to know the beauty and greatness of our country, I doubt whether five years could be better employed.

The Indians that I have met with since we entered the territory, are fine looking fellows, stout and athletic, excellent riders, well armed and well mounted. Many of them speak pretty good English, and they are shrewd and wary in their dealings with the soldiers. They understand all the tricks of the white man; and some of our boys, who imagined themselves very sharp, were completely outwitted by the red skin traders. The Mormons say that they are very treacherous, and that their love of money frequently prompts them to commit terrible murders. But I opine they will be very careful about committing themselves now, as terrible vengeance will certainly overtake them, and the sabre of the dragoon and the bayonet of the infantry will sweep, with terrible fury, the hills of their forefathers, at the first villainous act they may commit. The outrages committed by the Oregon Indians[10] have rendered the officers here very watchful, and the first spark of war will be followed by floods of native blood. This the Indians know, and the unbearable insolence they displayed last winter is changed to meekness and humility.

The news that we receive from the seat of war is very discouraging, though I presume things are put in good shape ere they reach the States. I have heard that the Snakes, Black Feet and Spokans had attacked the First Dragoons, and butchered nearly the whole regiment, and that the red rascals were plundering and ravaging the Ter-

[10] For an account of the defeat of the forces under Colonel E. J. Steptoe see note 2, chap. 5. This disaster was subsequently avenged when the army forces defeated the Oregon Indians at the battle of Four Lakes on September 1, 1858.

ritory, without the least show of resistance on the part of the troops.[11] I saw an Oregon settler, yesterday, who told me that the United States Government had the most terrible enemy to deal with that had been encountered since the days of Brandt,[12] and that the puny force in the departments of the Pacific was about as useful as a company of militia would be in a war with United Europe. "They are passive murderers," said he, "every man butchered, ever house burned is to be traced to the neglect of the United States Government alone; that is the responsible source; there lies all the blame." He spoke harshly of Col. Steptoe. There was not an Indian, he said, who was not a better commander than Col. S., and he was the laughing stock of all the warriors in the Territory. From what I hear, I anticipate the arrival of orders for our regiment to proceed to Oregon, to do the work that others have failed to do. And I hope that we will have a warmer time there than we have had in making the "conquest" of

UTAH.

[11] The report was untrue. Four companies of the First Dragoons under Brevet Major William N. Grier were a part of the forces led by Colonel George Wright against the Oregon Indians in the battles of Four Lakes and Spokane Plain. See Utley, *Frontiersmen in Blue*, pp. 204–7.

[12] Joseph Brant, or Thayendanegea (1742–1807), was a Mohawk Indian whose sister, Molly, became the wife of Sir William Johnson, the sole superintendent of the northern Indians prior to the American Revolution. During the Revolution he went to Canada, accepted a commission as a captain in the British Army, and led the Mohawk Indians in battle against the colonial forces. To the Americans he was a fiend who reveled in killing noncombatants. After the war he lived in Canada where he worked for the welfare of the Iroquois Indians.

Camp Floyd, U.T.

October 13, 1858

[13]

Since I last wrote to you, I have been looking around for the notables of the "Army of Utah" — the men, who, "half froze, half starved," last winter, yet live to tell the tale. Only to-day, I succeeded in seeing, for the first time, the greatest of them all, *the* man who bore the brunt of the entire affair, the chief actor and the real hero of the drama — Gen. A. S. Johnston. The General is a tall, erect, finely formed man, who bears upon his manly face the stamp of heroism, honor and every trait that ennobles a soldier. 'Tis plain he is no carpet-knight, no newspaper hero, but one who has the will, the inward power, to do his duty, though whole hosts oppose. An open, pleasant countenance, full of amiability and manliness, "an eye like Jove's, to threaten and command;" he is the embodiment of what is deemed the real chivalry among military classes. His hair and beard are slightly tinged with the snow of age, just enough to render his appearance the more imposing and commanding. He is, I should think, about six feet two or three inches in height, and will probably weigh two hundred pounds. The men love him as a father, especially those who passed through the campaign of last winter at Camp Scott, and declare that no other man, save "old Scott," who is always an exception in matters of praise, could have conducted the affair so well as he did. "When we," they say, "had eight ounces of flour per day, General Johnston had the same; when an attack was apprehended, and we camped in the snow, Gen. Johnston shared the same cold comfort. In short, when we suffered, he suffered; and such a man is worthy of honor and esteem." That he deserves the highest praise and honor, is undeniable, and the Government will ever find the old Texan patriot one of its bravest, truest defenders, so long as liberty,

96

integrity and justice are its watchwords, and their sustenance its greatest aim and object.

Next to Gen. Johnston, as the hero and patriot of the Mormon war, is Col. P. St. George Cooke,[1] commander of the Second Dragoons. He is at present absent on furlough, and consequently, I can say nothing concerning him, save that he stands with his regiment as Johnston does with the army. In the interim our regiment is commanded by Lieut. Col. M. S. Howe.

The quarters for the troops are going up rapidly, the soldiers making mortar and carrying "dobies" to the masons, who are citizens hired by the Quarter Master, at the pretty fair figure of six dollars a day "and found." Here you see a party mixing mud; there a party carrying dobies; there a squad carrying lumber, and there another squad nailing on the rough roofs. Each man has his place, in the allotment of which your correspondent occupies the respectable and responsible position of hod-carrier for a Mormon. Many hands make light work, however, and the "fatigue duty" as it is called, is nothing more than healthful, pleasant exercise, and all day long the merry joke and joyous laugh go round, and all are grateful to heaven and the peace commissioners at the prospect of a better time this winter than was experienced last season. The buildings will be substantial and comfortable, and every exertion is being made to render them as pleasant as possible. Dobies are an article much more severe upon the fingers than types; "Mormon mortar," as the boys term the mud we use in the buildings, is worse than dry ink in winter time; but we breathe the pure uncontaminated air of heaven, and enjoy the glorious scenery of the Utah mountains, and on the whole, now that a few slight showers have laid the dust, I give soldiering the preference. "Who would'nt be a soldier?" Who would not roam over our own great and glorious western country; this summer in Kansas, the next in Utah, the next in Oregon, and the next, perhaps, in Mexico, establishing Sam Houston's protectorate? Who would not ramble through our gigantic forest, roll among the tall grass of our prairies, scramble over the mountain tops, sleep beneath the clear blue of the firmament, and follow the star spangled banner to "death or glory?"

[1] See note 7, chap. 12.

A view from Camp Floyd looking east across Utah Lake sketched by Albert Tracy for his Journal *on July 31, 1858. Tracy has indicated main points of interest such as the mouth of the Jordan River, American Fork, Provo Canyon, and Provo.*

For some time past the neighborhood of Camp Floyd — that is to say, the country for sixty miles around, has been in a state of great excitement, and rumors of awful butcheries by the Indians, and terrible retaliations by the troops, are flying around. I have left to others the painting of the dreadful scenes, and will give you a correct account of the matter. A low, worthless Indian, an outcast from his tribe, who had been employed by the government last winter as a spy upon the Mormons, and had learned all the sentiments of the soldiery towards the settlers of the territory, and, of course, imbibed them, committed a brutal outrage upon the person of a little girl nine years of age, the particulars of which are two horrible for pen to write, and three companies of Infantry and two companies of Dragoons, under the command of Brevet Major G. R. Paul,[2] were sent out to capture him.

[2] See note 3, chap. 4.

This body of troops marched upon a large Indian settlement at Spanish Fork, and attacked the inhabitants, who were busily engaged in harvesting their corn, little thinking that those whom they looked upon as friends and allies (they having opposed the Mormons when rebellion was spoken of) were plotting their destruction. Three Indians, one of them the son of the principal chief of the Utah tribe, were killed, and the residue fled to the mountains.[3] Having ascertained what the troops required, they caught the red rascal who had

[3] Major Paul's account of the affair, dated "Camp near Spanish Fork, U.T." October 3, 1858, was sent to the Assistant Adjutant General, Headquarters, Department of Utah. It is as follows: "I have the honor to report the complete success of the expedition against the Indians residing on the public farm. My command arrived here at break of day on the 2d Inst., having marched forty-five miles, and immediately on its arrival the Indian village was surrounded, and as the Indians were attempting to escape, they were pursued, and nearly all captured; one chief 'Piutarts' [Pintut] of Petetennt's band was killed. There were not more than a dozen men in the village, the others having left for the mountains on the morning of the 30th. September. By detaining one chief and several of his band in custody, and releasing the others, they promised to bring in the guilty young men, which

committed the crime, and delivered him up to the commander of the troops, expecting that in so doing they would be allowed to return to their homes. But no, that would not be allowed, and the poor people are now out in the mountains with their wives and children, without food or dwelling save that which nature affords. "And," writes an officer to his "chum" in camp, "they must stay there till we return, which will not be while there is a potato or an ear of corn to be found in their storehouses." Glorious, is it not, for the soldiery of a great and mighty republic to punish in this manner seven hundred innocent persons for the villany of one whom these very suffering people have delivered up to justice, and who did not belong to their tribe or settlement? But "might makes right," and so I presume the weak will have to suffer, so long as the potatoes, &c., to be found in their storehouses continue to furnish a "d——d good time," as the officer abovementioned says they are "having at present among the Indian luxuries." Need we be surprised if starvation should drive the Indians to plunder and violence during the coming winter? Need we wonder if the conduct of the soldiery on this occasion give rise to murders, massacres and butcheries, and the villages of the Mormons blaze and burn before the red man's brands; if the traveller be waylaid and scalped and his bones left to whiten upon the snow; if sentinels be shot down upon their posts, and all manner of "savage atrocities" be committed? No, emphatically, no. Nothing else can be expected, and though "I am neither a prophet nor the son of a prophet," I feel safe in saying that such will be the case. Retaliation will, of course, be attempted, but whether the troops can effect much against the Indian in this mountainous country is to me a matter of doubt. The sentiments that animate the troops are disgraceful in the extreme, and do not tell well

they did, and all were released except the two culprits; the *third* was not to be found, but it was conceded by all, that though present, he had nothing to do with the outrage committed." "AG Letters," roll 593.

The Muster Roll of Company G, Second Dragoons, contains the following entry under "Record of Events" for the period August 31 through October 31. "The Company started for the Indian Farm n.r Spanish Fork, U.T. 1.st Oct. 58 to demand the surrender of some Indians (Utahs) that had been committing depredations on the settlers, and returned to this Camp on the 16th of Oct. 58. having received the offenders and turned them over to the Civil Authority. The Company at the time forming part of the Command of Major Paul of Infantry." "Regular Army Muster Rolls, Inspection Returns, 1821–1860, Second Dragoons," box 112, R.G. 94, National Archives.

for the military arm of our nation. Such expressions as, "I'd butcher every papoose I met with, fur nits become lice;" "When I go out, I'll have a couple of buffalo robes from the red devils;" "I'll nail a pony, and then desert;" "I wish old Harney was here, he'd bang every one of them," "Lord! won't the squaws catch jessy," [4] are in the mouth of almost every man in the department. Not only do the enlisted men talk in this manner, but the officers seem actuated by the same spirit. When you read of the dreadful doings of the red man, hereafter, remember that it is but the natural effect of the actions of civilized Christian men upon his "untutored mind."

A short distance from Camp is a large Mormon village, the people of which supply the soldiers with milk, butter, eggs, and such articles, at reasonable rates. The people are quite friendly, and laugh at the idea of having intended any opposition to the progress of the troops. They declare that they would have given the soldiers good quarters last winter, had they asked for them; but "they were stiffnecked, and we were not going to beg them to accept our hospitality." If the Mormons are not the most consummate hypocrites beneath the sun, Uncle Sam has not a more faithful, loyal, liberty-loving people within his proud domains than they; and from my association with them I am convinced that they are not liable to the charge of false pretense. Some of the more ignorant and bigoted of the soldiery are continually berating them, calling them all manner of hard names, and telling what they "would have done if the Mormons had'nt caved in;" but the thinking and intelligent portion (a very small minority, I am sorry to say), appreciate their worth and treat them accordingly. I told you before that I am a hod carrier. The mason I attend is a well educated, intelligent man, a native of Massachusetts, and an advocate of the most glorious institutions of that sterling Commonwealth, many of which he expects to soon see flourish in the land of the Latter-Day Saints. He is a bishop in the Mormon Church, and last Sabbath I heard him preach one of the most eloquent and powerful sermons it has ever been my lot to listen to, and I have "sat under" Chapin,[5]

[4] See note 3, chap. 9.

[5] Edwin Hubbell Chapin (1814–80) was the pastor of the Fourth Universalist Society in New York City. His sermons were notable for the great emphasis he placed on Christ rather than Christianity.

Beecher,[6] Tyng,[7] and many of our most renowned divines. There was nothing of fanaticism or bigotry in his address, but an earnest heart-stirring appeal to all to rally around the up raised standard of Jehovah, and fight the good fight, whose warriors are rewarded in Heaven, though they may be down trodden and oppressed upon earth. And when he prayed it was not for the success of Mormonism or the glory of "our Church," but for all mankind, be they what they may. Had you heard him, you would have agreed with me that those who rant about the ignorance, bigotry and fanaticism of the Mormons are merely slanderers of the lowest grade.

He has explained to me much of the workings of Mormonism, and, of a truth, I must say that they set an example well worthy of imitation in Christian communities. The Bishop is the head man of his settlement or village, and he and the Elders settle all difficulties between the people of their districts. There is no fighting, no going to law in the Mormon creed or practice. If two men disagree, the dispute is referred to the Bishop and Elders, and they decide the matter in public before an assemblage of the people. From this decision an appeal may be made to "the twelve," but he says that he has never known anything of this kind to occur, and he has been ten years a Mormon. The tenth part of everything raised by the farmers, and the tenth of the profits of the traders, are paid into the hands of the Bishop, who applies it to the purposes of feeding travellers, bringing poor emigrants across the plains, building churches and school-houses, &c. A statement is published yearly of the disposition of this fund, to which no man need contribute unless he is satisfied. By such means as this, everything is made to work harmoniously, and peace and good feeling are preserved among those who have left their home in other lands and built themselves a new "abiding place" among the mountains and valleys of

UTAH.

---

[6] Henry Ward Beecher (1813–87) was a minister in the Plymouth Congregational Church in Brooklyn, New York, where his sermons drew large audiences and the printed versions of them reached thousands of others. He was a leader in the antislavery movement, but he was opposed to interfering with slavery in the slave states.

[7] Stephen Higginson Tyng (1800–85) was regarded as one of the two greatest preachers in the Episcopal Church of his times. People flocked to hear him. He served in Philadelphia from 1829 to 1845 and subsequently in New York City.

Soldiers at drill near Camp Floyd.

Camp Floyd, U.T.
October 27th, 1858
[14]

The great "scouting party" that went out to capture the rascally red skin who outraged a little girl, and while on this duty did such valiant deeds among the potatoes and grain of the Indians at Spanish Fork, have returned, laden with spoils, and exulting in their success. Every man has five or six bushels of potatoes, and the wagons of the officers are loaded down with large quantities of the same vegetable. They declare that the Indians "have not a potato or a kernel of wheat left; for," say they, "what we could not carry off we destroyed." Many of them have buffalo robes and blankets belonging to the poor red men, and as they wrap them around themselves, or display them to their admiring friends, they exultingly exclaim "wouldn't it be rich to see the copper colored devils shake and shiver these frosty nights, while we sleep in their warm coverings?" A pretty set of rascals indeed, these "gallant soldiers" of our great republic — murdering and plundering under the guise of maintaining the country's honor and the peace of the frontier!

While out upon this expedition, a most brutal and cowardly outrage was committed upon an Infantry man by a Lieutenant of the Second Dragoons. This person, who is not two years from West Point, and occupies the elevated position of Brevet Second Lieutenant in our army, while upon a frolic at a Mormon village near Spanish Fork, met with the injured man, whose name I did not learn, and for the purpose, as he said, of "showing his authority," attacked him and beat him terribly about the head with the butt end of a large army revolver, cutting him in several places, and leaving him senseless upon the ground. The attack was entirely unprovoked, as the man had walked past him quietly, giving the usual salute, and when he had done his worst, he said, laughingly, "Well, that's one dough-boy (the nick-

104

name of the Infantry) less anyhow." Yet, for this cruel and cold-blooded attack, there is no redress in a military court, as the testimony of enlisted men is without weight when given against an officer, no matter how low he may be.

Companies C. and H., of the regiment, who left here nearly three months ago on an expedition against the Humboldt River Indians, returned on the 23rd instant, without seeing a single red skin.[1] They were under the command of Captain Haus.[2] Callaghan, the fellow who so outrageously blackguarded Capt. Anderson, on the 18th ult., as I then informed you, has been tried by a general court-martial, on two different charges, "conduct subversive to good conduct and military discipline" and "using disrespectful language towards his superior officer," the heavier charges against him being waived by Captain A. He was sentenced by the court-martial, of which Bvt. Col. Smith,[3] of the 8th Infantry, was president, to be confined at hard labor for eight months, to forfeit nine dollars of his pay per month during that time, and to wear, attached by a chain to his left leg, an iron ball weighing twenty-five pounds.[4] A pretty hard sentence, but well earned, in my opinion. Had he been arraigned on the other charges, he could not have escaped death. At the same court-martial, an artilleryman, whose name I have forgotten, was tried for desertion, and was sentenced to forfeit all pay and allowances due him at the time he deserted, to receive "fifty lashes on the bare back, well laid on with a raw hide," to serve the remainder of his time (three years and

[1] On September 11, 1858, a correspondent of the *New York Times* wrote from Salt Lake City that "A squadron consisting of two companies of the Second Dragoons and one of the Fifth Infantry passed through this city on their way to the Humboldt river on Monday last — the officers in command are Capt. Hawes and Lieut Sanders of the Dragoons and Lieuts Lewis & Bristol of the Fifth." Article reprinted in the St. Louis *Daily Missouri Republican,* October 19, 1858. By the time these troops reached Oregon the campaign against the Indians there had ended with the battles of Four Lakes and Spokane Plain.

[2] James M. Hawes graduated from West Point in 1845 and was assigned to the Second Dragoons. He became a first lieutenant in 1850 and captain in 1855.

[3] Charles F. Smith graduated from West Point in 1820. He became a major in the First Artillery in 1854 and a lieutenant colonel of the Tenth Infantry in 1855.

[4] On the recommendation of his company and regimental commanders, Callaghan had the unexpired portion of his sentence remitted on February 5, 1859. See "Judge Advocate General's Office, Court Martial Records," HH–976, box 166, special order no. 8, Headquarters, Department of Utah, February 5, 1859, R.G. 153, National Archives.

nine months) at hard labor in charge of the guard, wearing a ball weighing twenty-five pounds attached by a chain three feet in length to his leg, to forfeit in the interim all his pay except fifty cents a month, and at the expiration of his time of service to be drummed out of the army. Pretty rough usage that, and telling very poorly for the merciful disposition of our military men. But its all right, I suppose.

A correspondent of the St. Louis *Republican* says that the "dragoons stationed in Utah should be sent across the country into Oregon to attack the Indians there, as they are well mounted and in a good state of discipline, well drilled and fit for service of this kind." [5] This fellow, whoever he is, pretends great wisdom, and lays down what he considers proper in the premises, with the air of a Solon; perhaps you think I ought to name some military genius, as I would do if his advice was confined to that sphere, but he is wise in everything. Now, I am a member of the Second Dragoons, the regiment referred to, and I must confess that this sage correspondent gives us more credit than we are entitled to. So far from being well mounted, we have but twenty horses in camp, and they would not sustain three days hard march. "Well disciplined" too, he says. Let the "discipline" displayed at Spanish Fork answer that, and to clinch the matter, I refer him to forty-seven general prisoners in our regimental guard house. As for drill, there has not been one day since Col. Cooke left here, that the men have not been drilled at passing "dobies," and making "Mormon mortar," and the majority of the regiment is now raw recruits, who have not sufficient practice in the use of arms to execute *moulinet*[6]

[5] This quotation has not been found in the issues of the *Daily Missouri Republican* between July and December 1858, but the Fillmore City, U.T., *Deseret News* of September 22, 1858, had an editorial that said in part: "The Army of Utah is as well and gallantly commanded and officered and efficiently disciplined as it is superiorly equipped and generously sustained." Earlier the correspondent of the *New York Herald*, writing from Camp Scott, U.T., on June 4, 1858, said: "The discipline of the troops is said by persons better capable of judging of it than I am to be very perfect. Major McCullock declared that he never saw troops better disciplined, better disposed or better prepared for the field." See the *New York Herald*, July 2, 1858.

[6] The moulinet was a saber exercise whose object was to make the joints of the arm and wrist supple and increase a man's dexterity. It was done as a preparation for other exercises. At the command the dismounted trooper extends his arm to its full length in front of him and swings the unsheathed saber in a circular motion downward and over his head to the starting point. In the case of a rear moulinet the saber was swung in a circle from left to right in front of the trooper.

properly. These writers, who pretend to know so much about matters and things in general, found their remarks on hearsay — a very poor guide I take it. No man should write about what he has not thoroughly acquainted with, in the style of these would be sage individuals, and the only way they can discover the true state of affairs at Camp Floyd, is to come and see, or subscribe for the BULLETIN. I am well aware that our regiment enjoys a good reputation among military men, and *has* deserved it: but the men who earned its glory are nearly all gone, and the few that remain are too old to be effective. Moreover, our greatest officers are absent: Gen. Harney no longer belongs to us, Col. Cooke is not here, Col. May is at Fort Kearney, Capt. Steele[7] is away and many others are too far distant to reach us before next summer. In fact the only officers we have here are Capts. Howe, Campbell[8] and Anderson, (and good men too,) and a squad of inexperienced Lieutenants, the batch of whom would not be worth a continental, if assailed by a score of Spokanes or Blackfeet.

Some reckless slanderer, destitute of either honor, honesty or truth, says that "Brigham Young remains secluded, never leaving his house, but concealing himself from the rage of the Mormons, who can now see his duplicity and falsehood." [9] This is untrue, entirely without foundation. Brigham has been here several times, since I came to Camp Floyd, and the Mormons show him the utmost respect wherever he goes. He is still their head man, and his word is omnipotent wherever Mormonism has a foot-hold. My worthy friend, the Bishop, of whom I spoke to you in my last, introduced me to him, adding that I was a printer; "Ah!" said Brigham, "then I presume you have often put in type 'our own correspondent's' accounts of affairs out here. Now, do you take me for the terrible, treasonable, anathematizing, many-wived[,] law-resisting rascal I have been represented?" And, of a truth I should say, no. He has an open, pleasant countenance, that speaks of benevolence, humanity and frankness;

---

[7] William Steele graduated from West Point in 1840 and was assigned to the Second Dragoons. He won a brevet captain's rank in the Mexican War and a regular promotion to that rank in 1851.

[8] Reuben P. Campbell graduated from West Point in 1840 and was assigned to the Second Dragoons. He rose steadily and was promoted to captain in 1851.

[9] For similar accounts see the St. Louis *Daily Missouri Republican*, August 12 and 19, 1858.

there is nothing in his appearance to indicate the bold bad man that the race of Drummonds have represented him to be. I am not much of a physiognomist but I take it that Brigham Young is one of the *best abused men* we have within our large domain. He is not very well liked by some of our officers, I admit, but the cause of it is this: He holds the opinion that "the rank is but the guinea's stamp, the man's the gold for a' that," [10] and an honest, upright, sober, private soldier is a better man by far than a king without these qualities. Consequently he "cuts" the drunken loon with the epauletted coat, and takes to the plain shoulder and sleeve of an honorable enlisted man. This may account for the lying propensities of some of the worthies who "do" the correspondence for the New York *Herald* and kindred sheets,[11] who finding that though they do write for the papers, Mr. Young will not countenance their indulgence in low, vulgar freaks, while he has a voice among the people, the "galled jade winces," and Brigham's sturdy application of the lash to the favorite sports of some of the scribbling geniuses is the cause of the slanderous reports they so industriously circulated. I am no friend of Mormonism, or the policy of Brigham Young, but I approve of giving "the devil his due." He is no longer Governor nor is he vested with any civil authority; but Young's moral powers remain unaltered and unweakened with the Mormon settlers of

UTAH.

[10] Robert Burns' poem, "For A' That and A' That," published in 1800. "Is there, for honesty poverty/ That hangs his head, and a' that;/ The coward-slave, we pass him by,/ We dare be poor for a' that!/ For a' that, and a' that,/ Our toils obscure, and a' that,/ The rank is but the guinea's stamp,/ The man's the gowd for a' that."

[11] In his book on Salt Lake City Burton uses a quotation from the "correspondent of that amiable and conscientious periodical the 'New York Herald.'" See Burton, *City of the Saints*, p. 424n. See also the St. Louis *Daily Missouri Republican*, September 8, 1858.

A detachment of soldiers from Camp Floyd on a wood gathering expedition.

Camp Floyd, U.T.
November 10th, 1858
[15]

We have at length, thanks to Heaven and Colonel Howe, got into our quarters and discarded for this winter, at least, the miserable protection of Sibley's patent tent,[1] in which our army suffered so much last winter. We are well supplied with fire-wood, and I think we will be quite comfortable during the coming season. To each room twenty feet square, we have twelve men, so that there is no scarcity of companions; and although you might think it somewhat crowded, to us who have lain so long in tents, it is quite commodious. We moved in on the 1st inst., and on that night I slept for the first time beneath a roof since we left Carlisle Barracks — the third day of May last. To many of our men it is the first time that they have had any better covering than a canvass tent since June, 1857. You may well imagine then how gladly we took up our abode in our "doby" houses, though to the eye of some of my friends they would appear very poor dwellings, scarcely fit for cattle pens. We, however, are far away from civilization, unless we count the small speck at Salt Lake City, and deem our mud buildings the most comfortable structures in creation. It is strange how things change when viewed in different lights. Ere I assumed the character of a soldier, I would no more think of living in such an edifice than I would of taking a position in the penitentiary as

---

[1] On the other hand, Assistant Surgeon E. J. Bailey at Camp Scott, U.T., wrote to Lieutenant William W. Burns, the regimental quartermaster of the Fifth Infantry, on February 5, 1855, that the Sibley tent was "one of the greatest blessings the present age has given the soldier." See "AG Letters," roll 575. Burton says that the Sibley tent gave universal satisfaction at Camp Scott in the winter of 1857–58. He quotes Captain Marcy that none of the tents used by European armies compared to the Sibley in point of convenience, comfort, and economy in cold weather. But in summer, like all conical tents, it had disadvantages including a lack of room for comfortably disposing of one's kit. See Burton, *City of the Saints*, pp. 108–9.

An early view of Camp Floyd.

wool-carder or shoe builder; but when I took up my arms and moved into it on the first, I felt thankful that I was fortunate enough to obtain such a winter residence.

A rich case was tried at a general court martial in our camp a few days since. Lieut. Gay[2] — one of those good natured, fun-loving fellows, who delight in baulking and baffling such consummate old women as Col. ——,[3] was put under arrest for some trifling offence. The day after this event the Colonel received the following note:

"LIEUTENANT COLONEL —:

"Sir: This morning I lost a very valuable dog, and as I am unable to search for him, being under arrest by your order, I

---

[2] Ebenezer Gay graduated from West Point in 1854, and the following year was given a regular commission as a second lieutenant in the Second Dragoons. By March 1861 he was a first lieutenant and less than two months later a captain. While serving in the Union Army during the Civil War he won two brevets for gallant and meritorious service.

[3] This was Lieutenant Colonel Marshall Saxe Howe. For a note on his career see note 8, chap. 12.

ask you to detail fifty or a hundred men to hunt for him among
the mountain passes of Utah,

"Yours, very respectfully,

"Lieut. Gay, 2d Dragoons."

Of course the old fellow was very wrathy on the receipt of the
note, and he instantly prepared charges against Mr. Gay, for disrespect and contempt towards his superior and commanding officer.
Gay was arraigned, and pled guilty, urging that he always spoke what
he felt, and that it was utterly impossible to feel ought save contempt
towards the Colonel. Of course the Court had to pass *some* sentence
upon him, and he was accordingly sentenced to be reprimanded in
general orders, the lightest they could possibly give.[4] General Johns-

---

[4] The first charge against Gay was "Conduct to the prejudice of good order
and military discipline." According to the specifications of this charge Gay left
Company G, Second Dragoons, on or about the evening of September 16, without
written authority, and did not return until the next afternoon; that in his absence
he neglected his duties as company commander and by failing to report his return;
and finally that while under arrest with charges pending against him he wrote an
insubordinate, disrespectful, and offensive letter to Colonel Howe. The second
charge was that Gay showed contempt and disrespect toward his commanding
officer. The specifications of this was that he made both a verbal and a written
request for a search for his dog. According to the court-martial records, the letter
read as follows: "Sir, I have the honor to report that this morning I lost a very
valuable dog, and being unable to search for the same, (being in arrest) I most
most respectfully suggest that a party be sent out to endeavor to recover it."
     Gay pleaded not guilty to the charges and specifications. He argued that
officers regarded the dragoon camp as a part of the camp occupied by all troops;
that officers were in the habit of visiting other regimental camps without permission; and that Colonel Howe had told his adjutant that only one officer had to be
present for reveille. As for the letter, he did not intend it to be trifling or disrespectful, and as soon as he heard that it was so regarded he attempted to withdraw it.
To support the story of his intentions, he called as witnesses James Livingston, a
sutler, Corporal Richard Mansel, who actually wrote the letter dictated by Gay,
and First Lieutenant William A. Webb of the Fifth Infantry.
     The court found Gay guilty of the three specifications of the first charge, but
omitted the description of the letter as "insubordinate, disrespectful and offensive."
It found him guilty of the specification of the second charge, omitted the char-
acterization of the letter, and not guilty of contempt and disrespect for his commanding officer. He was sentenced to be reprimanded in the General Orders of
the commanding officer of the Department.
     Brevet Brigadier General Albert S. Johnston, commanding the Department
of Utah, did not approve of the court's finding Gay guilty of sending the letter and
not guilty of the charge of contempt and disrespect for his commanding officer.
But he did approve of the verdict. In his reprimand Johnston said in part: "Educated by his country, he [Gay] owes her the benefit of the talents she has developed,

ton gave a long lecture about the duty of officers, etc., and the "high tone of the members of the military class of our country." By "high tone" I suppose he meant the *loud noises* they are in the habit of making about camp — but so far as I could see, his order hit the Colonel much harder than it did Gay's, and I saw the old fellow bite his lip in rage as the Adjutant read some cutting remarks too plainly aimed at him to be misunderstood. When the specification containing the obnoxious note was read to the troops, a general laugh broke out all along the line, while here and there the crys of "good," "brave," etc., were heard. It was some moments before the adjutant could proceed with the reading; meanwhile the old Colonel fretted, foamed and roared, pale with rage and baffled vengeance. Mr. Gay, who is a great favorite with the men, stood calm and unmoved during the entire reading of the order, but when the soldiers gave such evidence of their approbation, he turned around and bowed to the parade. The Colonel vowed vengeance but has as yet done nothing.

On the night of Tuesday last, our company was thrown into a terrible excitement by the cry of "get your sabres and fall out." It was about ten o'clock and I was awakened by the cry, having just fallen asleep. Springing up and putting on my clothes, I rushed out with my sabre in my hand. In a moment, half a hundred men in their shirts and drawers, with naked sabres in their hands, were upon the Company parade. "Follow!" shouted the first Sergeant, and off we went on a run. A sentinel tried to stop us, but he was knocked down and run over; the guard, twenty-eight strong, ranged on the bridge to oppose us, but they soon gave way before the fierce onset. I rushed on with the rest, not knowing what was the cause of the outbreak, but with an indistinct idea that there was fighting to be done somewhere. At length I asked what was up. "Oh," said one, "the dough-boys (Infantry) are beating one of our men." Finding that it was merely a drunken row, some of us turned to go back, but were stopped with

selected for and maintained in a position which few are fortunate in obtaining and thousands are desirous of filling, she claims the time and devotion to her interests to which she is entitled and can procure from others; sustained in a profession which is characterized by the high tone of its members, it ought to be his first care to maintain in all their integrity, his conduct and example, those elevated principles and that courtesy which marks its excellence." "Judge Advocate General's Office, Court Martial Records," HH–976, box 166, R.G. 153, National Archives.

the cry of "Lieut. Gay is killed!" At this a yell of vengeance was raised, and all hands pitched in to avenge their favorite officer. Scarcely, however, had the crowd burst in the door of a house where the row was, than we heard Gay's voice from the opposite side of the run: "Hold on, boys; wait til I come over." This from him was enough. All was quiet. When he reached us he told us that he was neither killed nor hurt; that he was not out of his room that evening, and had been in no danger. We then went in to see what was the cause of the noise, when it was discovered that Lieutenants B—— F—— and L——, of our regiment,[5] were having a three handed fight, and that there was a prospect of its ending like the battle between the Killkenny cats. As the boys did not care which whipped, we went home to bed, wishing the combatants were all in a place not to be mentioned in the presence of delicate individuals. How the battle ended, I do not know, as I have seen neither of the three since, but I understand that they spoiled one another's countenances beautifully.

The rascally conduct of the soldiers at Spanish Fork is beginning to have its effect, and the Indians are already in war paint. They have danced the war dance; They have unburied the hatchet, and soon the war whoop will ring through our valleys and along our mountains. But this is what I expected, what everyone expected, who is acquainted with the circumstances of that villainous proceeding. They are robbing and plundering the settlers, and six men are reported killed at Salt Creek. The man who has charge of the Government herd and others, have appealed to General Johnston for protection, the former declaring that he will abandon the herd unless soldiers are sent out immediately. As yet, however, nothing has been done on our side, and every day brings news of some fresh Indian outrage.[6] Why

[5] Probably Second Lieutenant Thomas J. Berry, Brevet Second Lieutenant Samuel W. Ferguson, and Second Lieutenant H. Brock Livingstone.

[6] The Salt Lake City correspondent of the St. Louis *Daily Missouri Republican* reported on October 22 that Indian disturbances had resulted in the deaths of two white men from Fillmore City, U.T. See the *Republican* of November 18, 1858. A letter from Camp Floyd, signed "Reporter" appeared in Kirk Anderson's *Valley Tan* (see note 5, chap. 16) on November 19, 1858, which said in part: "On Saturday last 3 companies of Infantry left here for Rush Valley to join the companies of Dragoons there, for the protection of the U.S. herds, against the Indians, which threaten to drive the same off. I do not doubt that if the Indians should venture such a thing, they will be duly punished for it."

measures to prevent the red skins from keeping up their work of vengeance are not taken I cannot say. There seems to be a strange fatality hanging over this Territory, that now when anarchy is hushed, the red man is at his savage work, and towns and settlements are threatened with destruction. But on the men who had command of the Spanish Fork expeditions the blame must fall. They are the cause of all the bloodshed, robberies and burnings. They killed innocent, inoffensive Indians, and permitted their men to rob them of their winter's provision, and the work now begun is but the natural consequence of such conduct. The Indians were faithful so long as they were properly treated, but when the foot of oppression and wrong is set upon them they turn and sting. Who can blame them? Not I, for one.

When I spoke favorably of the Mormons generally, I did not mean to say that there were no fools, etc., among them, and as a faithful chronicler of passing events, I feel it is my duty to give their bad as well as their good side, to the public of my far-off eastern home, when I write of the people who have made their homes among the mountains of this almost unknown Territory. I called a few days since upon a thorough-bred Mormon, one of the fellows who were going to "play the devil and break things," if Uncle Sam meddled with their domestic institutions. Among other things that he showed me, was a file of the *Deseret News*, the home organ of the Latter Day Saints.[7] It contained many wicked things, together with much that was foolish and ridiculous. I observed, however, that neither Young, Kimball,[8] or any of the leading Mormons were cited to sustain its treasonable doctrines; but that all were the mere opinions of the editor of this delectable sheet. As a specimen of the kind of stuff it contained, I quote the following, which was published under the head of "Resistance no Rebellion:"

"It is a well known fact, that since ever the prophet and patriarch, Joseph Smith, received his inspiration from the God

[7] Albert Carrington (1813–99) established the *Deseret News* as a Mormon newspaper in 1850 in Salt Lake City.

[8] Heber C. Kimball (1801–68) was one of Brigham Young's chief counselors. Together with Young and Willard Richards he constituted the First Presidency — the executive head of the Mormon church. He was elected chief justice and lieutenant governor of the State of Deseret, and later served as a member of the legislature. When Utah became a federal territory he served as a member of the council and as its president in 1855–58.

of Heaven, the United States Government, and the blood-thirsty mob who are the 'free and independent sovereigns' of that *bastard Republic*, have persecuted the members of the Church of Jesus Christ of Latter Day Saints, everywhere and on every occasion.

"Their hands are red with the blood of martyrs who suffered for their religion.

"They murdered the modern Messiah, Joseph Smith, and deserve a more terrible curse than has fallen upon the Jews for their sacrifice of Jesus.

"They have sent an armed body of murderers and land pirates to plunder our cities, butcher our men and ravish our women.

"They have dared to insult God's chosen people with low epithets, even though the Lord of Heaven has sent famine and suffering upon them.

* * *

"Under these circumstances our duty to ourselves, to our families and to our God is to kneel and pray for Heaven's assistance, and then march on to meet these fanatical cut-throats, and forever put an end to their diabolical workings, even though we have to push through to Washington and hang the unhallowed villian who is at the head of that nation of robbers and murderers — the United States." [9]

This is but a single specimen of which I might send you thousands, but that, I think, will suffice. Under the head of *"The Public Treasurer,"* and bearing the signature of "John Jacques," I found the following exquisite gem of Mormon poesy:

> "When Uncle Samself wisely stands,
> With usurped powers in his hands,
> And issues forth unjust commands;
> And when God's kingdom, little known,
> At best a little mountain stone,
> Which Uncle Sam thinks all his own;
> Then James Buchanan is the man,
> With his Tom-foolish Utah plan,
> To drain the public treasury.

[9] The editor has been unable to find this article in the *Deseret News.*

"When Sam and Buch lay down and rot,
And their posterity's forgot,
But not their hellish Utah plot;
And when God's kingdom takes its stand,
In this his people's promised land,
To rule, to govern and command;
Then Brigham Young is just the man,
By many a wise and happy plan,
To fill the public treasury." [10]

Who will say that we have not, out here in the wilds of Utah, many "mute inglorious Miltons" and "Cromwells, guiltless of their country's blood." [11] I rallied my friend, the doby-laying Bishop, about the matter, and he assured me that Carrington of the *News* was not and never had been a member of the Church, and that by some he was considered insane, while others shrewdly suspected that he was a tool of their enemies to bring contempt upon them. Be this as it may, he has very few supporters among the settlers of this Territory.

I notice in the papers a statement that the "Gentiles have elected a member of the Territorial Legislature from the Green River County District." This is right, except in a few particulars. There is no "Gentile" elected to the Legislature; there is no such district as that named, and there is no such County in the Territory as Green River county. Whence this report originated I do not know, but it will give you an idea of how reliable the "advices" of some of your contemporaries are. I, as a typo, am sincerely sorry to see such rediculous statements in the newspapers; but it cannot be otherwise so long as they manufacture their own correspondence, as I feel certain some of them must do, or such blunders could not possibly occur. As well might the papers of distant States attempt to get up Philadelphia news without the BULLETIN, as for a journal to pretend to give correct accounts of what is transpiring here without having a correspondent in the Territory, or to make a passable falsehood without a knowledge of the customs, manners and society of

UTAH.

[10] *Deseret News*, February 24, 1858. There are minor differences between "Utah's" quotation and the version in the *Deseret News*.

[11] Thomas Gray, "Elegy Written in a Country Churchyard," lines 59–60.

Camp Floyd, U.T.
Nov. 20, 1858
[16]

With politics I have nothing to do — it is not at all in my line — being now a "military man" (Private Thing-um-bub, U.S.A.) and having as yet never had the right to exercise the freeman's privilege of the elective franchise. To be sure, I have hurrahed for Taylor, for Scott, and for Fremont; have marched in political processions and helped to swell the chorus of campaign song, when "Rough and Ready," "Old Chippewa" and "The Pathfinder" were before the people of "our great Republic;" [1] but this was all but my voice; "my *vote* was beyond my reach, until I reached the period that is called "of age." That period has not yet arrived, and when it does, I still, having sold my birthright for a striped jacket and a cockade, will not be able to make myself felt in our national contests. But, be this as it may, I have got hold of a precious piece of political trickery that is being attempted by the office-holders of this Territory, and for the management of which Judge Eckles,[2] of the Supreme Court, now in the States, is the agent.

A certain party of the "unterrified" are opposed to Governor Cumming,[3] who is possessed of rather more honesty than is generally met with in Democratic office-holders, and they wish to have him removed and a more pliable tool appointed in his stead — somebody that has no conscience, will do, if a sufficiently soft dough-head cannot

---

[1] General Zachary Taylor, "Old Rough and Ready," was the Whig Party's successful candidate for president in 1848. General Winfield Scott, "Old Chippewa," was the unsuccessful candidate of the Whigs in the presidential election of 1852. John Charles Fremont, "The Pathfinder," ran unsuccessfully for president on the Republican party slate in the election of 1856.

[2] Delana R. Eckels was the chief justice of Utah Territory.

[3] Alfred Cumming of Georgia was President Buchanan's appointee as governor of Utah Territory. See Introduction, p. 6.

be found. Judge Eckles, as agent and grand master of this conspiracy, sets out for Washington, to lay before the President "charges and specifications" against Governor Cumming, among which the most prominent one is, as the judge confessed, to a soldier who accompanied him to Fort Bridger, that his Excellency has turned Mormon, and set up a harem in Fillmore city. Others are, that he is neglectful of his duty, drunken, dissolute and unpopular. All of which are "false as fiends." But the judge must needs have backing for his sweeping denunciation of the Governor; so he gets a creature of his to wait upon Dr. Forney,[4] the Superintendent of Indian Affairs, with what is represented to be a simple note to the Hon. Mr. Bekles, inviting him to partake of a public dinner at Salt Lake City, ere he returns to the States, and asks the Dr. to sign it. An opportune moment is chosen, when Dr. F. is busily engaged with the duties of his office, and he signs the note without looking at its contents. The Judge declines the proferred honor, but puts the note in his pocket. Before long, however, the worthy Dr. discovers that he has appended his name to an article that severely censures Gov. Cumming, and in which it is hoped that "the efforts of your Honor (the Judge), will succeed in remedying the evil, and have this traitor removed from our camp." Accordingly a note, signed by the Superintendent of Indians Affairs, appears in the *Valley Tan*, the "Gentile" paper of the Territory, disclaiming any knowledge of such matters being contained in the invitation, and giving the Judge and his co-workers a pretty severe rap over the knuckles for their contemptible rascality.[5] The trick played upon Mr. Forney is a very scurvy one among gentlemen, but probably it is all right among politicians. For my part, I do not care which side whips, though I would prefer seeing the battle fought honorably. But this is the matter as we have it, and you may draw whatever conclusions you see fit in the matter. I have done my share.

[4] Jacob Forney of Pennsylvania was appointed the superintendent of Indian Affairs in Utah Territory. Previously the post had been included with that of the governor.

[5] Kirk Anderson established the non-Mormon or "gentile" newspaper, the *Valley Tan*, in Salt Lake City in November 1858. It derived its name from a term first used in connection with leather made in the territory in contrast to that imported from the United States. Gradually the term came to apply to any article of local manufacture. The article to which "Utah" refers appeared in the *Valley Tan* of November 6, 1858.

120

When Mr. Howell Cobb,[6] in the plentitude of his wisdom, bought in the bonds of the United States Government at sixteen percent premium, he probably thought he was doing an act of great financial sagacity, that would reverberate to his fame through succeeding ages, and bring upon himself the admiration of the American people, as one of the most clear sighted men that ever occupied the chair first filled by Alexander Hamilton.[7] But if he did, he was egregiously mistaken; for I can certify that one portion of his fellow men, at least, feel severely the fact that Mr. Cobb, when he emptied the Treasury, acted the part of a —— I was going to say fool, but that would be improper language towards so high a dignitary. Here we are in Utah, soldiers teamsters and employees of the Government generally, without a cent of money in our pockets — I have not been paid since I enlisted — and not the least prospect of getting any.[8] Yet we cannot even procure a cigar without the cash, and a notice at the post-office tells us that "all letters must be pre-paid." Now, how in the name of sense — if the administration knows such a thing — can they expect men to protect the frontiers, to keep the Mormons under subjection, and prevent the Indians from committing outrages, if they are denied even the paltry pittance of twelve dollars per month that we are legally entitled to?

Many of us have no other real pleasure than the occasional receipt of a letter from those we have left behind, and yet three cents required for postage cannot be got from the Government. In this state of affairs, who can wonder if desertions are frequent, and men are continually giving illustrations of the text, "you shall all look for me in the morning, and shall not find me?"[9] I would that Cobb were a soldier

[6] Howell Cobb (1815–68) of Georgia was the secretary of the treasury in James Buchanan's administration. His humor and companionship were prized by the president. He had no particular financial ability. In the early part of the Panic of 1857 he attempted to stabilize the situation by offering to redeem various classes of government bonds in gold at a premium if they were presented immediately. He took other steps to try to ease the demand for specie. The response was so great that within three weeks Cobb had to cease redemptions and disbursements.

[7] Alexander Hamilton (1755–1804) was the secretary of the treasury during George Washington's first term.

[8] This was not true. Members of the company were paid on June 30 for the period since April 30. See Muster Roll, Company A Dragoon Recruits.

[9] Prov. 1:28.

himself for a short time; I think he would not be guilty of such folly when the next "panic" arises.

Camp Floyd is "coming out" now. We have a "Dramatic Association," and "An Ethiopian Opera Troupe," that give nightly exhibitions for the delight of the motley population of this post. I am always favorable to whatever tends to promote good humor and drive away "dull care;" but I cannot give a word of favor to these performances, though "Headquarters" smile benignly upon them. The plays are of the most vulgar and degrading character, the managers appearing to think that the soldiers are the "scum of the earth," and as a matter of course, *filth* is the most palatable to them. I have seen officers at these performances, out of uniform, of course, who appeared to relish the low slang of the actors and actresses with great gusto, and I notice that they always lead off in the "applause," which will be easily accounted for in the fact that they are all "dead heads." Notwithstanding the low character of the pieces played here, the theatre is doing a great business — as tickets are sold on credit, an order being given on the paymaster for the amount.[10] Singular, is it not, that our officers cannot make an arrangement of this kind with the sutler and postmaster, so that things more necessary to our comfort and happiness may be obtained? Iago declares that "a soldier's a man," [11] but I doubt very much whether our officers entertain the same opinion. A soldier is a dog to them, a mere nothing, and woe betide the enlisted man who shows the least idea of *their* worthlessness.

To show how sensible and considerate our officers are, this will serve: The Adjutant of our regiment has issued an order making it a criminal offence for men to appear on parade without having their boots blackened, the belts varnished, and every thing in good condition; yet we can get neither blacking or varnish in camp, and not a man in the regiment has been issued a leathern stock — a thing also required in the order. But this is only a specimen of the way we do things out here. Fellows are let loose from West Point, full of the idea that they are born to rule, and soon they let out their dignity in everything that affects their subordinates. Men, in many cases better men

[10] Notices of the theatrical activities at Camp Floyd began appearing in the *Valley Tan* of December 10, 1858.

[11] William Shakespeare's *Othello*, act 2, scene 3.

a view to avoid, or obviate that the examination was y to more extensive ones summer. The reconnois-made so far as the lateness fied; and although it has not its realization of the hopes yet he was so fortunate as Spring to those which are o exist in that region, and made with his wagons, is ted by the California Mail Chorpenning, as affording the oid the Goose Creek moun-the Humboldt; whence the sible in winter the rest of lfornia. Next spring it is irther discoveries and im-be made on this route.

he late papers, that an ova-iven in St. Louis, to Mr. iis very quick trip of be-days with the Mail from o that City, by the Fort Fort Smith routes; and that route was 2765 miles. The is must not be surprised to carried by our northern as short, if not shorter ance by this route cannot —From St. Louis to Fort) miles; Fort Leavenworth, y Bridger's Pass and Tim-120 miles; and thence to ty 800 miles: in all 2420 or, *outhern route by 345 miles.*

ersonal.

ptain John Radford, and ins, two old St. Louisans, ok their departure for Cal-first named gentlemen in-rom thence to the States. shortly after they left, that

Theatre—Camp Floyed.

We made a hasty visit to Camp Floyd a few days since, and while there took a daylightpeep into the Theatre. Al-though not yet completed and the work-men still busily engaged, yet we could not but admire the taste displayed in the whole arrangement, especially when we took into consideration the difficulties they have had to encounter. The stage scenery and "properties" generally, ex-hibit a degree of skill and energy that is certainly commendable. We saw with our own eyes, and what may ap-pear a little astonishing to our friends in the "United States of America," scenery and fresco work painted from the most ordinary materials. Mustard common chalk, and blacking used for boots, were the elements from which palaces, cottages, gardens, and land scapes generally, were brought out upon the canvass, while Shakspeare himself, the patron saint of the Dramatic Tem-ple the world over, loomed out above the curtain drop done up in common chalk. The scenic effect is certainly very creditable and exhibits a degree of artistic skill which is most praiseworthy, and the Bard of Avon, could he see his face sketched between the prospenium, even though in *chalk*, would not *redden* or blush at his likeness. We shall take the earliest opportunity we can spare to make another visit to the Camp and see the performance.

Court adjourned over until when Judge Sinclair charge ed to the Grand Jury.

Gen'l David H. Burr was bar, a position he once occu but from the privileges an which he was lawlessly dep going into the history of the trated against his fair fam shafts of malice that were when he was powerless, we c: his traducers missed the mar unscathed, while his enemies As a part of the proceeding the following forms an inte charges preferred against the bar named, and which will when the Court meets:—

I beg leave to submit to th owing motion: That Ja Hosea Stout, and J. C. Litt ed to show cause why thei iot he striken from the roll his Court, for the follow vit:

Firstly—For preferring fa nd infamouse charges, agai the Bar in this Court, when to be false; thus imposing and showing that their asser of the Bar, cannot be relie

Secondly—For threatening ing a Judge of this Court—in the discharge of his offi coercing him to adjourn th great detriment of the pub hindrance of justice.

Signed,
DAVI

GREAT SALT LAKE CIT
November

KIRK ANDERSON —
Editor of the "Valley Ta
We had Conference in Z bath, I want to know if you so, I did not see you, as I myself. I should like to kn is about your *Phiz.*, that

---

This description of the theatre at Camp Floyd appeared in the Valley Tan *on November 19, 1858.*

than themselves, are treated as brutes by these new fledged cadets, and they lord it over the veterans of the service with rods of iron. Our army is a miserable affair — totally unfit for the purpose for which it is intended — and will continue so until the officers — or at least a portion of them — are chosen from among the enlisted men who show themselves fit for the position. Let our "military men" serve a year or two in the ranks, then go to West Point and "finish off," and if we do not have a corps of officers that will outshine those of any other army in the world, I am much mistaken. No one can under-stand how to manage soldiers without having some experience from association with them, and the young West Pointers who come out here to command, are entirely too "green" for the responsible positions they have to occupy. As our older officers are not very fond of these "wild western scenes," the command of companies is often entrusted to young Brevet Second Lieutenants, who are as ignorant of the duties of the position, as the renowned Pillow was of the art of trench digging.[12] This is the state of three of the dragoon companies at present, here.

The Indians are proving quite troublesome throughout the territory, and the army is kept constantly on the *qui vive*. Two companies of dragoons under the command of Capt. R. P. Campbell,[13] have gone in the direction of Fillmore City, the seat of government — the savages in the vicinity threatening to execute deeds that would throw Judge Drummond's tale of Mormon rascality entirely in the shade. Another party of fifty dragoons, under Lieutenant Thomas J. Berry,[14] have been sent to Levere [Sevier?] Valley to settle the red-skins in that locality, but as yet, nothing has been heard from either. By the way, I should not be surprised if Mr. Berry's party was never heard of again, the Indians being very strong in the valley to which he has been sent, and not at all likely to allow fifty men to pass through their

[12] Gideon J. Pillow, a former law partner of President James K. Polk and a Democrat, was appointed a major general and assigned to the armies under General Zachary Taylor and General Winfield Scott during the Mexican War.

[13] For a sketch of Campbell's career, see note 8, chap. 14. The Muster Rolls and Inspection Returns of Campbell's Company E show that it left Camp Floyd on November 7, 1858, and took a position on Johnson's Creek. It returned to Camp Floyd on December 5, 1858. The other unit was an infantry company.

[14] See note 4, chap. 9.

country without showing fight. Is it not positive folly to send such puny forces against hundreds of well armed desperate red men, who are now excited to vengeful feelings by the brutal conduct of our soldiers at Spanish Fork? More than this; Berry is utterly unfit for a charge of this kind. He is an inexperienced young man, not long loosed from the bounds of West Point, and as yet has tried his "prentice hand" at nothing save boxing the ears of his inferiors *in rank*. But he is a fair specimen of our young officers, and may do "something for his country," though I doubt it.

We are in constant expectation of receiving orders to march for Oregon, or Washington Territory to take the red-skins there in hand; and it is generally reported and received that we will take up the march early in the Spring, traverse the Territory of Oregon and winter at Fort Walla Walla in Washington. This may or may not be so; but I have no doubt we will have plenty of rolling round to do next summer, though the plan may not yet be laid out. But though I would rather travel to other scenes, next season, I do not see the sense of taking us from this Territory so long as the Utah Indians continue troublesome. However, if the "powers that be" will it, it must, *per se*, be right.

The 12th inst. was a gala day in Camp Floyd. The different regiments and corps stationed here, were paraded under arms and in full uniform, to witness the unfurling of the first United States flag raised in Utah.[15] A hasty flag-staff had been erected, and everything pre-

[15] The *Valley Tan's* account of the ceremony, reprinted in the St. Louis *Daily Missouri Republican* of December 10, 1858, was as follows: "Twelve o'clock was the time fixed for the exercises, and about half past eleven the different regiments were on the ground in the following order: the 10th regiment, commanded by Col. C. F. Smith, and the 7th by Major Lynde on one side; the 5th commanded by Maj. S. Eastman on their right, and the 2nd dragoons commanded by Col. Howe, with Major Reynold's Battery opposite to the 5th. Thus forming three sides of a square. A few minutes before twelve, Gen. Johnston rode up to the scene of action accompanied by his staff, and took a position near Capt. Phelp's battery.

"At precisely twelve, Col. P. Morrison, in command of the camp, waved his sword, the signal for the salute to commence. Simultaneously with the report of the first piece, the band struck up Hail Columbia, and the flag was raised by Lieuts. Dudley and Murray, of the 10th Infantry, which ceremony was performed by these gentlemen in a exceedingly creditable manner. The Star Spangled Banner was then given by the different bands, and after the firing of the last gun, Col. Morrison gave the request for three cheers for our flag, which was given by all present with a will which showed with what interest the troops took part in this interesting performance. After which they marched to their respective quarters to the tune of Yankee Doodle."

pared to make the occasion an impressive as possible. At eleven o'clock A.M., the flag was run up by Col's. Morrison and Crossman,[16] the bands of the four regiments here playing the "Star Spangled Banner," and the artillery forming a national salute, one gun for each State in the Union. "Hail Columbia" was then played amid the cheers of the soldiers, and we were then marched off to the tune of "Yankee Doodle." When we reached our quarters, a gill of whiskey was issued to each man, and the lovers of that beverage wished we had a flag raising every day. Col. Howe was out in full uniform, and perfectly astonished, us all by his martial appearance, which contrasted greatly with his ragged dirty every day fit-out. But he was "Old Howe" withal, and nothing can change him to us who have to soldier under his command in

UTAH.

---

[16] For a sketch of Morrison's career, see note 6, chap. 12. George Hampton Crosman graduated from West Point in 1823 and was assigned to the Sixth Infantry. During the Mexican War he won a brevet major's rank for gallant and meritorious conduct in battle. A regular promotion to major quartermaster came in 1847, and within nine years he was deputy quartermaster general with the rank of lieutenant colonel.

Camp Floyd, U.T.
Dec. 1, 1858
[17]

In this far off region, it is many days ere we receive intelligence from the head-quarters of our nation, and as a natural consequence, there are always rumors circulating that such and such things have been done; that Thing-um-bob has been removed, and What-do-you-call-him appointed in his stead, &c., &c. The latest rumor is that Governor Cumming has been removed, and is to be taken to the States to be tried for high treason and gross misdemeanor in office; that Brigham Young, Heber Kimball, "Gen." Wells,[1] of the "Destroying Angels,"[2] are to be treated in the same manner; that the territory is under martial law, and that Gen. Johnston is clothed with absolute power, gubernatorial, legislative and military. This may all be true; and is no doubt the wish of the party, who have no great love for any man, who, like Governor Cumming, refuses to aid their schemes of rascality and robberies; but it strikes me that Mr. James Buchanan will find himself in a tight place if he undertakes the task of taking Messrs. Young & Co., to *his* capital for trial. The people of Utah are as much opposed to "transporting persons across the high seas to be tried for offenses committed here," as our forefathers were, and if he calls upon the military arm to aid him in his tyranny, he will find many of his best soldiers liable to be tried for treason.

[1] David H. Wells was superintendent of the public works and commander of the Nauvoo Legion.

[2] A name given to the Sons of Dan or Danites, a secret Mormon organization associated in gentile minds with the cold-blooded murder of those who disagreed with the Mormon hierarchy. For more information on the Danites see Harold Schindler's *Orrin Porter Rockwell, Man of God, Son of Thunder* (1966), pp. 42–49, 54–55, 63–64.

But perhaps you are not aware of the most serious objection to Governor Cumming, and the principal reason why his removal is so anxiously desired by the official worthies here. Well, he is accused of the fearful crime of anti slaveryism, and as the majority of our national appointees are Southerners, this is unpalatable, and they, in the language of our sublimity, "can't get along without our niggers." It is to be hoped that civil war will be averted from us.

As yet nothing has been heard from the detachment of dragoons that went out with Lieutenant Berry, or from the two companies under Captain Campbell, that I mentioned in my last, though I presume they are laying over in some pleasant valley, taking it easy. The Indians, however, continue troublesome, and one company of dragoons (A) is going to Salt Creek, about thirty miles from Camp Floyd, in a few days. Captain R. H. Anderson,[3] an able officer, will have command, and it is to be hoped that he will succeed in doing something for the quietude of the country. But if he goes to fight, it is perfectly absurd to send such a trifling force against the red skins, now that they are ready for the field. A troop or a squadron may do well enough to pounce upon an unsuspecting body of Indians, while wrapped in slumber, or busy with their domestic occupations, but to attack them when their rifles are unslung and they are keeping "watch and war" throughout the forest, requires a somewhat greater force, if I know anything of the red man. The Indians of the Utah vallies are peaceably inclined, and wish to foster amicable relations with the whites; but the butchery at Spanish Forks, which will in history as

---

[3] For a brief sketch of Anderson's career see note 2, chap. 11. The second issue of the *Valley Tan* said that: "We understand that information has been received at camp [Floyd] that the Indians in the neighborhood of Malad Valley, under the leadership of Tintic, are assembling in considerable numbers and threaten mischief." The paper noted that a delegation of these Indians had recently visited the Navajo's to urge a cooperative effort against the white men, but that the outcome of this overture was not known. "Arapine, one of the principal chiefs of one of the bands of Utes, has lately returned from that country, while crossing Green River, his wife was drowned. The women and children have been removed to Green River, and the men are congregating in the southern portion of the Territory, doubtless with the intention of stealing Government cattle and other stock belonging to the people of that vicinity. Gen. Johnston, in view of the threatened danger, has sent out several military squads to protect the valleys, where the Government stock is hearded, as well as the people in the vicinities generally." See the *Valley Tan*, November 5, 1858, reprinted in the St. Louis *Daily Missouri Republican*, December 10, 1858.

128

greatly tell to the glory of our army as the bombardment of Greytown to our navy,[4] has aroused their savage nature, and the war-whoop re-echoes through the canons, and the war dance is performed in the valleys, and from far and near the blackened warriors gather in council to decide the fate of our young settlements.

Assistant Surgeon Cuvier,[5] of the Second Dragoons, was shot and seriously wounded at Salt Lake City a few days since. Two pistol bullets penetrated his shoulder, and he lay for a while in a critical condition but is now happily recovering. Of course, this is another atrocious deed of the bloody-minded, rascally, rebellious Mormons! To be sure it is! How else could it be? The doctor is a very fine man; in fact he is beloved and respected by the soldiery, and I yield to none in admiring his good qualities. Yet I must admit that he is entirely to blame in this affair, and you will agree with me in the opinion that he was rightly served, when I tell you the circumstances. It appears that a young gentleman, in the employ of the government, was taken into custody for violating an ordinance of the city against persons being "drunk and disorderly in the public streets." Dr. C., being himself liable under the ordinance, undertook the man's rescue, and in his zeal drew his revolver on the police officers. One of the latter immediately fired upon the doctor, and wounded him as before-mentioned. I presume that you will have this matter in horrible colors from some of the voracious newspaper correspondents out here, but I can assert that my account is correct, and dare anyone to prove the contrary.[6] The doctor is an excellent gentleman, and I would be very sorry to say anything to his disadvantages; but the truth must be told, and I have no interest in doing otherwise. I do not pretend to

[4] The city of Greytown on the eastern coast of Nicaragua was maintained by the British as a part of their protectorate over the Mosquito Indians. Across the bay the American owned Accessory Transit Company established a settlement and officials of the company had difficulties with the pro-British settlers of Greytown. When the United States minister failed to get redress for damages to the company and injuries to himself, an American naval vessel destroyed Greytown by bombardment on July 13, 1853. No lives were lost as the inhabitants heeded a warning and left.

[5] John M. Cuyler of Georgia was commissioned as an assistant surgeon in 1834. Promotion to the ranks of captain and assistant surgeon came in 1847, major and surgeon later in that same year, and lieutenant colonel and medical inspector in 1862.

[6] Apparently the story did not get published in the newspapers.

equal any of my contemporaries as a writer, but I can claim at least the charm of veracity.

Desertions are quite frequent among the soldiers at this fort, and scarcely a night passes without one or more taking "French leave." They all strike for California. The roads to that State being thronged with travellers, they obtain a passage there without much trouble, as they are active as guards at night and look out by day. No pursuit is made, and the fellows who are dissatisfied walk off in open day without the least fear of being retaken.[7]

The state of health in camp is very low, and every day we hear the solemn notes of the dead march, and the roll of musketry over the grave of some poor fellow who has ended his earthly career in this distant region, far from the soothing hands of kind relatives.[8] It is sad to see the sick lying upon their beds, with no one to soothe their pillows but rough soldiers, whose awkward attempts to be gentle almost excite a smile in the midst of sorrow. Thank Heaven, I have, as yet, borne up well, and I hope that Providence will carry me safely through, that my dying hours may be amid more genial scenes and my last rites performed by gentler hands.

A light artillery company now here is to be stationed in Salt Lake City, and it is making preparations to start immediately. It is under the command of Captain Phelps,[9] and will remain until next spring, when it is to go to Oregon. The recent attack on Dr. Cuvier is the cause of this movement, and I presume that we will soon have trouble there from a collision of civil and military authorities. "We will see what we will see."

This morning an order came for our company to prepare for a month's scout, and we are to be supplied to-morrow with the necessary tents and other equipage. From the large amount of ammunition that we are receiving, I should judge that we [are] expected to do some fighting, and that some unfavorable intelligence has been pri-

[7] In 1853 the secretary of war reported that past experience showed that in an army of 10,000 men nearly 1,500 would desert each year. See Utley, *Frontiersmen in Blue*, pp. 40–41.

[8] When Camp Floyd (later called Fort Crittenden) closed on July 27, 1861, a total of 84 officers and enlisted men were buried there.

[9] John W. Phelps graduated from West Point in 1836 and was commissioned as a second lieutenant in the Fourth Artillery. He rose to the rank of first lieutenant in 1838, captain in 1850, and resigned in 1859.

130

vately received from the other parties now out. I should like to "smell powder" in a regular "pitch-in," merely for the novelty of the thing. As yet, I have never had the pleasure of participating in a fight of any consequence, and I would should like to see how the Indians would receive a charge of dragoons in a case where the chances were equal. That the red-skins are intent upon a fight is clear, as old Tich Nich, the chief of the Utahs, has declared that the death of his son, who was killed at Spanish Fork, demands the extirpation of every "blue jacket" in the Territory, and that if the good Spirit gives him the power and length of life, he will revenge the murder. In contests with these Indians, the Infantry are entirely useless. The natives are all well mounted, and scud away over the plains, to the great annoyance of the "double quick." The dragoons can pursue them mounted, with fair prospects of bringing them under the sabre, and when they seek the shelter of the canons, can be speedily dismounted, and with their Sharp's Rifles and revolvers do effective service on the spot, much more than can be done with the unwieldy muskets and bayonets of the Infantry. But such small parties as are sent out cannot avail much, and if we do fight, it will be to our loss, unless our superior arms give us the advantage. However, by the time I next write, I will have to tell you of blood-shed and battle.

So good old Pennsylvania has redeemed herself, and even "Ault Berks" has shaken off her ancient allegiance to Democracy, and sent J. Glancy Jones up Salt River.[10] "Like thunder from a cloudless heaven" this news came upon us, and although I am certain it was entirely unexpected here, the soldiers who served in Kansas declare that they "knew it would be so as soon as the people got their eyes open to the way things were done in '56, when they put honest men in jail and let thieves run at large." The Gentile settlers in this country

[10] Jehu Glancy Jones (1811–78) had a legal career in Easton, Pennsylvania, before entering politics. Elected as a Democratic congressman, he served from 1851 to 1853, but declined reelection. Later he was elected to fill a vacancy caused by the death of the incumbent and served from 1854 to 1858, when he resigned. He was an unsuccessful candidate in the election of 1858. Political intrigue supposedly kept him out of the Buchanan cabinet. He was a supporter of the president, and in 1858 was appointed minister to Austria. Berks County, Pennsylvania, was known as "Ault Berks," and by virtue of representing that district in Congress, the term became Jones' nickname. See Charles H. Jones, *The Life and Public Services of J. Glancy Jones*, 2 vols. (1910).

are nearly all Democrats, and they do not much like the downfall of the party in *their* Keystone, as they took it. Nor is it relished by the ultra Mormons, who have not lost sight of the Republican declaration of war against the "twin relics of barbarism — polygamy and slavery." Why is it that you, in Philadelphia, have re-elected that handsome specimen of Democracy, "the widow's friend?" [11] Was the Navy Yard too strong for freedom, or is it the result of opinion? He of all others, I should have wished beaten. But on the whole I am heartily glad of the result, and more especially, of the election of S. S. Blair, Esq.,[12] from the Somerset District, than whom a better, more honest, upright, and straightforward man does not march in the phalanx of freedom. You have done rejoicing over this, in Pennsylvania, I presume; but you must excuse me for joining the hallelujah at this late hour, in shout of triumph and three times three for my native State, from the far-off [land?] of

UTAH.

[11] This was Thomas B. Florence, whose reelection in 1858 was described by the *Bulletin* of October 12, 1858, as "the only exception to a clean sweep of the [pro-Buchanan] Lecompton Democracy within the bounds of the consolidated city." Florence (1812–75) was first elected to the House of Representatives in 1850 and served until 1861.

[12] Samuel S. Blair (1821–90) was a lawyer in Hollidaysburg, Pennsylvania, who was active in Republican politics. He served in the House of Representatives from 1859 to 1863.

From Utah Salt Lake City.
Jan. 25, 1859
[18]

The condition of the army is very quiet and comfortable.[1] Now and then detached bodies are ordered to move to some point to suppress Indian insurrections, but they invariably find but little to do. I think and know that about the most use for them will be to quell *white insurrections*. It is not supposed at present by most people here, that the Mormons are reduced to a state of quietness, and you need not be astonished, ere long, to hear that we have a fuss. There is a constant bickering going on, which may yet terminate in what you least expect. Many of us here hope not, but the action of some of the

A view of the Wasatch Mountains.

[1] Although this item was printed with the name "Utah" at the end, it does not seem to be of the same character as those that came before and afterward. Assuming that it was written by "Utah," its brevity must be attributed to the fact that the author was then supposedly suffering from a gunshot wound in the arm. See chap. 19.

132

Mormon people seems to encourage the like, but not by any means the majority. A little time will be required to develop their course.

Even the Secretary of State, Mr. Hartnett,[2] who has heretofore been considered rather lenient to these people, has been threatened, on the streets, with violence, as has also Mr. Kirk Anderson, of the *Valley Tan*. Their lives, however, are not in imminent danger as yet, but this and other actions show but little congeniality of feeling between the Mormon people and *the people of the United States*.

The merchants have all bare shelves in their stores. Many have sent to California for goods in order to replenish their exhausted stocks. Their profits have been very good.

The Legislature has adjourned for this session. They ask, by a memorial, to be admitted as a State in the Union, but I promise that Governor Cumming has not yet given his signature to the document, and if I know him intimately, and I think I do, he will "sca[r]cely."

UTAH.

[2] John Hartnett held the office of secretary in the territorial government of Utah.

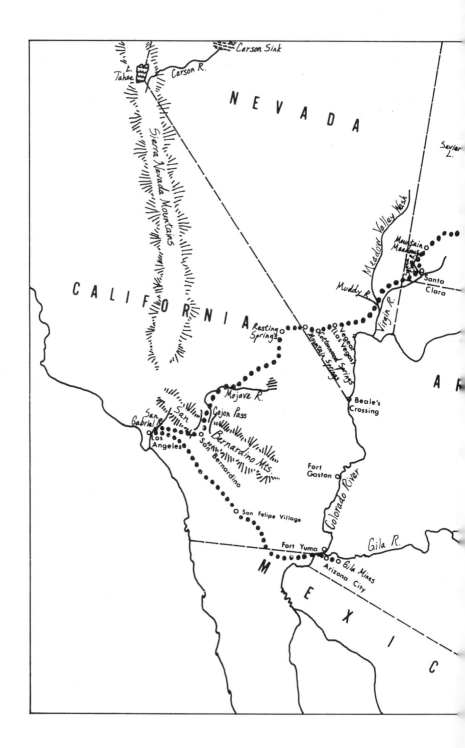

"Utah's" Approximate Route
from Camp Floyd to
the Gila River, New Mexico Territory,
via Los Angeles in 1859

Map information on "Utah's" route
was researched by Todd I. Berens.
The map was drafted by Mark Takemura.

SCALE 0   50   100   150   200 MILES

Los *Angelos, Cal.*
March 15, 1859
[19]

Do not, when you recognize the hand-writing, drop this as an epistle from the grave, or a manifesto from the internal regions, for your correspondent, though silent for more than three months, is still in the "land of the living" — considerably shattered, it is true, crippled for life, emaciated, ragged and pen[n]iless, (when the post-age on this is paid) but still alive.

I left Camp Floyd as I apprised you in my last, and when two days out we had a skirmish with the Utahs, in which I received a gun-shot wound in the right forearm, which caused a compound fracture of that member, and lacerated it from the wrist to the elbow. The affray lasted but a few minutes, and I was the only one of our party injured. The Indians fled after losing three men. I was taken to our camp, and the attendant surgeon pronounced amputation necessary. To this operation I refused to submit, so he bandaged my arm in a kind of way that reflects no credit on his surgical skill, and pronounced me unable longer to do the duties of a soldier. *Three days* afterwards I was discharged and received as my pay a check on a St. Louis Bank. This check, as I had no money, I had cashed by submitting to a shave of *fifty per cent.* The "shaver" was a Mormon. Hearing that there was a party about to start for California from Fillmore city, I went to that place to engage a passage, but the train was gone when I arrived. I concluded to stay there a few days and then worked my way towards the southern settlements, in hopes of getting a chance to go to California. The day after I arrived there I was robbed of everything I owned, except what clothing I had on and $8.50 that I had in my pocket. There were none but Mormons in the town. A lively plight

136

the villain left me in, surely. But I can tell you more of the "honesty" of some of the followers of the "Modern Messiah." (D. News, v. 6, No. XXIV.)[1]

While at Fillmore, a party of five Government-men came there with authority to search for Government property. There were mounted on mules, and "put up" at a Mormon hotel. The mules attracted the desires of our pious "Saints," and they resolved to steal them. I became aware of the plot, and informed the leader of the party of the danger. He took the alarm, and left, as I supposed, for Round Valley, twenty miles distant where there were some soldiers stationed. Judge of my surprise when I saw the mules pass through Fillmore next morning, under the charge of two deserters. He had only gone as far back as Cedar Fort — nine miles — where he had been followed by two Mormons named Giles and Huntsman, who stole the mules and then turned them over to the deserters. Evans, the person in charge, had been guilty of great carelessness, not even putting a guard on his animals. The mules were taken to the lower settlements, where a Mormon named Bruce purchased them and brought them through to the States.

From Fillmore, I travelled through all the Mormon settlements, and reached Santa Clara, the extreme southern village, on the 12th of February. There I met a man who had some cattle to drive through to California, and as, with my right arm in a sling, I could not do much service, I agreed to do my best for my grub and passage. On the 16th, we set out; our trip from thence to San Bernardino, sixty miles from this place, was the most trying I have ever experienced. Three days brought us to the "Muddy," a turbid stream that rolls through filth and mire to the Rio Virgin. There we struck "the desert." Filling our water kegs, we rolled on, travelling through a country where

---

[1] This apparently refers to a discourse by President Heber C. Kimball on June 29, 1856, in which he told how he and Brigham Young once set out on a five-hundred-mile journey with $16.50 between them. They paid out $82.00 en route but still had money left at the end of their journey. Kimball said that the additional funds were supplied by angels. He asked if angels could not also bring flour. "Can they not go and take it from those who have plenty and put it in the empty bins, sacks and barrels belonging to good men, and that too without our knowing it? It is very common for one to increase, and for another to decrease." See *Deseret News*, August 20, 1856.

even the hardy sage will not grow. 73 miles brought us to the Vagear [Las Vegas], a little oasis in the desert, where we got a fresh supply of water, eat a little and allowed our animals to roll. Large numbers of Indians gathered around us, and not wishing to be an[n]oyed by the filthy wretches we took the road again. This is the country of the Par-Utahs — the most disgusting and villainous looking Indians I have ever met with.[2] They have in them the filthiness of the Pawnees, the powerful physical development of the Sioux and the ferocity of the Cheyennes. They are inveterate thieves and outrival the Pawnees in beggary. Numerous and well armed, they bully and browbeat small parties, taking what they want, despite all remonstrance; but with native cunning they change their mode when the whites are strong, and "how do you do, sir? how do you do?" with the greatest suavity in hopes of allaying suspicion that they may pilfer such articles as are convenient, which they do with a skillfulness that would do credit to London pick-pockets. A trick of one of them will serve to show this. Coming up to us while we were eating, he commenced to tell one of our party who had a large knife in a scabbard on his belt, how sorry he was that the Indians were such thieves, and growing warm on the theme, he concluded with, "my hands are clean — we never steal." M. F. was so pleased with him, that he reached for his knife to cut the fellow a piece of bacon. It was gone. "Search the Indian," said one. He did so, and behold! the clean-handed individual had the knife concealed in a fold of his blanket.

From the vagee [Vagear] we marched sixty-five miles to Cotton-wood Springs, there rested two hours; forty-seven miles from there are the Mountain Springs, where we halted, and were about to un-

[2] A corruption of Paiute, a term often applied to most of the Shoshonean tribes of western Utah, northern Arizona, southern Idaho, eastern Oregon, Nevada, and eastern and southern California. Supposedly the name originated from the Indian word *pah*, meaning water, and Ute. According to John Wesley Powell, the name properly belongs exclusively to the Corn Creek tribe of southwestern Utah, but has been extended to include many other tribes. The Utes are an important Sho-shonean division related linguistically to the Paiute, the Kawaiisu, and the Ban-nock. They formerly occupied the entire central and western portions of Colorado and the eastern portion of Utah, including the eastern part of Salt Lake Valley and Utah Valley. On the south they extended into New Mexico. They were apparently always a warlike people and when they first acquired horses they became more aggressive. See Frederick W. Hodge, ed., *Handbook of American Indians North of Mexico*, Smithsonian Institution, Bureau of American Ethnology Bulletin no. 30 (1912), pp. 186–88, 874–76.

harness, when, from behind a clump of cedars, six arrows were shot into one of the mules belonging to our team. This is a favorite trick of the redskins, shooting arrows into animals so as to disable them, that they may be abandoned and furnish a feast. They prefer "mule beef" to any other kind of meat, and driving a fat, sleek animal of this species through their country is about as safe as a bottle of whiskey would be in a Democratic meeting. This act changed our purpose, and we drove ninety-six(?)[3] miles further to the Resting Springs, where we halted, intending to rest a night there, as it was an hundred and sixty-four miles to the next water that is not too strongly impregnated with alkali to be fit for use. While lying there, and before any one had got asleep, two of our party got into a quarrel, and one gave the other a terrible wound in the thigh, with a butcher knife. From the effects of this wound he died, four days afterwards. The name of the deceased was Charles F. Smith. He was a native of Dayton, Ohio, and, I should think, about thirty years of age. The other calls himself Geo. Harris, is a carpenter by trade, and hails from New York. Both were deserters from the United States Army.[4] This lamentable occurrence induced us to continue our journey, and on the 25th we reached the Mohave, having travelled four hundred and fifty-five miles without sleeping or resting more than two hours in any one place. Talk about "Jordan" now, will you? The water at the places I have named, the Mohave excepted, and there is none other, is miserable, being all, more or less, impregnated with alkali; but when it's "Hobson's choice" with a man he will swallow anything.

[3] The question mark is in the original. All of these distances are questionable; from Las Vegas to Resting Springs the total distance is approximately 65 miles.

[4] The "Register of Enlistments" in the National Archives does not contain information which exactly fits "Utah's" description of these men. There was a Charles A. Smith, a boatman, age twenty-four, of Port Byron, New York, who enlisted in New York City in November 1857, and who deserted from Company B, Third Artillery, on January 29, 1859. Another possibility was Prussian-born Charles Schmidt, a weaver, age twenty-seven, who enlisted in New York City in April 1858 and deserted the following July. A third possibility was Josephus Smith, a laborer, age twenty-two, of Michigan, who enlisted in Chicago in March 1858. Assigned to the Seventh Infantry, he deserted in June 1858. As for the name Harris, there is a James Harris, a sailor, age twenty-two, who enlisted in New York City in November 1857 and deserted from Company F, Eighth Infantry, in September 1858. Another possibility was William Harris, a farmer, age nineteen, of Schuylerville, New York, who enlisted at Albany, New York, in March 1858, and who apparently deserted from Company D, Second Dragoons, in May 1858.

The Mohave is called a river, but it is not to outward appearance such. We travelled along it for forty-five miles, and in no place did I see it a stream. It is a succession of water holes, in some places ten or twelve miles apart, and I could nowhere discover aught that indicated a subterranean connection; but that some such connection exists I do not doubt, as the water is very good, pure, clear and cool, whereas, were it what it appears to be, mere stagnant pools, this would not be the case. You may well suppose that we were glad when we came to these holes, and that we felt as though Gough's splendid apostrophe to water was not mere "jingling syllables." [5]

Here we took it easy and gave up our rapid mode of travelling, being out of the Par Utah range. The red rascals sometimes come to the Mohave, however, and the second day after we struck it we overtook a party whose mules had been stolen; but whether by the Mohaves or Par Utahs, I cannot say. We loaned them cows to put the harness on instead of their lost animals. On the 28th we met Lieut. Beale with a number of camels on his way to St. [Ft.] Yuma.[6] He was escorted by a platoon of the 1st Dragoons. On the 2d inst. we met three companies of Dragoons en route for the Colorado, where the Indians are very troublesome.[7]

[5] John B. Gough (1817–86), a bookbinder and a reformed drunkard, was a popular temperance lecturer between 1843 and 1886. He emphasized individual reform.

[6] Edward F. Beale (1822–93) entered the United States Navy as a midshipman in 1836. He achieved fame prior to, during, and after the Mexican War when, as a bearer of important government dispatches, he made six ocean to ocean journeys between California and Washington, D.C. He resigned from the navy in 1852 with the rank of lieutenant, and served as the superintendent of Indian Affairs for the state of California. He was also a brigadier general in the California militia. In 1857 President Buchanan gave him the command of an expedition to survey a wagon road from Fort Defiance, New Mexico, to the Colorado River. For his transportation he used camels especially imported at the request of Secretary of War, Jefferson Davis, for use in the Southwest. The camel experiment was a success, but the coming of the Civil War stopped further development of the idea. By 1858 it was expected that Beale's Route and Beale's Crossing on the Colorado River would be a major path to the West Coast, but hostile Mojave Indians stopped the first sizeable emigrant party to try the route.

[7] Lieutenant Colonel William Hoffman set out from Los Angeles with a company of dragoons in December 1858 to reconnoiter the country around Beale's Crossing on the Colorado River. The Mojave Indians harassed him and fought a skirmish with the troops before Hoffman returned to California. Later two companies marched overland and in March 1859 met other companies that traveled by water to Fort Yuma. See Utley, *Frontiersmen in Blue*, pp. 164–65.

Rev. Mr. Boardman,[8] formerly of your city, is here, permanently located, I believe — and is quite a lion. He is much pleased with the country and people, and the people with him, and they are continually telling one another so, consequently all is harmonious. He has a large field to work upon, as neither stores, grog-shops or gambling houses are closed on the Sabbath; and the Manager of the circus had his complimentary benefit last Sunday afternoon. I hope Mr. B. will see these matters straightened up before he praises the Los Angelos folks too much.

The climate of this section is most delightful; The hills are clad with everlasting verdure, and nature's choicest gifts grow spontaneous in the valleys. Kansas, glorious Kansas! land of tall grass and Free State men! to you alone need the southern part of California bow the knee. But not only is the region great in an agricultural view, but gold — "the god of this world" — is found among its hills and along its rivers' banks, though the precious metal was heretofore supposed to belong entirely to the upper country.

This is the first effort I have made to use my arm since it was injured, and though I have received no medical aid, nature seems to be restoring it. As it is, however, it will be many a day before I will lose the token of respect given me by the redskins of

UTAH.

---

[8] Henry Augustus Boardman (1808–80) was the pastor of the Tenth Presbyterian Church in Philadelphia and a director of Princeton Seminary.

Los *Angelos*, Cal.
March 28th, 1859
[20]

"Ho! for the Gila mines!" is the cry of the day in this part of our "great Republic." The palmiest days of '49 are cast in the shade by our new "diggings" — Frazer River is nowhere, and Pike's Peak a mere *bagatelle*.[1] "The Gila!" "Gila Mines!" "Great Diggings!" &c., &c., are heard wherever you turn. Grave judges discuss the matter; lawyers wrangle about it; gamblers bet on it; our city papers crow lustily over it; and Rev. Mr. Boardman, our only preacher, delivered a sermon yesterday on the subject, from the text, "Search, and you shall find." All classes are infected, from Don Andress Pico,[2] the wealthy ranchero, who once commanded the California army of Mexico, and who would have hung, but for the clemency of the great John Charles,[3] down to your humble correspondent. I have been employed by a company of miners as *cook-and bookkeeper*, (a queer combination, is it not?) and will set out for the new El Dorado in a few days. These new mines are situated on a little stream known as the Gila River, about three hundred miles southeast of this place, in the country of the Apache Indians, and from [what] I learn, are unsurpassed by any yet discovered. The gold is of much finer quality than that of the old mines, being worth $19.83 per ounce, and is found in

[1] Gold was discovered in the Fraser River in British Columbia in the spring of 1858, at Pikes Peak, Colorado, in the early part of 1859, and on the Gila River in Arizona in late 1858. See Rodman W. Paul, *Mining Frontiers of the Far West, 1848–1880* (1963), pp. 38, 39, 157.

[2] Don Andreas Pico was a Californian and an officer in the Mexican Army who fought against the Americans in the Mexican War. It was he who led the attack on Colonel Stephen W. Kearney's force at the battle of San Pasqual. Subsequently he signed a surrender document for Lieutenant Fremont which ended the Mexican War in California. See Robert G. Cleland, *A History of California: The American Period* (1930), pp. 211, 213, 219, 224.

[3] See note 2, chap. 9.

142

the shape of nuggets, varying in size from $1.60 to $48, and upwards. I have seen some specimens brought to this place by miners, that, I am assured by experienced men, indicate an almost boundless extent of the precious "dirt." The matter has been thoroughly investigated by men who understand the business, and the Gila mines are a fixed fact. The country has been prospected for one hundred and sixty miles along the river, and gold in abundance found everywhere — not dust and nugget here and there, but shining bright all along the banks, like gold coin through a net purse. It is not far from the coast, and the necessaries of life do not command the exorbitant price they did when the gold regions of this State were first opened to the world.[4] To young men of energy and industry, there is no better field. Should any persons in your portion of creation wish to visit these mines, the best and shortest road for them would be the Southern Overland Mail Route. Taking this road at Fort Smith, Arkansas, they would have excellent travelling to Fort Yuma, on the Colorado, fifty miles from the new diggings. There are several deserts to cross on this route, but at no place more than seventy miles without water.

There are other diggings on the San Gabriel, about ninety miles from this place, but the yield is not very great, and the place is so difficult of access, that but few are heading that way. I am inclined to think, from what I have seen from these mines, that they are more valuable than is generally supposed, and that they will some day prove to be of great wealth.

The Mojaves and other Indians along the Colorado are raising "particular thunder" just now, stealing cattle, robbing emigrants, and threatening the soldiers. A large force, under the command of Col. Hoffman,[5] is already at the scene of trouble, and last Tuesday, Brevet Brigadier General Clarke,[6] the able and energetic commander of the Military Department, passed through this place on his way there, intending to take the field in person. It is rumored that the Par-Utahs

[4] See Paul, *Mining Frontiers*, pp. 155, 157.

[5] William Hoffman graduated from West Point in 1829 and rose steadily to the rank of major in 1851, but during the Mexican War he won two brevets, one as major and the other as lieutenant colonel, for gallant and meritorious conduct.

[6] Newman S. Clarke began his military career in the War of 1812, and in 1846 was commissioned as a colonel in the Sixth Infantry. During the Mexican War he was breveted for gallant and meritorious conduct.

Los Angeles, California, as it appeared in 1857.

are assisting the Mojaves, but I do not credit this. When I came
through their country, Tussygoveth,[7] their principal Chief, an Indian

---

[7] Evidently "Utah" meant Chief Tutsegabit.

of more than ordinary intelligence, told me that he and his tribe were going to the Buckskin Mountains to hunt deer and antelope, and I am inclined to think that this will account for their absence from the road at present. Small parties of the Par-Utahs may be on the Colorado, but I do not think that any considerable number will be found there. They are entirely different from the Colorados, Mojaves, Yumas, &c.,

speak another language, and have never, in any way, affiliated with them.

There is a strong movement going on in this part of California, to obtain a division of the State, and have the three Southern counties of Los Angelos, San Bernardino, and San Diego, placed under a Territorial government.[8] The members of the Legislature from these districts have introduced bills for that purpose; the press is unanimous in its favor, as are also the majority of the people. Some see in this movement an attempt to form a new slave State, but in this view I think they are mistaken. The people generally are opposed to slavery here, and besides this, California is not suited in any respect for a slave State. That it may be the hope of some of the leaders in the movement; I do not deny; but the native Californians form by far the greatest portion of the voters of this district, and they are as good antislavery men as ever "headed" a Free Soil ticket.

There is a great excitement here concerning the Pacific Railroad, and great indignation is displayed at the defeat of the bill contemplating its continuation.[9] Many are loud in denouncing the Federal Government, and talk about secession, rebellion and revolution. This, of course, is all talk, as they will not rebel until they get strong enough to protect themselves against the Indians, or resist an invasion by the

[8] In February 1859 Andreas Pico of Los Angeles proposed that the six southern counties of California be set up as the separate Territory of Colorado. On April 19, the California legislature passed an act giving its consent to this separation provided that the people in the counties concerned voted for such at the next election and provided that Congress would create a new territory or state. The people so desired and in January 1860 Daniel Rogers introduced a resolution in the state assembly to form a separate territorial government for these counties. This passed in both houses but before it could be implemented the southern states seceded and shortly afterward the Civil War began. In the midst of the struggle to save the Union the separatist proposal of the California counties seemed unwise if not treasonable. See Theodore H. Hittell, *History of California* (1897), 4: 241, 260–61, 265.

[9] The rapid development of California made it imperative that a railroad be built to connect the West Coast with the rest of the Union. It was assumed that the federal government would help build only one route. A northern route would benefit the northwestern states. A central route would aid Missouri and make St. Louis a key point. A southern route would funnel trade into New Orleans and the South. A House committee recommended the central route, but in late May 1859 the House of Representatives voted to send the bill back to committee. The Senate did nothing. For a brief account of the struggle see Nevins, *The Emergence of Lincoln*, 2: 195–96; and Roy F. Nichols, *The Disruption of American Democracy* (1948), pp. 17, 42, 44, 53, 71–72, 94, 99, 104, 137, 192, 231–32.

"Destroying Angels" of Brigham Young, which will require some years yet.

The approaching election for State officers promises to be an interesting one, three parties being in the field, whose strength is estimated to be about equal — the Republicans, Administration Democrats and Douglas Democrats.[10] There are quite a number of gentlemen spoken of in connection with the nomination as candidates by the different parties, prominent among whom are Mr. Stanley,[11] (Rep.); John Nugent,[12] (Ad. Dem.), and J. W. McCorkle,[13] (Douglas Dem.)[.] It is currently reported that Don Andress Pico, a wealthy ranchero, who is now a member of the State legislature, will be an Independent, Native California Democrat, Free Soil, Pacific Railroad candidate; but I do not know how much truth there is in the rumor. Gov. Weller,[14] I presume, will be a candidate for re-election, though I have heard nothing positive. If Don Pico should be a candidate, there will be a rich time during the coming political campaign.

I stated that the natives were mainly Free Soilers. This they are, most emphatically, though not many of them are yet enrolled as Re-

[10] Senator Stephen A. Douglas of Illinois had failed to win the Democratic party's nomination for president in 1852 and 1856. During the debate in the Senate on Kansas in 1857–58 he denounced the Lecompton constitution as a violation of "popular sovereignty." His stand led to a break with the Buchanan administration, and he became the enemy of proslavery groups in the Democratic party. Following his debates with Abraham Lincoln during his successful campaign to retain his Senate seat, he announced that he would be a candidate for president in the election of 1860.

[11] Edward Stanly (1810–72) was a member of the North Carolina bar who served as a Whig member of the United States House of Representatives (1837–43); a member and speaker of his state's house of representatives; and as the state attorney general. He returned to the House of Representatives (1849–53), but when he was defeated for reelection he moved to California where he ran unsuccessfully for governor on the Republican ticket in 1857.

[12] John Nugent was the editor of the San Francisco *Herald*.

[13] Joseph W. McCorkle (1819–84) was a member of the Ohio bar and served as postmaster of Dayton before moving to San Francisco. He was an unsuccessful candidate for judge, but was elected to the state assembly (1850–52) and to the United States House of Representatives (1851–53). After losing the next election he was appointed a judge of the ninth judicial district and served until 1857. Meanwhile, in 1855, he made an unsuccessful bid for the United States Senate. Thereafter he practiced law in San Francisco, Virginia City, and Washington, D.C.

[14] John B. Weller (1812–75) served as a Democratic Congressman from Ohio; an officer in the Army during the Mexican War; a member of the Mexican boundary commission; a lawyer in California; a United States Senator from California (1852–57); and as governor of that state (1858–60).

148

publicans, that party lacking an advocate to explain its principles in contra-distinction with those of the Democracy. Lately, however, Don F. Ramirez, a young man of considerable talent, has commenced the publication of a Republican paper under the title of *El Clamor Publico*,[15] which has already gained an extensive circulation. It is edited with ability and wears at its mast head, as its candidate for the Presidency, the name of John C. Fremont, a name immensely popular among the native citizens.

Although California is one of the United States, its position is analogous to that of New Jersey — as that State is said to be by would be wags and small jokers — and I presume a few words in regard to this region of country would not be unacceptable. Los Angelos is a town of about three thousand inhabitants, including gamblers, Indians, Chinese, etc., and is situated about twenty-nine miles from the Pacific coast — the nearest seaport town being an insignificant village called San Pedro. There are no manufacturers there, the inhabitants being merchants, vine-growers and wealthy landholders. It is situated in a beautiful valley, well watered, in which are grown the best wine-producing grapes in California. The houses are mainly one and two story brick and adobe buildings, many of them old fashioned, flat-roofed Mexican structures, that give the town a low, squatty appearance when viewed from a distance. Asphaltum is used for the purpose of roofing, and is an excellent article for uses of that kind.[16] The town is quiet and orderly, but the inhabitants possess very little energy or enterprise. There are three papers published here — two weekly and one semi-weekly.

Twelve miles from here is El Monte, a pleasant fertile valley, in in which there are some fifteen hundred inhabitants, not concentrated together, but scattered all over the plain. Kokomongo is twenty miles from this, and occupied by a few Mexican rancheros, who occupy

[15] Francisco P. Ramirez, a compositor for the Spanish page of the Los Angeles *Star*, resigned that position in 1855 and began to issue a one sheet weekly newspaper in Spanish called *El Clamor Publico*. See chapter 11 of Leonard Pitt's *The Decline of the Californios* (1966).

[16] This refers to a bituminous pitch that oozed to the surface of the La Brea pits in what is now Hancock Park in Los Angeles. The Indians used it to waterproof their canoes and baskets. The Spaniards and later settlers used it on the roofs of their adobe houses.

their time in raising grapes and big horned cattle. The wine raised in this valley is second only to that of Los Angelos.

Eighteen miles further brings us to San Bernardino, an old Mormon town, situated in the most beautiful valley that I have ever seen; where eternal green appears on all sides, pure water rolls in crystal streams, and birds of all kinds fill the air with music. Coming into it, as I did, after a long desert march, it appeared doubly charming, and seemed to me to be a realization of some of the Mormon ideas of heaven. The Mormons abandoned this glorious valley by order of Brigham Young, when he stood in a hostile position towards the Federal government, and it fell into the hands of a lot of loafers, gamblers and drunkards. I was there two days, and can safely say that I saw nothing done by the inhabitants but drink whiskey and play cards. Gambling is carried on in open day with perfect impunity; in fact there is no one to arrest the gamblers without being liable to be accused of being "spiteful because he lost." It is to be regretted that this magnificent valley has not fallen into better hands, as those now [here?] will never profit by its great natural advantages.

The principal productions of the country are grapes, corn, and barley, though oranges, peaches, and others of the most delicious fruits are grown here; and some small "patches" of wheat are cultivated. From the grapes, is made some of the best wine I have ever tasted — superior, in my opinion, to that of Mr. Longworth, of Ohio.[17] The hill-sides furnish pasturage for immense herds of cattle, which grow to a great size, and are valued more for their hides and horns than their flesh. The climate is mild and genial, such a thing as ice and snow being unknown in this part of California, while the cool sea breeze that is always in motion kindly tempers the heat of summer.

Among the inhabitants are many Indians of the Kowee tribe,[18] but they have abandoned their savage habits, and have adopted a civilized mode of living, some of them being quite wealthy. They speak the Spanish language and appear to have forgotten that they ever had any other.

UTAH.

[17] Nicholas Longworth (1782–1863) was an Ohio lawyer who, in 1828, produced a marketable wine and retired from the law to cultivate grapes and manufacture wine. He won prizes for his Catawba and Isabella wines.

[18] Possibly the Korekins who formerly lived at the mouth of the San Joaquin. See Hodge, ed., *Handbook of American Indians*, p. 454.

Stodart's Diggings, Gila Mines
April 6, 1859
[21]

We arrived day before yesterday at this new land of promise, and squatted upon a claim named after one of the members of our party. Taking advantage of the first opportunity — one of our company returning to Los Angelos to-morrow, disheartened already — I send you my impressions of this region of [the] country, and what other items I have been able to gather. We left Los Angelos two days after I last wrote to you, and pushed on rapidly to our destination. Nothing of interest occurred, until we reached San Felipe, an insignificant village, one hundred and thirty-five miles from Los Angelos, inhabited by Greasers and Indians, and a few white men in the employ of the Butterfield Overland Mail Company.[1] There I had my first experience in earthquakes — not a very agreeable, nor much to be wished for visitant. I had just commenced cooking our breakfast, when I noticed the coffee pot tremble, and the frying-pan performing a "bolero." Ere I had time to think of the probable cause of this unique performance, I found myself stretched out full length upon the ground and a sort of top-heavy, sick at-the-stomach sensation come over me. I looked around and saw my company sprawling upon the earth in every possible variety of posture, some of them going through motions that would astonish the "india rubber man" himself. "It's an earthquake" thought I. "It's an earthquake, by thunder" cried one of the party; and the rest chorused "earthquake," affixing every word

[1] In September 1857 the Butterfield Overland Mail Company agreed to run a semiweekly service from St. Louis and Memphis to Fort Smith, then through El Paso, Fort Yuma, Los Angeles, and San Francisco in twenty-five days or less for a Post Office Department subsidy of $600,000. The first coach left St. Louis on September 16, 1858, and arrived in San Francisco on October 10, for an elapsed time of twenty-three days and twenty-three hours. For a history of the venture see Roscoe P. and Margaret B. Conkling, *The Butterfield Overland Mail, 1857–1869* (1947).

that could well follow "by." The shock lasted about forty seconds and was very severe, demolishing two Indian huts and a pig-pen, the largest building in the place. It was followed by eight other separate and distinct shocks, but they were all very slight. "Rather numerous the shocks this morning," said I to an old greaser. "Oh! that's nothing here," he replied. "We had *fourteen* of them on the twenty-fourth." (of March). Rather an agreeable place to live, where earthquakes are accounted "nothing." From thence we pursued the "even tenor" of our way until we reached the mines, and now we are preparing to search for that which is greater, in the "eyes of the world," then talents, virtue or valor, that god of these, the "latter days," (vide the Mormons) — gold.

The face of this country is the most singular I have ever seen, and in the little while I have been absent from Philadelphia I have seen "considerable, if not more." The surface appears to be in a state of decomposition; everything is assuming a new aspect, and ten years hence people who pass through this region now will not be able to recognize it. The land, which has long been desert, probably since the day the horses of the sun ran away with the wayward son of Apollo,[2] will ere long, if I do not mistake the work going on, be transformed into as fair and fertile a region as can be found between the Androscoggin[3] and the South Pole. That some marked and important change for the better is taking place, cannot be denied; and from what I know of geology, I am inclined to think that what I have written above will fall, if anything, below the mark, and that, instead of "as fair and fertile," it will be *the most* fair and fertile beneath the "American sky." (Dan'l Ullman is my authority for this last expression.)[4] You will probably smile at the idea of the desert becoming an Eden; but remember it was once said, "can any good come out of Nazareth?"[5]

[2] In Greek and Roman mythology Phaëthon, the son of Apollo or Helios, the sun god, borrowed his father's sun chariot and drove it in so careless a fashion that he would have set the world on fire if Zeus, the father of the gods, had not struck him down with a thunderbolt.

[3] A river in Maine.

[4] Evidently a member of the expedition.

[5] John 1: 46.

An unfortunate accident occurred on the 16th of March, which has thrown a gloom over mining operations in this section, as the miners were thereby deprived of a machine for supplying water, a thing much wanted here. The schooner Arno, which had on board the engine and machinery intended for that purpose, was wrecked at the mouth of the Colorado, on the day named, and her entire cargo lost. The passengers and crew escaped. To us, this is a matter of small moment, as it is probable we would never need its assistance, being near the Gila; but to many other companies it is a serious drawback, as it is impossible to go on without its aid, unless they take to the tedious mode called "dry washing." [6] The company who owned this machinery, however, have assured the miners that they will not abandon the enterprise, but that a new engine, etc., will be sent on as soon as possible.

The expedition against the Mojaves is marching up the Colorado river, having left Fort Yuma the 26th ult. It is composed of six companies of the Sixth Infantry, and is commanded by Brevet Lieutenant Colonel Hoffman.[7] Among the officers I recognize my old friend Lieutenant Bootes, who marched along, looking as serious and determined as ever. Gen. Clarke has abandoned his patriotic intention of taking the field in person.

To-day, I saw a letter from S. A. Bishop, Esq., who has charge of the Central Overland Mail route (Lieut. Beale's) party, and who left Los Angelos on the 28th of February, with forty men and a number of camels, to meet another party, who are, it is supposed, making their way from the East.[8] They had moved on without interruption, though threatening messages were marked in the sand along the route by the Indians, until he reached the Colorado, when he found the course

[6] Dry washing was a method of extracting gold from auriferous earth without water. It consisted of shoveling sand or dirt into a large cloth which was then shaken until pebbles and large particles of stone and dirt rose to the surface.

[7] See note 5, chap. 20.

[8] For more on Beale see note 6, chap. 19; Utley, *Frontiersmen in Blue*, pp. 164–65; and Hubert H. Bancroft, *History of Arizona and New Mexico, 1530–1888* (1889), pp. 496–97, 501. Samuel A. Bishop was associated with Beale in the explorations. On this occasion he was taking supplies to meet Beale who was coming from the East with a party of about thirty-five men and some twenty persons from an emigrant train turned back by the Mojaves the previous fall. See the San Francisco *Herald*, May 17, 1859.

blocked by about six hundred red skins, who informed him that he could not cross. Mr. Bishop laid down his arms and made signs to the Indians that he wanted their chief to do likewise, and come and meet him and they would have a talk. This the Indians agreed to, and Mr. Bishop went out to meet the chief. He explained to the red skin that his intentions were peaceable, that his men would not steal or kill, and that all he wanted was to pass through their country. The chief agreed to allow the party to pass, on condition of receiving a large quantity of tobacco and a shirt to each of the minor chiefs. To these terms Mr. Bishop acquiesced, and the "toll" was paid. Next morning, he prepared to cross; a rope was stretched across the river, and the boat, an india rubber affair, launched and freighted. Just as the boat was about to move, a large number of Indians, estimated at about eight hundred, appeared on the opposite side of the river and coolly informed the mail party, that, by order of the chief who had treated with the whites the previous day, they could not cross unless they supplied every red skin present with a shirt. This was more than could be done, even though the mail party were to strip themselves, and, after some parley, Mr. Bishop concluded that the Indians did not intend to let him pass on any terms. Consequently, he sent two men across to cast off the rope and prepared for a retreat or defence, as circumstances would direct. The men cast off the rope without being molested, but when they set out to return, the red villains commenced sending showers of arrows after them. The men escaped without injury, but the boat was pierced in many places, and was nearly full of water when it regained the shore. Simultaneous with the attack on the boat, a terrific fire of arrows was commenced from behind upon the main body of the mail party, but a few well directed shots sent the red rascals beyond range. Mr. Bishop then retired with his party to a place where he could defend himself, and corralled his wagons.

Early next morning the Indians made their appearance, and commenced sending arrows into the mail party's camp. Mr. Bishop waited until the fellows, receiving no reply, grew bold and insolent, and had presented themselves in considerable number in the open ground near his camp, when he told his men to "let it rip," and a hot fire from Sharpe's rifles was opened upon the enemy, who returned it with considerable vigor. The fight continued for three hours, when the In-

154

dians retired, leaving nearly half their number dead on the field. Since then they have not made their appearance, and Mr. Bishop writes: "We have whipped the Indians on this side of the river, and I feel confident that could we cross *en masse*, we could whip them on the other side, too. But I cannot take more than half my party over at a time, and could not do much while crossing the river, which is nearly a quarter of a mile wide. Had I fifty more men I could do it with ease." [9] And for these fifty men he writes to Col. Hoffman, who will, in all probability, *not* let him have them, as that would diminish the gallant Colonel's glory in the expected conquest. Mr. Bishop's men behaved with great spirit in this affair, and he deserves much credit for his skillful action and prompt punishment of the treacherous rascals. He says that there was but little ammunition wasted, nearly every shot bringing down an Indian, and that his men have got a considerable amount of "Indian hair" on hand. None of the whites were killed or seriously wounded, though all were more or less scratched by arrows. I should be glad to hear that his request for assistance is granted, but I fear it will not be. Uncle Sam's officers like to whip a crippled foe; and here they have an opportunity to display their peculiar talents that is too good to be lost.

Mr. Bishop states that the Indians engaged in the battle were Mojaves, Yumas and Navajoes, but does not mention the presence of the Pan [Pah] Utah tribe.[10] This serves to confirm my opinion, expressed in my last letter, that Tussygoveth and his bands are hunting instead of fighting, and that this will account for their disappearance from along the Salt Lake Route. Some people think that all Indians are blood thirsty villains, and that they all delight in war dances and scalp collections. In this I differ with them, and think my doctrine will prove correct. I will risk my head on the Pan Utahs, however.

The Indians of the Colorado, the Mojaves, Yumas, etc., are a wily, treacherous set of villains, by no means "the mildest mannered men that ever cut a throat," or scalped a traveller, and are at all times ready for murder and robbery. The first named tribe, in particular,

[9] Bishop's letter appeared in the Los Angeles *Vineyard*, April 12, and the San Francisco *Herald*, April 17, 1859.
[10] Bishop's letter does mention "Pah Utahs." See the San Francisco *Herald*, April 17, 1859.

has an unholy reputation for rascality, and many a bloody tale is told of them, that makes the blood run cold and the hand instinctively grasp the revolver's butt. Their cold-blooded massacre[11] of an immigrant train last fall still remains unavenged, and I hope that, now that the Government has taken them in hand, they will be punished in a manner that will prevent them from such acts again. I hope to see no milk and water, tobacco and blanket policy, but to hear of them being converted by the stern logic of the musket and the cutting appeal of the sabre. But Mr. Buchanan pardoned treason in Utah, (though I observe he is not so lenient with "traitors" in office),[12] and he may pay a premium on murder along the Colorado.

I have said nothing in this letter concerning the richness of our Gila mines, for the reason that our party has not gone to work yet, and I wish to tell you of the matter from actual experience. There is considerable difference of opinion even here, concerning the wealth of the mines, and, of course, I cannot say as yet whether the workers are lazy or industrious. Some are full of life and joy, and are continually humming songs expressive of their feelings, which it would be almost impossible to transcribe, and declaring that California is the best State under the Star Spangled Banner, and the Gila Mines the glory of California. Others, again, are howling and lamenting and sing a doleful melody with the following refrain:

"Oh! miners! poor miners!
Hungry and cold!
Though poor, I'll return to my home far away,
So Farewell to the land of gold."

In my next I will be able to state more satisfactorily than I could now the actual prospects of these mines.

UTAH.

[11] For a report of the massacre, see John Udell, *Journal of John Udell* (1868), pp. 45–48.

[12] This apparently refers to Senator Stephen A. Douglas' break with President Buchanan on the Kansas question (see note 10, chap. 20). "Utah" may also have had in mind the investigation of the Buchanan administration by a committee headed by Congressman John Covode of Pennsylvania, which uncovered evidence of the misuse of public funds and the awarding of naval contracts for political purposes, as well as irregularities in the administration of the War Department. See Klein, *President James Buchanan: A Biography*, pp. 338–39.

Gila *Mines, California*
April 10th, 1859
[22]

I promised to write to you as soon as I had an opportunity to examine the part of creation in which my tent is, for the time being, pitched. In fulfilment of this, and also for fear lest I should never have another opportunity to do so, the Indians being threatening, and a number of our men returning to Los Angelos to-morrow, reducing our party to nine effective men and your crippled correspondent I send you this. Possibly it may be my last letter to you; but if you do not hear from me again, you will probably hear from one of my companions — certainly, if any escape — and I presume you will give —————— ————, Esq., ex-editor of the —————— *Herald*, ex-soldier, &c., the benefit of an "obituary" in your inimitable BULLETIN. [1] The Indians have informed us that, if we do not leave our claim in three days from the present time, they will be under the necessity of removing our scalps, and one intimated that the snarled locks that cover your correspondent's head would be very acceptable to him. As I said above, some of our party are about to return, frightened by the threats of the red rascals. I, however, will remain — come weal, come woe, I will not be driven from this ground as long as I can resist, even though I have to combat the Indians single-handed. Should it come to the worst, I will meet it manfully, and dying, leave no stain upon my honor. The base assertions of my foes will, in time, work out their own refutation. But to my task.

The Gila mining region commences about twenty-miles south by east of Fort Yuma, among the hills that come down to the Gila river on its southern sides, running north a distance not yet ascertained, and is from eighteen to twenty miles wide. There are but four points,

---

[1] For a discussion of "Utah's" possible newspaper connection see chap. 26.

beside our claim, where mining is and has been carried on successfully and with profit to the miners. Taking the start from Gila City, these four camps are scattered along the margin of the rivers Colorado and Gila. Within the first twenty miles of auriferous district, the last named river crosses it at its southern terminus, while the Colorado, in its crooked, winding, zig-zag travels, entwines its water through the range at four different points. Thus you will see that but a small portion of this district is out of the Indian country, where the richest mines only are capable of being worked without machinery for the purpose of raising water, and this desideratum will not be obtained for some time yet. Our claim is in the Indian country, right among the Mojaves, and well supplied with water. Since we commenced operations, we have averaged fifteen dollars per day to the hand, never working more than two hours per day, the intensity of the heat preventing us from doing more. The other claims do not average more than three dollars per diem to the hand, but they are in a part of the country comparatively safe. So you see if we do gather lucre fast, we run a big risk in so doing.

The Gila is an inconsiderable stream; but the water is now at its lowest stage, and yet furnishes enough to wash out our dust and for our use in cooking, which is all we ask of it. The water is muddy and disagreeable, but it is freer from unwholesome matter than any of the kind I have ever seen. Of the Colorado I need not speak. I presume the explorations of Lieut. Ives[2] have rendered it familiar to everybody. The climate is the most uncomfortable imaginable — very hot days and very cold nights. No day since we came here has the thermometer stood at less than 103 degrees, yet ice half an inch thick was formed several times during the night. And then those harrassing northwest gales that so frequently sweep across the plain, carrying vast columns

[2] In November 1857 a schooner from San Francisco brought Lieutenant Joseph C. Ives, United States Army, and his men to the head of the Gulf of California. With them they brought a fifty-foot-long, Philadelphia-built iron stern-wheel steamer named the *Explorer* for use in ascending the Colorado River. Ives and his men left Fort Yuma in the boat on January 11, 1858, and traveled upstream as far as Black Canyon, then rowed to Las Vegas Wash. They then retraced their route part way to a Mojave Indian village. The boat was sent downstream to the fort with a few men while Ives, a portion of his scientific corps, and an escort of twenty men traveled eastward by land to Fort Defiance, New Mexico. See Joseph C. Ives' *Report Upon the Colorado River of the West* (1861).

Rocky Mesa on the Gila River in 1864.

of sand that takes away our breath and fills our optical organs with its galling particles — rendering red eyes, galled and aching, rather plentiful. At times a volume of sand rises like a water spout, as these phenomena are laid down in geographies and travellers' tales, and whirls about on the horizon in such a manner that one soon comes to the conclusion that none but the Indians and the Bedouins can live here. Everything is sandy, scorched and shrivelled.

The country back of us, for the distance of some thirty miles, until it reaches the mountains, is a level plain, smooth and even as a sad-iron, interspersed with beds of salt and a few patches of rank, saline grass. It is in places covered with driftwood, that would seem to indicate that the entire country was overflowed at one time. There is not a drop of fresh water to be found upon it, all being of the most bitter alkaline quality. The soil is of heavy clay, that curls and twists in the sun's ray, yet shows that it is undergoing some most singular changes. The scenery would always present the same dry, parched appearance, were it not for the mirage, which is here seen in all its varied phantasmagorial phases, making rivers and lakes, with magnificent forests and gorgeous panoplies of flowers, and birds of every hue and shape, and men of every clime and nation, and beasts and fishes, sparking springs and jetting fountains, within a few yards of us — the driftwood changing shape to magnificent houses and palatial mansions, and the distant mountains to turretted castles, and, anon, like vast mounds of earth suspended in mid-air. The only natural products of the country appear to be cayotes and craw-fish, though we frequently see immense flocks of cranes, pelicans, gulls, geese, ducks and curlews flying to and from the Gulf.

The Indians are the Mojaves, Yumas and Apaches, and are the meanest and most treacherous red-skins I have ever met with. Murder and theft are their pastime, smoking and eating their only business. They have sworn eternal enmity to the white race, and though some of them pretend to be friendly, they are not to be trusted. The old men and the women frequently visit our camp and deport themselves very well for Indians; but the braves and warriors stand aloof, except when they come with a threatening message. Their appearance is filthy to an extreme, and their raiment as scanty as that of our first parents before they ate the forbidden fruit. Many of the women

160

who visit us wear nothing save a coat of river mud plastered on their heads for the purpose of keeping off the direct rays of the sun, and exterminating the somewhat super-abundant vermin. "Virtue" is unknown among them. Notwithstanding their degradation, I think they will fight, and fight fiercely, too.

I have heard a "rumor" here that appears, from the way things are being done, to be entitled to more credence than rumors generally are. It is stated that Gen. William Walker,[3] the "grey-eyed man," is in California, having smuggled himself in under the name of James Wilson; that he will proceed secretly to the frontiers of Sonora, and there be joined by Gen. Henningsen[4] and his Arizona "emigrants." Sonora will then be invaded, and Walker will do his best to keep from fighting, merely disturbing the country, marching and counter-marching, issuing proclamations, etc. When the work is fairly under way, and the chaldron is bubbling over, the large body of troops now on the Colorado, under Col. Hoffman, nominally for the purpose of punishing the Mojaves, though actually for an entirely different service, will march into Sonora, arrest Walker and his leading men, enrol[l] his soldiers or volunteers, and take possession of the country. Thus we will obtain possession of this coveted territory, without the stain of filibusterism, prevent Walker from falling into the hands of remorseless foes, and give this portion of Mexico a stable government and a substantial protection. Being so far away from the civilized portion of California, I cannot say anything concerning the movements there, but my friend who takes this letter to Los Angelos will send you, as a postscript, whatever news can be gathered there concerning this

[3] The rumor was untrue. William Walker (1824–60), the American filibuster and adventurer, made an unsuccessful effort to establish an independent republic in lower California, which included the paper annexation of Sonora, in 1853–54. After he was driven out he and his followers went to Nicaragua, where he became president before being overthrown in 1857. He returned to the United States, prepared a new expedition, set out for Nicaragua, but was arrested and sent back. In 1860 he landed in Honduras with another force, intending to go to Nicaragua, but was arrested by the British, turned over to the Hondurans, and executed. One of Walker's former associates was interested in schemes to seize Sonora in 1859, and this undoubtedly was the source of the rumor heard by "Utah."

[4] Charles F. Henningsen (1815–77) was a soldier of fortune who had served with Louis Kossuth in the Hungarian revolt of 1849. He came to the United States with Kossuth, married a niece of Senator John M. Berrien of Georgia, and served under Walker in Nicaragua. Returning to the United States in 1857, he settled in Georgia and subsequently served briefly in the Confederate Army.

matter. That the rumor is plausible cannot be denied by those acquainted with the current of events here. Col. Hoffman has done nothing that has as yet been made known. Walker *is* in California, and *did* come as "James Wilson." Sonora is a rich prize, and our Government would like to have it. Moreover, it *might* be made, by careful working, a slave State.

A word for Sonora itself. General Pesquiera,[5] a sort of guerrilla revolutionist, is forming a separate republic, kingdom, or empire for himself, on the Gulf of California. He has routed all his opponents; holds possession of Guaymas and Mazatlan, and all the other important points on the Gulf; has fitted out a naval armament and proclaimed Sonora independent of Mexico. The latest news was that he had routed the Church party, taking more prisoners than he had men in his army, and that the entire population of Sonora were crying "Viva Pesquiera!" Of course, under the circumstances, it will be a contested point, and one offering great inducements to a filibustering government. Mexico will claim it; Pesquiera will want protection in his independence; Walker will invade it; Hoffman will rush to the rescue, and the Administration will, taking this and the "Mormon war," go down to posterity with an eclat second only to that achieved by Franklin Pierce, when our navy bombarded the strong castles and impregnable walls of Greytown.[6]

UTAH.

[5] Ignacio Pesqueira was a colonel and inspector of guards in the Mexican Army. When an American named H. A. Crabb attempted to establish a colony in Sonora in 1856, the scheme was opposed by Jose de Aguilar, the governor. But Aguilar's enemies accused him of plotting to sell the state to the filibusters, so he was arrested and replaced as governor by R. Encinas. Pesqueira went to the aid of Aguilar and overthrew Encinas. Pesqueira then ruled Sonora as governor and was chosen for that post partly by popular vote in 1857 and 1861 and partly by an appointment by Benito Juarez, the ruler of Mexico. He had a reputation for administrative ability. See Bancroft, *History of Texas and the North Mexican States*, 2: 693–701.

[6] See note 4, chap. 17.

Gila Gold Mines, Cal.

May 7, 1859

[23]

For the first time since my last, I have an opportunity to send you a note. The Indians have not as yet molested us, being all collected on the Colorado to meet Col. Hoffman's army. Our claim is paying well, even better than I at first expected. If Col. Hoffman's expedition be not a failure, I shall, ere this time next year, be on Chestnut street with a pocket full of "rocks."

Mr. Bishop, of whose fight with the Indians I wrote to you some time since, crossed the Colorado a few days after the fight. He effected this at Aubrey's Crossing, some forty miles above that of Mr. Beale. When I last heard from him, he was about one hundred miles east of the Colorado, and has not been again attacked. He lost no men in the fight.

From Sonora, I learn by a mining party just arrived, that Gen. Pesquiera has upset all opposition, and is now supreme ruler of that portion of Mexico. He has told the people that he is neither Liberal, Constitutionalist, Reactionist, or Churchman, but a Pesquieraite, and an advocate of "independence and honesty." I am much mistaken if the last term (honesty) does not prove his ruin as the "Greasers" are opposed to every thing of that sort.

From this State I learn that the war between the Broderickites and the Gwinnites is waxing very fierce, and that there will be two Democratic State Conventions and two Democratic State and Congressional tickets.[1] Two separate and distinct Conventions have al-

---

[1] The Democratic party in California was divided between the followers of Senator David C. Broderick, who supported the principle of "popular sovereignty" on the matter of slavery in the territories, and those who rallied behind Senator William M. Gwin, a supporter of the Buchanan administration, who was demanding the protection of slavery in the territories. After a bitter election campaign which saw the administration forces win by a narrow margin, Broderick was chal-

ready been called, and each will make a ticket. Very few think that
any thing like a reconciliation can be effected, and the Broderickites
swear by the beard of John Fremont and the neck of James Buchanan, that there is only one way of settling the difficulties, to which
they will agree — and that is on a Broderick platform, with a Broderick ticket, and Broderick men in all the offices now filled by Gwinnites. And they will stick to it. Whatever may be his failings, David
C. Broderick is an honest man; and rather than swerve from his
course, when convinced of its propriety, he would sacrifice his wealth,
his life, or aught else, save truth and firmness, that can be of value
to a man; and of such material are his backers composed. Of course,
while this "war of roses" is going on, the "Black Republicans" are
not idle. They are beating the drum and sounding the trumpet
throughout the State, and are preparing for a fierce struggle with
the "unterrified." Should they and the Free Democrats unite,
Lecompton-Buchananism will receive a clubbing in the Golden State,
that will make the Slaveocracy howl from Maryland to Florida. If
they do not unite, the result cannot be foretold.

The bill, consenting to the formation of the Territory of Colorado,
has passed the Legislature, and received the approval of Gov. Weller.
It is as follows:

SECTION 1. The consent of the Legislature of this State is hereby given to
the effect that all that part or portion of the present territory of this State, lying
all south of a line drawn eastwardly from the western boundary of the State,
along the sixth standard parallel south of the Mount Diablo meridian east to the
summit of the Coast Range; thence southerly, following said summit to the
seventh standard parallel; thence due east on said standard parallel to its inter-
section with the northwest boundary of Los Angelos county; thence northeast
along said boundary to the eastern boundary of the State; including the counties of San Luis, Obispo, Santa Barbara, Los Angelos, San Diego, San Bernardino, and a part of Buena Vista, be segregated from the remaining portion of
the State, for the purpose of the formation by Congress, with the concurrent
action of said portion — the consent for the segra[gat]ion of which is hereby
granted — of a Territorial or other Government, under the name of the "Territory of the Colorado," or such other name as may be deemed meet and proper.

lenged to a duel by David S. Terry, chief justice of the supreme court of California
and a hot-tempered Southerner. As a result of this encounter Broderick was shot
and died on September 16, 1859. On his deathbed Broderick said that his enemies
had killed him because he opposed the extension of slavery and a corrupt administration. For the most recent account see David A. Williams, *David C. Broderick:
A Political Portrait* (1969).

164

SEC. 2 says that the Governor shall, in his Proclamation for the next general election, direct the voters of the counties proposed to be segregated at such general election to vote, "For a Territory," or "Against a Territory;" and in case two-thirds of the whole number of voters voting thereon shall vote for a change of Government, the consent hereby given shall be deemed consummated.

SEC. 3 provides for the counting of these votes and directs that, if two thirds, or more, favor the segregation, it shall be the duty of the Governor to transmit a certified statement of said votes, with a copy of this Act annexed, to the President of the United States, and to each of our Senators and Representatives in Congress.

SEC. 4 provides that the consent to segregation, granted by this act, if sustained by a two-thirds vote, shall continue in force until a separate and distinct Government is formed.

SEC. 5 provides for the adjustment of the portion of the State debt to be assumed by said new Government, and for the division of public property.

It is sincerely hoped that Congress will act favorably in this matter, as the counties proposed to be formed into a separate government have interests entirely at variance with the other portion of the State. One is almost exclusively mineral; the other is exclusively agricultural; and there are now on the statute books of this State, two separate and distinct code of laws — one for the Northern part and another for the Southern. This conflict of interest should be obviated, and we look to Washington in hope.[2]

From Col. Hoffman's expedition we have very satisfactory *official* news, and very unsatisfactory, though more probable and truthful, *unofficial* intelligence. Col. Hoffman's dispatches to General Clarke, the Chief of this Department, are to the effect that the Mojaves have humbly sued for peace, and that he has made a treaty with them and taken nine of their chiefs as hostages for the faithful performance of their part of their contract. The terms of the treaty are, that "the Mojaves will offer no opposition to the building of posts and roads in and through their country, and that the lives and property of whites passing through their land, shall be held sacred." The Colonel is my authority for this abstract of the contract, and he does not say what *he* promised on the other hand. The Colonel states further, that the Mojaves were *very anxious* for peace; and declared that they would not fight, and that if the Americans wanted to kill them, they would offer no resistance; that they asseverated that they never harmed an

2 See note 8, chap. 20.

emigrant, nor were connected in any way with the murders laid to their door, and that they "manifested great alacrity to comply with my demands, which gave evidence of their sincerity!" Innocent and much slandered Mojaves! Sincere, honest and worthy redskins! Peaceable and harmless fellow creatures! Wise and immaculate Hoffman! Great combination of Napoleon, Wellington, Murat, Jonah and Bob Acres![3]

So much for Col. Hoffman's story; now for the others. A gentleman whom I know to be worthy of all confidence — honest, upright, and straightforward — told me to-day, that the Mojaves did not seek peace, did not beg for mercy, but that, on the contrary, they set Col. Hoffman, and his seven hundred bayonets at defiance; and when the Col. talked of war and blood, one of the chiefs took his bow and arrows and said: "The white man is a coward. Does he remember me?" drawing himself up to his full height. The Col. immediately recognized him as one of ten Indians who had caused him and fifty dragoons to retire from the Colorado on a former occasion. This appeared to make the Col. more anxious for peace, and he finally offered to withdraw his soldiery from the Mojave country, to present them (the Indians) with blankets and guns, and assured them that if they consented, they would never again be molested. After some consultation, the Indians agreed to this, and the seven hundred soldiers of the Mojave expedition retired amidst the jeers and taunts of a band of red-skins, who had been whipped by Mr. Bishop's party of forty. Well might Owen Lovejoy want the army reduced to a skeleton![4]

The event to which the Indian referred, when he asked Col. Hoffman, "Do you remember me," is this: Col. Hoffman, with an escort

[3] The reference is to the French Emperor Napoleon; to his brother-in-law, Joachim Murat, a famous general in Napoleon's army; to Sir Arthur Wellesley, the Duke of Wellington, the leader of the British Army that defeated Napoleon; and to Jonah of the Old Testament, who was rescued from the sea by a great fish so that he could preach a doctrine of repentance in the city of Nineveh. Bob Acres is an eccentric character in Richard B. Sheridan's comedy, *The Rivals*, first produced in London in 1775.

[4] Owen Lovejoy (1811–64) was an ordained Congregational minister who served as a Republican Congressman from Illinois from 1857 to 1864. He was the brother of Elijah Lovejoy, an antislavery editor who was murdered for his views. As a prominent abolitionist in Congress, Owen felt that the Army was the instrument of the slave power. For the speech referred to see the *Congressional Globe*, 35th Congress, 2nd session, part 1, p. 1132. See also Edward Magdol, *Owen Lovejoy: Abolitionist in Congress* (1967), pp. 221–22.

of fifty dragoons, was sent out by Gen. Clarke to examine the route to the Colorado. While engaged in this duty, they were met by a party of Indians, ten in number, who made "hostile demonstrations," and being, like Johnny Coup, anxious to sleep in a whole skin, they hastily retired without firing a shot, never pausing to rest until they reached San Francisco!

I think that Mr. Bishop has conferred a lasting favor on his country by his brave and determined stand against the Mojaves, for which too much praise cannot be bestowed upon him. Forty against nearly fifty times that number, encumbered with his camels and wagon train, he fought them, beat them, and crossed the river in the very face of their opposition. Had Col. Hoffman followed up with a vigorous blow, no further trouble need have been apprehended from these murderous red-skins. But, now, all is rendered worthless. I hope, however, that when Mr. Bishop meets Lieut. Beale, and their parties are united, they will "pitch in" and make Mojavedome tremble.

An old Pah-Utah brave, whom I knew in the land of "Latter-Day Saints," called on me a few days since, and told me that they were having troublous times in Utah. That you are aware of ere this, I presume, but still my opinion of the cause may not be out of place. It is this:

There is a desire on the part of certain individuals to have Gov. Cumming removed, and Judge Cradlebaugh[5] and Gen. Johns[t]on are in the plot. This resurrection of old troubles is for the purpose of bringing about a collision between the citizens and soldiers, that may render the Governor liable to a charge of mismanagement. This, I think, is all the *actual* trouble there. Gov. Cumming, however, has no lack of supporters, and I understand that Dr. Forney, Superintendent of Indian Affairs, unequivocally endorses his position. It is a Democratic fight, however, and, like the Western lady, I don't care which whips.[6]

A few days since, I paid to visit to Chucuana valley, and had a talk with some of the Chucuana Indians. This is a splendid race of

---

[5] John Crandebaugh was an associate justice of the Supreme Court of the United States and ex officio judge of the Second Judicial District, Utah Territory.

[6] See Bancroft, *History of Utah*, pp. 574–75.

7

aborigines — quiet, orderly and honest, *for Indians*.[7] The chief assured me that he had nothing against the white man, and could not afford to lose men fighting for fun. Some of his men were with the Mojaves, he said, but they were volunteers — a sort of red skin Lafayette, I presume. He showed me some glorious specimens of gold, but I could not induce him to discover where he had got them. He would do so, however, he said, if I would join his people: and as a further inducement, would permit me to select any two squaws I choose from his tribe for my wives. I did not accept the tempting offer, however. Whatever weight the gold might have had in inducing me to turn Indian, was entirely counterbalanced by the last offer — one woman having upset my calculations once before, I did not feel inclined to risk two now. I think my visit to this tribe will benefit us, as the chief promised to use his influence to induce the Mojaves to allow us to remain unmolested.

I, while looking over the country a few days since, discovered a large number of human bones — of about eighty persons, I should think — but nothing to give a clue to who they were. Some of the bones were those of quite young children. Our party buried them in the sand. The mysteries of these desert wilds are as great as those of the ocean.

I will give a few words of advice, and my reasons therefore, to those who may have correspondents in California. When you write mark your letters *"Overland via Butterfield routes"* and you will save from ten to twenty days in the time of transportation; *id est* your correspondent will receive it that much sooner than if not so marked. To illustrate my position, let me tell my own experience in this matter. I received a letter by the Butterfield route on the 3d inst., postmarked Pennsylvania, April 10. Now, had this letter not been so marked it would have went to New York and laid there until the 20th of April, and I would have received it about the 27th of this month, a difference of twenty days. And thus it is in all cases. The mail never fails to reach Los Angelos in the twenty days from St. Louis, and sometimes it accomplishes the journey in eighteen days. Even this is a consider-

---

[7] The reference is to the Chiricahua Apaches who roamed the Chiricahua Mountains straddling the emigrant route to California. For insights into "Utah's" qualifications about these Indians see Utley, *Frontiersmen in Blue*, pp. 82–83.

168

able saving, but when we consider that this is a semi-weekly, instead of a semi-monthly mail, the gain is still greater. There is no mail conveyance across our continent that does its duty so effectively as this does, and it would be a great gain to the country if the patronage that is bestowed on the steamship lines, and the Salt Lake overland routes were given to this. But of what possible service to the country, now impoverished and bankrupt, thanks to Buchanan and his backers, is the money paid to that soulless monopoly, the Pacific Mail Steamship Company? If the new Congress wish to commence well, let them, immediately after electing Mr. Green Speaker, take this great bonus from the Steamship Company, and give it to the Butterfield route.[8]

UTAH.

[8] The Pacific Mail Steamship Company, controlled by William H. Aspinwall and William H. Davidge, carried passengers and mail from Panama to California. It also built the Panama Railroad to carry passengers and mail across the Isthmus from the Atlantic to the Pacific side. Traffic from New York to the Isthmus was handled by the United States Mail Steamship Company. The railroad and the two steamship companies were referred to by the public as "The Monopoly." Between 1847 and 1859 these companies had a government contract for the delivery of mail to California. The Mr. Green referred to is James S. Green (1817–70) who was elected as a Democratic Congressman from Ohio and served from 1847 to 1851. After diplomatic service in Colombia, he was elected as a Democratic Congressman from Ohio to the 35th Congress but did not take his seat. Instead he was elected to fill a vacancy in the Senate and served there from 1857 to 1861.

Los Angeles
May 17, 1859
[24]

It is but little over a week since I wrote to you, full of hope and flattering myself with dreams of golden pleasures in the future; now I am as poor as though I never saw a gold mine. That unfortunate wound I received at the hands, or rather bullets of the Utahs has "laid me on the shelf" again; and my mining days are over — at least so the doctors say. Well saith the poet, "The best laid plans of mice and men gang aft aglee." [1]

I find the rumors concerning the *actual* result of Col. Hoffman's mission prevalent here, and with even more glaring features of failure. But I shall not say more till I have positive proof that it is not as the Colonel represents. The Col. established what he calls a "post," on the Colorado, at Beale's Crossing, a distance of two hundred miles by land, and three hundred miles by water, above Fort Yuma. It is named "Camp Colorado" and is garrisoned by two hundred men, consisting of companies F and I, 6th Infantry, and a detachment of the 3d Artillery, with two howitzers. Officers — Brevet Major L. A. Armistead,[2] commanding; Assistant Surgeon J. Milham,[3] Medical Department; 1st Lieut. Levi C. Boots (our old friend of the "Utah

[1] From Robert Burns' poem, "To a Mouse," published in 1785. "But, Mousie, thou art no thy lane,/ In proving foresight may be vain:/ The best-laid schemes o' Mice an' Men/ Gang aft a-gley, [awry]/ An' lea'e us noght but grief an' pain,/ For promis'd joy!"

[2] Lewis Addison Armistead graduated from West Point in 1836, won two brevets in the Mexican War, and received a regular commission as captain in 1855. During the Civil War he was a brigadier general in the Confederate Army and was killed at Gettysburg.

[3] John J. Milhau was commissioned as an assistant surgeon in 1851.

170

Army"), 1st Lieut. E. G. Marshall,[4] 2d Lieut. M. Bryant,[5] 6th Infantry; 2d Lieut. Tipton,[6] 3d Artillery.

From Col. Hoffman's report of the expedition I extract the following, concerning the navagation of the Colorado river.

"The steamer Jessup, drawing about two and a half feet of water, reached Beale's Crossing in twenty-seven days from Fort Yuma. At one point it was found necessary to lighten her, and in many places she had to work her way through the bars of quicksands which obstruct the navigation. The difficulties between Fort Yuma and Fort Gaston are greater than those higher up the river — the Jessup having been nearly eleven days between these two points, a distance of only forty-five miles. For forty miles below the crossing the navigation is free from obstructions. At the time the Jessup went up, the river was at a remarkably low stage." [7]

The Colonel is now in town, awaiting the next coasting steamer to take him up to San Francisco. He is accompanied by his adjutant, First Lieut. I. L. Comly,[8] Sixth Infantry. Col. Hoffman is apparently about fifty years of age, with grey hair and beard, his face is rather long and very thin, approaching very closely that peculiar cut of v[i]sage known as "hatchet face." He appears to be a man of considerable shrewdness, and is very a[m]iable and gentlemanly in his manners. He asserts that the Mojave expedition is a success, and I hope he is correct, though these are the most villainous Indians I have ever met with.

[4] Elisha G. Marshall graduated from West Point in 1850 and was promoted to first lieutenant in 1855.

[5] Montgomery Bryant was commissioned as a second lieutenant in the Sixth Infantry in 1857.

[6] John Tipton graduated from West Point in 1856 and was commissioned as a second lieutenant in the Third Artillery in 1856. He was promoted to first lieutenant in 1859.

[7] Hoffman's report is printed in the annual report of the secretary of war for 1859.

[8] Apparently "Utah" meant James L. Corley, of South Carolina, who graduated from West Point in 1850. He became a first lieutenant in 1855, the regimental quartermaster later the same year, and the regimental adjutant from November 1855 to April 1861.

172

The troops composing the expedition, besides those at Beale's
Crossing, are disposed of as follows: —

To be stationed at San Bernardino, (now *en route* there from
Beale's Crossing,) Companies E and K, Sixth Infantry. Officers —
Captain R. B. Garnett,[9] commanding; Surgeon W. B. Edgar,[10] Medi-
cal Department; First Lieut. D. D. Clark,[11] Second Lieut. J. A.
Smith.[12]

To return to the Presidio of San Francisco, now *en route* from
Beale's Crossing to San Pedro, thence on steamer Senator, 24th inst.,
Companies C and H, Sixth Infantry. Officers — First Lieut. B. S.
Smith,[13] First Lieut. S. O. Higgins,[14] Second Lieut. McCleary.[15]

En route for Fort Yuma from Beale's Crossing, Companies G,
Sixth Infantry, and F, Third Artillery. Officers — Capt. W. S.
Ketchum,[16] Sixth Infantry; Capt. H. S. Burton,[17] Third Artillery;
Second Lieut. Orlando Moore,[18] Sixth Infantry.

From Fort Yuma it is understood that Company 6th Infantry,
with the officers belonging to it, will proceed to San Diego.

I notice in the N. Y. *Herald* a note from some Californian, intended to set the people of the Atlantic States right in regard to the

[9] Richard Brooke Garnett graduated from West Point in 1840 and by 1855
was a captain in the Sixth Infantry. He later became a brigadier general in the
Confederate Army and was killed at Gettysburg.

[10] William Francis Edgar was commissioned as an assistant surgeon in 1849.

[11] Darius D. Clark graduated from West Point in 1849 and in 1855 was commissioned a first lieutenant in the Sixth Infantry.

[12] James A. Smith graduated from West Point in 1852 and was commissioned
as a regular second lieutenant in 1855 and as a first lieutenant in 1859.

[13] Benjamin F. Smith graduated from West Point in 1853 and received his
regular commission as a second lieutenant in 1855. In 1856 he was promoted to
first lieutenant.

[14] Silas Parsons Higgins graduated from West Point in 1853, was commissioned a second lieutenant in 1855, and a first lieutenant in 1856. He died in
1860.

[15] John McCleary graduated from West Point in 1854, was commissioned as
second lieutenant in 1855, and as first lieutenant in 1860.

[16] William S. Ketchum graduated from West Point in 1834, was advanced
regularly, and in 1846 was commissioned as a captain in the Sixth Infantry.

[17] Henry S. Burton graduated from West Point in 1839 and attained the rank
of captain in 1847 and major in 1861.

[18] Orlando H. Moore was commissioned as a second lieutenant in the Sixth
Infantry in 1856.

Congressmen from this State.[19] He is rather "off his eggs" concerning the matter. The two gentlemen referred to were elected by the people in obedience to official proclamations, and though it is now attempted to upset the election, the decision as to their right to seats will be decided by Congress itself, that body being the judge of the rights and qualifications of its own members. From present appearances, I think there will be three sets of Congressmen clamoring for admission, and Congress will have no small trouble deciding in the premises. The two gentlemen elected last fall are Democrats. There is no lack of candidates for the various offices to be filled at the ensuing election, especially on the Administration side of the house. Prominent among the candidates for the Gubernatorial nomination on the Buchanan ticket are Messrs. Weller, Latham, Nugent and Denver, — the tug will be, I think, between the first and the last named, though it is hard to tell, they "checker things so now-a-days."

The steamer Santa Cruz arrived here a few days since from the mouth of the Colorado via Guaymas and Mazatlan. She brings positive intelligence of the capture of all the towns of Sonora and Sinaloa by Gov. Pesqueira. It appears that the Miramon's officers[20] deserted their posts at the approach of the Liberals, and that the two States named were revolutionized without blood. Among the passengers by the Santa Cruz were a large number of Generals, Colonels, Captains, &c., belonging to the Miramon faction. Immediately after capturing Mazatlan, Gov. Pesqueira issued a decree opening all the Mexican ports on the Pacific Coast and Gulf of California to all vessels propelled by steam, on the simple condition that they carry the "mails free of charge." This shows the wisdom of the hero of "Constitutional Liberty," as his friends style him. It is difficult to arrive at a solution of Gov. Pesqueira's intentions, but I think he has abandoned his "independent republic" idea, and will adhere to the Liberal cause.

[19] The two Congressmen were Charles L. Scott of Sonora and John C. Burch of Weaverville, both Democrats. This item has not been located in the files of the New York *Herald*. Perhaps it appeared in another newspaper.

[20] In 1855 a liberal Mexican government began a program of religious and political reform that resulted in a new constitution adopted in 1857. The reforms led to a civil war between the conservatives and liberals that lasted until 1860. Lieutenant Colonel Miguel Miramon was a supporter of the conservative forces and later president of Mexico. Colonel Ignacio Pesqueira was a liberal and a long-time governor of the Mexican state of Sonora.

174

When Comonfort was overthrown, and the Church party seized the reins of Government, Pesqueira opposed the revolutionists, but deeming it impossible to sustain his anti-church power doctrines throughout Mexico, he resolved to "go on his own hood." [21] Since the defeat of Miramon by the Juarez forces, however, he has announced his adhesion to the Liberal party, and "conquered" two States to his doctrines. If he is sincere, I say success to him.

We have not got to go to the Gila or the Colorado for gold, as it appears that on the San Gabriel river, a mountain stream, about forty miles from this place, mines of considerable wealth have been discovered. [22] At the mines there is no scarcity of water, and its proximity to this place, when the cost of provisions, etc., is considered, renders mining much more profitable there than at more remote points. I clip the following from one of the Los Angeles papers, of to-day:

"The diggings on the San Gabriel river are exciting a good deal of enquiry, and many persons have left the city within

---

[21] Ignacio Comonfort was a former minister of war who became president of Mexico in December 1855 upon the resignation of President Juan Alvarez. He was a liberal and committed to a policy of no dismemberment of the national territory; the avoidance of civil war; and the calling of a constituent congress to frame a constitution. His government was beset with financial problems and the United States tried unsuccessfully to use this need to acquire the Mexican state of Sonora. In January 1858 Comonfort was overthrown and General Felix Zuloaga became the new president of a conservative government. Liberal forces led by Benito Juarez established a rival capital at Vera Cruz and kept alive the struggle against the conservatives. Zuloaga dismissed army officers who had served with the liberals, struggled with the financial problems, pondered the question of liquidating territory for money and decided against it. His failure to provide a new constitution led to his undoing. He resigned in January 1859 and Miguel Miramon became president. Miramon marched against the liberal stronghold at Vera Cruz, but abandoned the siege in March and returned to Mexico City where he defeated a liberal army that tried to take the city. After the battle Miramon ordered the execution of captured officers, but a subordinate applied the order against some civilians and children as well. Thereafter the liberals retaliated by killing captured conservative officers. The United States sent a confidential agent to Mexico to study the question of recognition. In March 1859 the United States recognized the government of Juarez and entered into negotiations on matters relating to claims, the grant of transit rights across Mexican territory, and the cession of lower California for a price. A treaty (the McLane-Ocampo) was negotiated but was not ratified by the United States Senate. See Hubert H. Bancroft, *History of Mexico, 1824–1861* (1885), 5: 666–776.

[22] Los Angeles *Star*, May 17, 1859. The San Gabriel mines are not discussed in Hubert H. Bancroft's *History of California, 1848–1859* (1888), vol. 6, nor in Paul's *Mining Frontiers*.

the past few days to engage in business. There has been about sixty persons at work along the banks and spurs of the mountain, near the river, for some weeks, who are making, on an average, from four to five dollars per day. Although gold was discovered on this river some years since, and men have been almost constantly engaged there in working, it appears that until recently, the most profitable digging have remained undiscovered. The prospect is that a large amount of gold will be taken this season from those mines."

Lieut. E. F. Beale, of the "Great Central Overland Mail Route," arrived here on Thursday, 12th inst. He reports the road good to the San Francisco mountains, about two hundred miles east of the Colorado. At this point he met Mr. S. A. Bishop and party, and as his provisions were nearly out, he pushed on to the Colorado — where Mr. B. had *cached* a quantity of the "needful," when he sent his wagon train back — taking only a part of his men with him. When within about thirty miles of the river the Mojaves attacked the party, and *intimated* their intention to prevent its passage, (this was since Col. Hoffman's "treaty" was made), but when the heavy, muscular figure of Mr. Bishop appeared from a wagon in which he had been riding, they fled in dismay. The party moved on to the river, but when they arrived there they found the *cache* had been "raised." Lieut. Beale then left the party and hurried to this place to obtain the necessary supplies. Accompanying his party are some twenty of the emigrants who were robbed by the Mojaves last fall. After Mr. Bishop's appearance, and before the red skins got out of range, the party killed four of their assailants. Lieut. Beale remained here but a few hours, and then returned to his men. When he makes his report I will transmit it by the first mail.

Arizonia has "got her dander up," as you will see by the following "preamble and resolutions," adopted at a meeting in Arizonia City on the 7th inst., which I have been permitted to copy in advance of publication.[23]

"WHEREAS, For a series of years, we have in vain humbly knocked at the portals of our National Government; in vain have we annually sent our duly

[23] For background on Arizona's effort to achieve territorial status in this period see Bancroft's *History of Arizona and New Mexico*, pp. 503–8, and Howard R. Lamar, *The Far Southwest, 1846–1912: A Territorial History* (1966), pp. 423–26. Arizona City became known as Yuma in 1873.

176

constituted delegate to Washington; in vain have we petitioned, supplicated and implored Congress for relief; and in vain have we invoked protection of persons, property and life — a guarantee of the ordinary rights and privileges of every American citizen. Facts have been heaped upon facts, instances have been added to instances, showing conclusively our utter destitution, and our absolute inability to defend ourselves without the protective influence of a government. We have shown that we are wholly without government; that, in the entire country from the Rio Grande to the Colorado, a distance of six hundred miles east and west, and a like distance north and south, there are no Courts, no civil officers, no law; and that crime stalks about in our midst in open day. We have shown that immigrant trains have been attacked by ruthless savages, and driven back, with great loss of life and property, leaving destitute women and children to wend their way back in doubt and dread through our almost trackless country; and that others, less fortunate, have been slain *en masse*. Men and children have been brutally murdered while struggling in defence of wives and mothers, and the wives and mothers have been ravished to death. We have shown that armed Mexicans have invaded our territory, and stained our soil with American blood; that Mexican cut-throats and outlaws, under cover of night, have brutally murdered and mangled the bodies of our citizens in charge of our mail stations; and that marauding parties of ruthless savages and barbarous Mexicans infest our entire territory, deluging the country in blood, driving off our herds, producing constant dread and alarm in our midst — preventing immigration, impoverishing our people, and depopulating our country. Not withstanding all this, the doors of Congress, to us, have been closed; the ears of those high in power have been deaf to our cries for relief; and to the scenes of blood and carnage here presented, they have shut their eyes with seeming indifference and evident contempt.

"Therefore, be it Resolved, That we, the citizens of Arizona city and vicinity, invoking the guidance and protection of Divine Providence, do hereby solemnly determine, with the consent and operation of our citizens throughout the Territory, to establish and maintain a government for ourselves.

"2d. That we earnestly request our fellow citizens in all parts of the Territory to unite with us in this effort to redeem our adopted country from the ravages of crime and supine negligence.

"3d. That we hereby recommend to our fellow citizens, that an election be held at suitable places throughout the Territory, on Monday, the 30th inst. for the election of Delegates to a Territorial Convention, to be held at Tucson, on Monday, the 27th day of June next; and that Arizona City elect six, and Gila City four delegates to said Convention.

"4th. That we also recommend that said Territorial Convention, when convened and organized, shall have full power to adopt an organic law for the future government of the Territory, to apportion the Representation, and, if deemed necessary, to elect temporarily the various officers of the Territory, and to do such other acts and things as said Convention shall deem meet and proper.

"5th. That this Territory now contains a larger population than did either Kansas, Nebraska, or Washington at the time of their organization; and that the opposition to our Territorial organization, on the ground of a deficiency of population, must be regarded either as the result of ignorance or fanaticism.

"6th. That if our population is less than represented, we are the more entitled to governmental protection; for the many can protect themselves, the few cannot.

"7th. That United States Tax Collectors are located almost everywhere in our midst. Thus is the Government asserting the odious, repudiated English doctrine of "Taxation without Representation."

"8th. That our sincere thanks are tendered to the Hon. Sylvester Mowry,[24] our Delegate to Congress, for his unremitting perseverance in our behalf.

"9th. That these resolutions be published, etc." [25]

Meetings have been held in all the towns of Arizonia, and these resolutions unanimously endorsed, so that the spunky youngster appears to be in earnest.

Some time since I wrote that there was a "Rev. Mr. Boardman, of Philadelphia," here. Well, this gentleman displayed his eloquence for some time before the people got stirred up. Finally, a meeting was held and a society organized, called "The First Protestant Association of Los Angelos," of which the keeper of a gambling saloon is President, and the proprietor of a dance house Secretary, with a Board of Trustees who are all notorious "sporting gents." If your enlightened city can produce anything to beat this in the shape of a religious association, I should like to hear of it. But to make it more emphatically a gamblers' institution, the worthy gentlemen comprising the management refused to furnish one of the city papers with a copy of the proceedings, because its editor belonged to the anti gambling faction. Yet Mr. Boardman accepted a salary that is made up from the earnings of vice, and the gains of those who deal out misery.[26] Verily for clerical curiosities, we need not go to

UTAH.

[24] Sylvester Mowry (1830–71), a West Point graduate in 1852, became a first lieutenant three years later; in 1858 he resigned from the army to devote himself to development of mines in Arizona. Chosen by the people of Arizona to represent the area in Congress, he was not admitted. His *Arizona and Sonora*, 3rd ed rev. (1864), and *Memoir of the Proposed Territory of Arizona* (1857, 1964) informed Easterners about these areas.

[25] Signed by L. W. Hastings, chairman of the committee, this appeared in the San Francisco *Herald*, May 18, 1859, with the city referred to as Arizona.

[26] The *Bulletin* published a correction of "Utah's" comments August 31, 1859, saying it was now convinced the report was "wholly untrue" and regretted it had been deceived by its correspondent. It added that Mr. Boardman and other Association members are "gentlemen of the highest respectability."

Los Angeles, California
May 23th, 1859
[25]

Verily, this is a world of changes. When I last wrote to you Liberalism was rampant in Sonora, and Linaloa [Sinaloa] Pesquiera was victor[i]ous, the Church party was in the dirt, and everything was going on "swimmingly." Now, I am apprised by a friend of mine, who is there, that Mazatlan is besieged by the forces of the Miramon faction, and that Grandara (Reactionist) is up in arms in Sonora, backed by the Indians of that State, who constitute two-thirds of the inhabitants. My friend is a Liberal, as all Americans in Mexico seem to be, and is sanguine of the ultimate success of his party. He says that Pesquiera will annihilate Grandara and his copper-colored in "less than no time," and that by the next mail he will have the pleasure of informing me that "the banner of the Constitutional party waves in triumph over the last vestige of fanaticism and bigotry." Well, we will see. I prefer waiting, though I sincerely hope he is correct in his opinion.

Among the notables of the Liberal party is a fine specimen of Young America, one Charles B. Norton, between whom and the commander of a British ship-of-war some spicy correspondence passed a short time before the abandonment of Mazatlan. Mr. Norton was formerly a school teacher at Guaymas, and when the war of parties began, joined the Liberal forces, and ere long was appointed Grand Admiral of the Mexican fleet of the Pacific — a schooner and two fishing boats. Under his management the Mexican naval forces have obtained a respectable size, and rendered some efficient service to the party he supports. Here is the correspondence:

178

(COPY)

H. B. M. S. ALARM, MAZATLAN,
JAN. 4, '59.

To the Person Commanding the Schooner Iturbide:

My attention has been called to an outrageous act committed yesterday upon a French vessel in the neighborhood of this port, by you. She having been fired at, brought to, and ordered away. Were it not that I have to think you have so acted in ignorance, I should at once take possession of your schooner. And I hereby give you notice, that should you again venture to pursue — fire into, bring to, or in any other way molest any foreign vessel, upon any pretence whatever, I shall at once, and without further warning, consider it my duty to take or destroy the said schooner, and such other small craft which act along with her. I have the honor to be, sir, your obedient servant,

(Signed)   DOUGLASS CURRY,
Captain of H.B.M. ship Alarm.

(COPY.)

H.B.M.S. ALARM, JAN. 5, 1859.

To the Person Commanding the schooner Iturbide:

SIR: — It having been officially reported to me that you have detained two launches (under Mexican flags) but having foreign property on board (copper ore), I request that the said launches be sent into this port, this afternoon, or I shall take other steps to have the launches and property restored. I have the honor to be, sir, your obedient servant.

(Signed)   DOUGLASS CURRY, Captain.

To these peremptory epistles Admiral Norton replied in the following spicy and laconic strain:

M. C. SCHOONER ITURBIDE, NEAR)
MAZATLAN, JAN. 5, 1859)

To the Person Commanding H.B.M. ship Alarm:

SIR: — Not having, at anytime, fired at or committed any outrage upon any vessel, the statements in your communication of yesterday are false, and can only be excused by attributing them to your ignorance of the facts.

The general tone of said communication, I consider as uncalled for and insulting, not only to the Government under whose orders I am, and to whom *alone* I am responsible, but to me, personally, and unworthy of respect, and I do, hereby, inform you that I shall proceed in all cases, as heretofore, until orders to the contrary are received from my superiors.

As regards your threat of destroying my vessels, I would merely recommend you not make any premature calculations. I have the honor to be, sir, your obedient servant,

CHARLES E. NORTON

Com. the Mex. Naval Forces in the Pacific.

P.S. — in respect to your note of this morning, permit me to state that I cannot reply definitely until advice from my superior officers at the camp.

NORTON.[1]

Political matters are growing quite warm here, and there will be a "nice time" for the "unterrified," when their State Convention meets. Weller is apparently somewhat scared at the looks of things, and has issued a circular to his friends and Democrats generally, setting forth that he was an able, faithful and patriotic Senator; that the reason he was not returned to the United States Senate, was not because he was unpopular, but because Broderick *was* popular — "not that I love Caesar less, but that I love Rome more,"[2] you see; that he has been an upright, impartial and worthy Governor, and that, all things considered, the people ought to re-elect him. This neat piece of self-praise and petty begging for popularity, is signed John B. Weller, and franked by him to all parts of the State. The Denver men are calmly and coolly laying their wires, and doing all they can in a quiet way to secure the nomination of their pet. My opinion is that Denver leads the crowd now; but there is no telling what effect the pathetic appeal of the Governor will have upon the mind of the masses of the Democ-

[1] Norton's force was subsequently obliged to surrender to the British. See the *New York Herald,* May 1, 1859.

[2] William Shakespeare, *Julius Caesar,* act 3, sc. 2. In Shakespeare love is in the past tense.

racy.[3] Next comes Latham, the Custom House pet, the candidate of the Southern gentry,[4] who fill the majority of the Federal offices here. He will probably secure the vote of the San Francisco delegation, but I doubt if he gets another vote. Then John Nugent, late Special Commissioner to Frazer River, the man who would not go to Bogota.[5] He has the support of the San Francisco *Herald*, of which he is "editor and proprietor," and of the most prominent anti-Vigilance Committee men in the State, including Phil. Herbert and "sich like." There are a number of others in the field, but these are the most prominent.

The "Broderickites" are now a regularly recognized party in the State, and maintain the doctrine that the people of a Territory are the only persons, the only power, who can say whether slavery shall exist in their midst or not. They do not call themselves "Douglas Democrats," as do the anti-Buchananites of the Atlantic States, nor will

[3] James W. Denver (1817–92) studied engineering, practiced law, and edited a Democratic newspaper in Ohio before settling in Missouri. During the Mexican War he raised a company, was commissioned its captain, and served with General Scott's army. He resumed the practice of law and newspaper editing in Missouri briefly before moving to California in 1850. Without his knowledge or consent he was elected as a state senator and served in 1852–53. In 1853 he became the secretary of state for California, and while holding that office was elected to the United States House of Representatives. As a Congressman he introduced a bill for the building of three transcontinental railroads, but this ambitious project did not meet with the approval of the House. In 1857 he was appointed commissioner of Indian Affairs but shortly thereafter he was sent to Kansas as the territorial secretary. By 1858 he was made governor of Kansas, but served only until the fall of that year when he resumed his work as an Indian commissioner. In 1859 he retired from that post, returned to California, made an unsuccessful bid for the United States Senate, and then moved back to Ohio. During the Civil War he was appointed a brigadier general of volunteers and served with the Army of Tennessee. He resigned his commission in 1863 to resume the practice of law in Washington, D.C., and in Ohio.

[4] Milton S. Latham (1827–82) practiced law in California; became clerk of the circuit court for Russell County (1848–50); clerk of the recorder's court of San Francisco (1850); district attorney for the Sacramento district (1851); and a Democratic member of the United States House of Representatives, 1853–55. He declined renomination and became collector of the port of San Francisco (1855–57). Elected as governor of California in 1859, he served only six days when he resigned as a result of being elected to the United States Senate to fill the vacancy caused by the death of David C. Broderick.

[5] John Nugent apparently was offered the position of consul at Bogota but declined. A gold rush in the Fraser River region of British Columbia in 1857–58 drew a number of Americans there who complained about their treatment at the hands of the British. John Nugent was sent as a special agent to the region in August 1858 to ensure that American citizens received fair and liberal treatment. He reminded his countrymen that they had duties as well as rights.

182

they bind themselves to follow any man upon whom the utmost reliance cannot be placed. They are arrayed upon a fixed platform, to that platform they will stand, come weal or wo[e]; and that platform is, as I have stated, freedom for the Territories. Mr. Broderick is not their *leader*, he is their champion, their standard bearer; the chief exponent of *their* principles, not they the followers of *his*. They are men of mind — in fact all the Democrats of any intelligence, save the Federal office-holders — and do not require a President or a Senator to mark out a course for them, being capable to manage that matter for themselves. Mr. Broderick's friends have challenged the honorable Doctor William M. Gwin to meet their champion on the stump to discuss the principles at issue, but the challenge has not been accepted. In regard to Gubernatorial matters, they are keeping rather quiet, but they will have a ticket in the field, with Hon. J. W. McCorkle at the head.

The Republicans are very silent. They have called a State Convention, and will no doubt nominate a ticket — either "straight" or in conjunction with the "Broderickites." Mr. Stanley will probably be their candidate for Governor.

Mr. McKibben, M.C.,[6] made a speech in San Francisco, a few days since, in which he said — "I have been called a Broderick Republican, but I care not for names. I am in favor of freedom in the Territories, and they may call that Broderick Republicanism or Black Republicanism, as they choose."

I am now convinced that the Mojave expedition is a failure, an utter, complete, total failure; in fact, what my old friend Major Raymond[7] would call "a magnificent fizzle." The Mojaves are at their old tricks again. A party of five belonging to Lieut. Beale's company were attacked one day last week and compelled to retire to the main body, with the loss of one of their number. The Indians making the attack numbered about thirty, and were all Mojaves, some of whom

[6] Joseph C. McKibbin (1824–96) was born in Pennsylvania, attended Princeton College in 1840–42, went to California, where in 1852 he was admitted to the bar, and served as a state senator (1852–53). In 1857 he was elected as a Democrat to the United States House of Representatives, but failed in his bid for reelection.

[7] There is no Major Raymond listed in the official records who matches this identification. It was apparently a militia rank.

were wrapped in blankets bearing the United States mark. I have not learned the name of the man killed. Now, if Col. Hoffman actually made a treaty with the Indians and took some of their numbers as hostages, of what possible benefit is it? If men are butchered in this manner so soon after this boasted treaty is made, what are we to expect when they cease to miss the hostages the Col. has for their good conduct? An Indian cares nothing for another unless he can fight; those taken by the Col., so I am assured by a man in the government employ, who acted as a translator, that they were got by promises from Hoffman to feed them well, give them blankets and guns, and send them back on the steamer, are mere boys, and have never done service in the field. Again, an Indian soon loses his love for his fellows if separated from them for any length of time, and these hostages will, ere long be, if they are not already forgotten. But, supposing they are hostages, and were obtained in the manner claimed by Colonel Hoffman, what will he do with them now that the faith for which they were pledged has been broken? Kill them? That would be murder — aye murder, to punish these boys for the offences of others. The worthy Col., I am inclined to think, is somewhat in the condition of the man who won the elephant in the raffle — he has got the Mojaves, or rather three of them, on hand, and he has now no way of disposing of them. But the Colonel contends, contrary to the statements of all except the soldiers, that the Mojaves came to his camp with proffers of friendship, and absolutely begging for peace. What if they did? Do they not do so even towards those whom they mean to most foully murder at the first unguarded moment? Has the Colonel grown gray in Indian service without knowing this? And more, if officers are in pursuit of a criminal, and he, finding escape impossible, comes to them in humiliation and begs forgiveness, will the hand of justice be stayed by his piteous appeals? Not that I wot of. In these days, when pusillanimity pervades every branch of our Government, the coarse of Col. Hoffman may meet official approbation. Against this I do not contend. But I hold that he has failed in the real objects of his expedition — the punishment of the Mojaves for their numerous crimes, and the assurance of safety to persons passing through their country hereafter. Suppose Lieut. Ives had, when sent to explore the Colorado, anchored at the mouth of the river, and sent information to the

Government that the Indians had reported it unnavigable, would that have been deemed satisfactory? I think not. And what more has Hoffman achieved? He arrived at the Mojave country and sent the gratifying intelligence to his superior, that the Indians were very sorry, and promised to behave better in [the] future! That is the amount of his accomplishment.

Speaking on this subject, the *Southern Vineyard*, the leading paper of the lower part of California, edited by a gentleman who has resided here for nearly a third of a century,[8] and who knows by sad experience what the Indians of this portion of America are composed of, says:

> "Since the attack on the emigrant party on the Colorado river, last fall, and the massacre of one entire family, and the killing of others of that party, by the Indians, we have urged the importance of inflicting a severe chastisement upon those engaged in that inhuman outrage. When these same Indians had the hardihood to resist the United States troops, who, under Col. Hoffman, last winter, were making a peaceful visit to the country inhabited by them, we flattered ourself that the time had arrived when that chastisement, however much delayed, would be administered. When we heard the sound of preparation that was made in the latter part of winter to send a force equal to any emergency that might arise, and sufficient to crush out all opposition that might present itself, we required a confident belief that the day for the humiliation of those perfidious savages was nigh at hand."

(The editor here expresses his sorrow at the failure of the Mojave expedition, and comments upon Col. Hoffman's course in a manner rather more severe than you would care to publish, and continues:)

> "If an exemplary course had been pursued, it would have had an effect upon the Mojave Indians, and their numerous allies and tributaries, which would have been productive of great good, and the preservation of many valuable lives, which will necessarily be offered upon the shrine of Indian barbarity

[8] J. J. Warner established the semiweekly *Southern Vineyard* in Los Angeles in 1855. The paper became a daily in 1867 and failed in 1873. According to Winifred Gregory, ed., *American Newspapers, 1821–1936* (1937), only three issues for 1859 are known to exist.

185

before these Indians are forced into an obedience of those laws of fidelity and integrity, of which they have no knowledge." [9]

Am I not right, then, in saying that the whole thing is an abortion, and that matters are as bad, if not worse than before? In the course of the same article, the *Vineyard* gives an account of a tribe of Indians being humbled in an effectual manner — a tribe of precisely the same nature as the Mojaves:

"More than thirty years since, when American trappers, with careful step, first trod the banks of the streams and rivulets of Northern Mexico, in pursuit of the beaver, a company of Missourians, of French descent, followed down the Gila river below the Pimo [Pima] villages. While all but a solitary camp sentinel were asleep, they were fallen upon by a large number of the Pimo Indians, who, during the afternoon, came into the camp. The Indians were unarmed, and as they proffered their friendship no suspicion was excited. Early in the evening the Indians brought into the camp a quantity of poles, for the pretended purpose of keeping up fires during the night. As soon as the fatigued trappers were asleep, and the poles, with which the Indians kept up their fires, were burned into a sufficient number of clubs, conveniently sized, the savages fell upon the sentry and the sleeping company, and murdered the whole party.

"The following year another party of trappers, mostly Americans, led by a native of Tennessee, arrived near the Pimo villages. The Indians approached their camp with signs of peace and friendship. When a large number of them, headed by their chiefs, had collected near the party, a scathing fire was opened upon them by the trappers, which caused many to bite the dust. Among those who fell was the head chief of the Pimos. The lesson taught those Indians at that time by that little band of hardy hunters, was effectual. They had been met and overcome by their own artifices. From that

[9] Another view of the Mojaves was expressed by Brevet Major L. A. Armstrong, Sixth Infantry, who wrote from Fort Mojave, Arizona, to Major W. W. Mackall, the assistant adjutant general at San Francisco, on June 14, 1859, concerning the outrages by the Paiute Indians. He added: "The Mohaves are the best behaved Indians I have ever seen, that I think *might* be civilized. As they live almost entirely, from what they raise from the soil they can be easily controlled. They number, I think, about five hundred warriors — at certain seasons of the years, after gathering their crops, wheat and corn, they can concentrate — ...." See "AG Letters," roll 595.

day to the present they have been the best Indians the continent affords, and they number themselves by thousands, when, if they had not been taught so salutary a lesson, which changed their very nature, they would ere this, no doubt, have become extinct.[10]

"If Colonel Hoffman could have treated the Mojaves in the same manner, it would have been the means of saving hundreds of valuable lives, and of working an entire change in the nature and disposition of those Indians and their allies, as well as enthroning *fear*, the only god whom they obey everlastingly in their minds."

From the State at large there is nothing of special importance. The same number of murders and robberies are daily chronicled, and Chinamen are still considered legal prey for whoever wishes to "run a muck." There is some excitement on the Chinese question now, news having been brought that there were ten thousand Celestials on their way here from the "Flowery Kingdom." It is a *canard*, however, I am inclined to think. The miners in some portions of the State are very hostile to the Chinese settling among them; why, I cannot say. Those who are living in and about Los Angeles are industrious persons — meddling with nobody, but rubbing along, eating rice and stewed rats with perfect satisfaction. They are principally washermen — willing for "tuo bittee to wash and ilon godd fol Mellikan man." [11]

Gov. Weller has been very merciful of late and has pardoned quite a number of convicts on "condition that they leave the State immediately." Where these fellows go to, I cannot say, but I deem it a very

[10] The American trappers described may have belonged to the party under James O. Pattie which was in the area in 1825 and 1826 and had clashes with the Apaches and the Mojaves. The situation in regard to Indian affairs in this early period is described in Bancroft's *Arizona and New Mexico*, pp. 401, 403–6. On American trappers see Robert G. Cleland, *This Reckless Breed of Men* (1950), and the multivolume work edited by LeRoy Hafen, *Mountain Men and the Fur Trade of the Far West* (1966). A sketch of James O. Pattie by Ann W. Hafen is in vol. 4, pp. 231–50.

[11] For an editorial critical of the anti-Chinese movement see the San Francisco *Herald*, March 21, 1859. The *Bulletin* later carried a report from San Francisco, dated November 7, 1859, that: "An association has been formed at San Francisco (with the purpose of embracing the whole State) for the purpose of excluding the Chinese from all employment, except the lowest kind." See the *Bulletin* of November 28, 1859.

impolitic business on the part of his Excellency to thus shove the villains of California off on other parts of the country.

The San Gabriel mines, of which I wrote in my last letter, appear to be quite profitable, and there is quite a rush for them at present. Some fifty persons came down on the steamer from San Francisco, yesterday, to try their luck at the new diggings. I wish them success, and would take a hand myself, were it not for my crippled condition.

Pike's Peak is generally regarded here as a humbug, or a delusion. Old California miners, who are there, represent it as all nonsense about the wealth of the mines there, and say that it is a story got up by speculators, who own the country thereabouts. They also represent that large numbers of filibuster agents are lurking about the mines, striving to entice adventurous spirits to follow their lawless banners on piratical incursions upon the country of our neighbors.

The Indians in the Northern part of California are represented to be somewhat troublesome, and several persons have been killed by them. A house near Red Bluff was fired by the red rascals some time since, and seven persons burned to death — two women and five children. The Governor has commissioned officers to commence a campaign against them. There will be no United States troops engaged in this matter, California doing her own fighting in such cases.

UTAH.

In Search of a Soldier
[26]

In mid-June 1859, a little more than a year after they began, the last of the letters signed "Utah" was printed in the *Bulletin*. "Utah" said then that if he were not incapacitated by his old wound he would be off to try his luck at the newly-opened San Gabriel mines.[1] The letter was made up of long quotations from other sources coupled with his own brief interpretation of events. Subsequent issues of the *Bulletin* carried news from California including some that touched on the Mexican civil war and California politics — subjects on which "Utah" had written — but no further by-lines. In the months that followed there was no explanation of the sudden termination of the columns and no obituary of the correspondent, despite "Utah's" previously expressed hope that if he died he would at least rate a notice. It is obvious that the editors did not appreciate "Utah's" comments about the Reverend Boardman, and the *Bulletin* later published a correction,[2] but this is the only known instance of any objection to anything in the letters. Perhaps the editors of the *Bulletin* decided that in view of the national attention being directed to such things as the coming election of 1860, there was little space or interest left over for news of the mines of California. National attention was also focused on the John Brown raid on Harpers Ferry in the fall of 1859, and on his subsequent trial and execution. The pages of the *Bulletin* reflect the concern over this event as well as over the results of Lincoln's election, the secession of the Southern states, and the attack on Fort Sumter. All of these things overshadowed the fate of a single correspondent in California.

Who was "Utah"? The question has intrigued the editor since he read the first letter of this man. In the beginning it seemed as though

[1] See chap. 25.
[2] See note 26, chap. 24.

the answer might be relatively easy to find through a process of elimination. From the comments about himself in his letters we know that he was a printer, apparently not yet twenty-one years of age, or at least not yet a voter, and a lightly built man. He called himself "a backwoods Pennsylvanian," but had close knowledge of, and interest in, Philadelphia. He had made it a point to hear sermons by three of the great preachers of his day — Edwin H. Chapin, Henry Ward Beecher, and Stephen H. Tyng. It would seem that he had some firsthand acquaintance with Great Britain and France, perhaps as an emigrant, or perhaps as the result of a visit. Intelligent and well read, he refers to himself as a former editor of a newspaper, the ———— Herald. Given his age, it would seem that this must have been a small-town paper, perhaps one published in the "backwoods" of Pennsylvania. On October 11, 1858, he wrote that he had been in the army nearly five months. This would put his date of enlistment in the Second Dragoons sometime in late March 1858. While on the march from Fort Leavenworth to Camp Floyd with Company A of the dragoon recruits, he held a temporary noncommissioned rank, probably a corporal. We know that he left Carlisle Barracks on May 4 and arrived at Camp Floyd, Utah, on September 25, 1858. He was assigned to a company of the Second Dragoons which he does not identify, but he speaks of a Lieutenant Gay in terms that suggest that they were in the same unit. In the early part of December 1858 his company was preparing to go out on a month-long scout. Later he tells us that he was wounded in a fight with the Indians only two days after they left camp. After refusing to let the surgeon amputate his wounded arm, he was discharged, and made his way to California, arriving there in March 1859. It seemed logical to assume that we would find our man among those discharged for disability between December 1858 and March 1859. If so, the rest of the information could be used to check the background of a particular soldier.

The records of the Second Dragoons showed only one disability discharge in the time period between December 1858 and March 1859. The date of discharge closest to that of "Utah's" was December 17, 1858, and the soldier was Alburtus Howerton of Company F. He was a twenty-three-year-old former clerk who enlisted at Richmond, Virginia, on March 2, 1858. Notations on the records indicate that he received a surgeon's certificate of ordinary disability. He was a "Rejected Recruit." Since the date of his enlistment he had been serving as a cook. Howerton was not "Utah." [3]

Perhaps there was a lapse of time between the actual discharge and the time the paper work made it official. Looking over the records of the sick and disabled men on the returns of the Second Dragoons at Camp Floyd (Companies A, B, C, E, G, and H) the editor discovered that there were eight possible candidates for the identity of "Utah."

Of these eight men, two were discharged in April and six in May 1859. Three of them were twenty-one years of age at the time of their enlistment; one was twenty-three; and one was twenty-eight. Two of these eight names were eliminated because their dates and places of enlistment did not fit the information in the "Utah" letters. These men were James Donnellon, who enlisted at Fort Leavenworth on September 1, 1857; and Patrick Crawley, who entered the Army at Nashville, Tennessee, on August 18, 1854. Both were given disability discharges on May 10, 1859.

Joseph Genther, aged twenty-two, looked as though he might be a likely prospect. He enlisted at Philadelphia on February 23, 1858. According to his enlistment record he was born in Germany, and his occupation was that of a tailor. Assigned to Company E of the Second Dragoons, the muster list shows him as "Left sick at Camp Floyd, U.T., April 21, 1859, ..." But Genther got better, served out his enlistment and was discharged in Virginia in February 1863. Clearly Genther could not be "Utah."

There were now five men whose dates of enlistment put them in the running. Two had enlisted in Buffalo, two in New York City, and one in Carlisle, Pennsylvania.

Two men who volunteered for the army at Buffalo, New York, were Charles P. Cole and John S. Gould. When Cole, aged twenty-two, enlisted on March 30, 1858, he gave his occupation as wagon

[3] Information on Howerton and other soldiers discussed in this chapter is drawn from "Regular Army Muster Rolls, Inspection Returns, 1821–1860, Second Dragoons," boxes 108–13, R.G. 94, National Archives, and from "Register of Enlistments in the U.S. Army, 1798–1914," microcopy 233, rolls 25 and 26, R.G. 94, National Archives.

maker and Chenango County, New York, as his birthplace. His service with Company A, Second Dragoons, terminated with a disability discharge dated May 16, 1859. No case could be made for considering him as "Utah."

John S. Gould, aged twenty-one, of Livingston County, New York, gave his occupation as a printer when he enlisted at Buffalo on March 22, or April 6, 1858. Assigned to Company E, Second Dragoons, he was given a disability discharge at Camp Floyd dated May 10, 1859. Except for the New York connection, Gould could have been "Utah." Further research in the pension records in the National Archives disclosed that after his discharge Gould was employed in the Quartermaster Department at Camp Floyd. Subsequently he went to western Texas where he carried the mails. He joined the Texas Rangers under the name of John Williams and served a few months. When the Civil War began he was living at Meridia, Basque County, Texas. The citizens there raised a company of soldiers to protect the frontier from Indians after the United States Army Regulars were withdrawn to fight the war in the East. This company did not wear uniforms. Later the company was organized as a part of the Eighth Battalion, Territorial Cavalry, Confederate States of America. Gould, again serving under the name of John Williams, was made a lieutenant, but claimed he never took the oath of allegiance to the Confederacy and served on the frontier. His unit later became a part of the First Texas Cavalry and was moved into Louisiana after the fall of Vicksburg in 1863. Unwilling to serve the Confederacy against the Union, he deserted in April 1864 and made his way to New Orleans, then in the hands of the federal troops. Here he tried to enlist in the United States Army but was turned down because of his Confederate service. Then, on February 7, 1865, he was accepted for service in the First Regiment of New Orleans Infantry and was discharged in 1866. He returned to Philadelphia and went to work for a newspaper. For many years Gould tried unsuccessfully to get a pension for his federal service, but was turned down because of his association with the Confederate cause. Gould's story did not match "Utah's" so he had to be rejected.

The two recruits who enlisted in New York City were twenty-one years of age and were both Irish born. One was John Mugan, a laborer, who joined the army on June 2, 1857. After service in Company E, Second Dragoons, he was given a disability discharge at Camp Floyd on May 10, 1859. The date of enlistment and the civilian occupation disqualified Mugan.

The other twenty-one-year-old Irishman who enlisted in New York was William Morrison or Morrisey, who gave his occupation as a porter. His service extended from February 23, 1858, to the date of his disability discharge at Camp Floyd on May 15, 1859. If one assumed that the occupation of porter was a mistake for printer, then Morrison might be considered. There was nothing to suggest any connection with Pennsylvania or journalism. It seemed as though he must be eliminated from consideration.

Henry W. Fischer, a painter, enlisted at Carlisle on April 13, 1858, and was given a disability discharge from Camp Floyd on April 28, 1859. Fischer was German born and his age was given as twenty-eight. This seemed to rule him out except there was the possibility that the German birth might account for "Utah's" knowledge of Europe. The five-year waiting period for naturalization might account for the fact that he had not yet voted. During that time he might have served as an editor of a small-town newspaper in Pennsylvania. He enlisted at Carlisle, and that city had a newspaper known as the *Volunteer Herald*. The few scattered issues for 1856, 1857, and 1858 in the Library of Congress gave no useful clues regarding any editorial work by Fischer. There was a weekly newspaper in Philadelphia called the *Saturday Morning Herald* at this time, but it went out of existence in 1857 and no numbers of it survive. There were other Pennsylvania cities and towns that used the word *Herald* in the titles of their newspapers, but in almost every instance only a few scattered issues survive for years prior to 1858. None yielded any clues to Henry W. Fischer or Fisher.

A Philadelphia directory for 1855 and 1856 shows "Fisher & Brother" of 15 North 6th Street among the "Printers-Book and Job." In the alphabetical listings we find two men named Henry G. Fisher. One was a printer who lived at 10th Street below Prime; the other was a painter whose business address was North West 10th Street and Locust Avenue, with his home at 14 Raspberry Street. By 1859 Henry the printer is no longer listed, but Henry the painter is. Then, in the 1860 directory, both the painter and the printer are listed. Henry the printer now lived at 1131 South 10th Street.[4] This seems to indicate that it was Henry the printer who was away from Philadelphia at least for the year 1859, but he was back for the 1860 directory. Possibly the middle initial is an error in the directory, or when he enlisted he disguised his identity a bit with a different middle initial and another occupation. On the payroll for the dragoon recruits en route to Utah the soldier signed his name Henry W. Fisher. This speculation about a mistake in a middle initial is undermined by the fact that a printer named Henry G. Fisher died in Philadelphia on May 7, 1866. His age is given as sixty-one, sixty-two, or sixty-seven.[5] In any case he would have been too old to qualify as the young recruit of 1858. The possibility of connecting Henry W. Fisher with any printing in Philadelphia immediately prior to 1858 must then rest on the assumption that he is covered by the entry for Fisher & Brother.

Fischer was assigned to Company A, Second Dragoons, at Camp Floyd on September 28, 1858 — a date that corresponds to "Utah's" transfer to an unnamed company. Still, there is no record of any pension in the Old Wars, Indian Wars, or Civil War indices for any Fisher or Fischer whose service record matches that of "Utah." No record of his death in California was found. Therefore Fischer could be "Utah" only if one accepts certain speculations about his age, citizenship, and occupation. Another unresolved question was how he got back to Philadelphia from California.

Thus, of all the people associated with the Second Dragoons who received disability discharges, the record of none matched the details given by "Utah." Only Henry W. Fischer or Fisher remained as a possibility, and there were many unanswered questions about him. The search must go on.

A decision was made to approach the identification problem on the basis of occupation. How many persons in the Second Dragoons gave as their occupation the trade of printer? Returns from that regi-

[4] *McElroy's Philadelphia Directory for 1855*, p. 171; *for 1856*, p. 811; *for 1857*, p. 833; *for 1858*, p. 838; *for 1859*, pp. 221–22; *for 1860*, p. 304.
[5] Death Records, 1860–1869, entry 122 for 1866, Philadelphia City Archives; *Bulletin*, May 8, 1866.

194

ment yielded three names: John S. Gould, whose history has already been given, Edward Walters, and Francis Clinton.

Edward Walters of New Bedford, Massachusetts, aged twenty-three, enlisted at New York City on June 24, 1857, and was attached to Company E, Second Dragoons. The record shows him as deserting on April 4, 1859, from Camp Floyd. The date of enlistment, the New England background, and the date of desertion ruled out Walters.

This left Francis G. Clinton, aged twenty-one, of Clearfield, Pennsylvania, who enlisted at Philadelphia on April 19, 1858. He was assigned to Company G, Second Dragoons, on September 28 of the same year. The records of Company G show him as being on detached service at Salt Creek Valley, Utah Territory, beginning on December 22, 1858. But they also show him as having deserted on January 21, 1859, from Chicken Creek, Utah Territory.

How could this tie in with "Utah's" account of his wounding and discharge? One explanation would be that for some reason his discharge was apparently in the field and was perhaps not properly recorded. Could it be that the attending surgeon did not note that this man was being discharged for a disability? "Utah" was critical of the way the doctor bandaged his arm. Perhaps his paper work was also bad. The only thing that can be said on this score is that there are indications that reports did get lost. For example, the Adjutant General wrote to Major Emory for the Morning Reports of the Sixth Column which he led part of the way to Utah. Emory replied that he had already filed two reports, and since he no longer had the records of the column, he could only submit a partial answer based on a single retained copy.[6] No instance has been found of any mishandling of a medical report. The post records of Camp Floyd show a special order number 121, dated December 15, 1858, assigning a medical officer to Nephi who was also to attend to the command on Chicken Creek. This may or may not have been related to the sequence of events relating to the treatment of "Utah's" wound.[7]

[6] W. H. Emory to Colonel S. Cooper, September 10, 1858 . "A. G. Letters," roll 578.

[7] "Post Returns, Fort Crittenden [Camp Floyd]," microcopy 617, roll 268, R.G. 393, National Archives.

"Utah's" letters say that on the march to Camp Floyd he broke his goggles, destroyed one pair of uniform pants, tore a shirt to tatters, lost a boot and possibly a horse. When Clinton was first reported as a deserter the muster rolls showed that he owed the U.S. Government $.81 for "Ord & Despt Roll"; $52.17 for ordnance — presumably his carbine; $42.31 for "H.[orse] Equipt."; $1.53 for "C & G [camp and garrison] Equipment"; and $31.44 for clothing.[8] Some of these charges match those facts noted by "Utah." Most appear to be charges for what he took with him.

Clinton's case became more intriguing when a further examination was made of the muster rolls and inspection returns of the Second Dragoons. That for Company G, covering the period April 30 to June 30, 1859, carries the following notation:

"*Deserters*, reported before but taken up for the purpose of placing charges against them.

Wilkes, Charles. Pvt
Clinton, Francis G.

Due Livingston & Co. Sutlers, Camp Floyd, U.T. $13.17 & to Mrs. Seidler Co G Laundress $4.50 as reported by [the] Council of Administration." [9]

The fact that this entry is made for the period when "Utah's" letters ceased made it of special interest. Was he picked up as a deserter? The company was then in Camp Floyd, and there is nothing on Clinton's enlistment record to indicate that he was apprehended much less tried. The above entry deals with Charles Wilkes, who deserted on October 13, 1858, and Francis G. Clinton, who deserted January 21, 1859. Additional charges were being added several months later as the paper work caught up.

On the other hand, in the few records of Camp Floyd preserved in the National Archives, there is a volume of "Guard Reports" for the period December 1860 to March 1861. Among the list of prison-

[8] "Regular Army Muster Rolls, Inspection Returns, 1821–1860, Second Dragoons," for Company G, October 31 to December 31, 1858, box 112, R.G. 94, National Archives.

[9] "Regular Army Muster Rolls, Inspection Returns, 1821–1860, Second Dragoons," for Company G, April 30 to June 30, 1859, box 112, R.G. 94, National Archives.

ers is a Clinton, but no first name is given. His unit is Company B, Fourth Artillery. On January 4, 1861, he was confined for deserting his post.[10] This was two years after Francis Clinton's desertion and a year and a half after a possible recapture. If the Camp Floyd record refers to the same Francis Clinton then we must assume that he was in trouble on more than one occasion since the first desertion would have been punished long before 1861. The letters of "Utah" do not indicate that he was the kind of man who was prone to desertion or to other disciplinary problems.

In his last letter "Utah" complained about his health; perhaps he died from the effects of his wounds. California was attempting to keep records of deaths in 1858, perhaps there was a Francis Clinton among the deceased. Today the County of Los Angeles has no records dating from the nineteenth century. Our Lady Queen of Angels Church operated by the Claretian Fathers preserves much of what remains from the previous century. Their records contain no information concerning the death or burial of a Francis Clinton during the period in question.[11]

Assuming that Clinton did not die in California, one might expect that he eventually found his way back to the East. Whether he did or not, it seemed as though he would eventually apply for a pension. Yet the pension files at the National Archives contain no record of any such request by him or from a widow or other dependent.[12]

None of the Philadelphia directories published between 1855 and 1860 shows any printer named Clinton. A Francis Clinton is listed as a carpenter, and his name appears in each volume throughout the period. The 1860 directory contains an additional listing for a Francis Clinton who was a machinist. If Francis Clinton was "Utah" he evidently did not work under that name as a printer in Philadelphia.[13]

10 "Guard Reports, December 1860–March 1861," Camp Floyd and Fort Crittenden, Utah, R.G. 393, National Archives.

11 Antonia Escanega of Our Lady Queen of Angels Church, Los Angeles, to H. D. Langley, October 23, 1969.

12 There is a pension record on file for a Francis G. Clinton, but he served as a second class boy in the United States Navy during the Civil War and after the war with the Tenth United States Cavalry.

13 McElroy's Philadelphia Directory for 1855, p. 94; for 1856, p. 108; for 1857, p. 115; for 1858, p. 116; for 1859, p. 122; for 1860, p. 163.

It is quite possible that he lived and worked in a small community near Philadelphia.

In all of Pennsylvania there were seventeen newspapers from the mid-1850's with *Herald* in their names.[14] Considering that those men associated with the Philadelphia *Bulletin* were presumed to have known of "Utah's" editorial days, it seemed logical to assume that the particular *Herald* with which he was connected was published in or near Philadelphia. There were *Herald*'s in Norristown, Frankford, and West Chester, as well as the previously mentioned Philadelphia *Saturday Morning Herald* which ceased publication in 1857 and for which no files are known to exist. The weekly *Frankford Herald* lasted from 1854 to 1915, but no issues of the 1850's survive. Issues of the Norristown *Weekly Herald* exist for the years 1855 to 1862, yet nothing was found to connect Francis G. Clinton with that paper. West Chester's weekly *Independent Herald* was published between 1854 and 1857. Scattered issues remain, but they contain no information on Clinton's editorship. A second weekly, the *Jeffersonian & Democratic Herald*, served West Chester from 1842 to about 1910. The files for the middle and later 1850's are reasonably complete, but nothing was found indicating that Francis Clinton was an editor.[15]

"Utah's" interest in the outcome of the Congressional elections in Somerset and Reading, Pennsylvania, suggests that there might be clues in the newspapers in those cities. The Somerset *Herald* (later the *Herald-Republican* and *Herald and Whig*) was published for a number of years. Now only one issue from 1854 is known to exist. That date seems to be too far removed from "Utah's" age in 1858 to be useful. Reading had no newspaper that used the name *Herald* on its masthead.[16]

[14] Gregory, ed., *American Newspapers*, pp. 589–630.

[15] West Chester's *Independent Herald* was established in January 1854 with Henry Bosee as publisher. From January 1, 1855, to May 1, 1856, Lewis Marshall was publisher with William Whitehead as associate editor. The paper became known as the *Independent Herald and Free American* on May 1, 1856, with William L. and Edwin F. James as editors and publishers. In February 1857 they sold the paper to Samuel E. Downing and John J. Pinkerton who published it until April 25, 1857, when it was renamed the *Chester County Times*. Information supplied by Dorothy B. Lapp, corresponding secretary, Chester County Historical Society, West Chester, Pennsylvania. West Chester's *Jeffersonian & Democratic Herald* was edited by John Hodgson. The Norristown *Weekly Herald* was edited by Robert Iredell and Loyd Jones.

[16] Gregory, *American Newspapers*, p. 622.

198

There were other newspapers with *Herald* in their titles in Butler, Carlisle, Catasauqua, Greensburg, Harrisburg, Wayne County, Johnstown, Lancaster, Pittsburgh, Scranton, and Towanda. Most have only a few issues for the years 1856 to 1858 and these have yielded no clues of Clinton.[17]

An argument for identifying Francis G. Clinton as "Utah" thus rests on seven points, his age; his place of birth in Clearfield, Pennsylvania, which qualified as a "backwoods" area; his civilian occupation as a printer; his date and place of enlistment in Philadelphia in 1858; his assignment to Captain Gay's Company G, Second Dragoons; his date of desertion on January 21, 1859, closely matching the chronology in "Utah's" letters; and his name and literary allusions suggesting a man raised and educated in a strong Anglo-American environment.

The case against considering Francis Clinton as "Utah" rests on the inability to connect him with printing in Philadelphia or with the editorship of any newspaper with *Herald* in its title. Furthermore, the character of "Utah" as revealed in his letters makes it difficult to believe that he would be a deserter. If he lived, one would assume that sooner or later he would have applied for a pension. Also, if he was unjustly accused of desertion we would assume that he would make the effort to clear his name.

Further searches in the National Archives brought to light a muster and payroll of Company A, Dragoon Recruits, dated June 30,

[17] Gregory, *American Newspapers*, pp. 589–630. There are only three issues of the Butler *Democratic Herald* for 1856–57 and these are in the Library of Congress. Carlisle's *Volunteer Herald* is represented by a nearly complete run for 1856, two issues for 1857, and three for 1858, all in the Library of Congress. The complete file of the weekly *Catasauqua Herald* is in the custody of the Historical Society of Western Pennsylvania, Pittsburgh, Pennsylvania. The Harrisburg *Daily Herald* was published from December 1853 to August 1858, when it merged with the Harrisburg *Telegraph*. The Pennsylvania State Library at Harrisburg has a nearly complete run for 1855, several issues for 1856, and two for 1858. The *Wayne County Herald* was published in Honesdale from 1832 to 1893, but only two issues, one from 1852 and one from 1853, are known to exist for the decade before the Civil War. There are no known issues from the 1850's of the *Johnstown Herald* or the *Lancaster Herald*. The *New Castle Weekly Herald* was established in 1857 and that same year changed its name to the *New Castle Courant*. Pittsburgh's *Morning Herald* was established in 1840, but no issues for the 1850's survive. Scranton had a weekly newspaper, the *Lackawanna Herald* for 1853–1856, when it changed its name to the *Herald of the Union*. Yale University Library has a broken series for 1853 to 1856. A single issue is in private hands. Towanda had the weekly *Bradford Herald* from 1859 to 1861. Broken runs of this paper are in the custody of the Bradford County Historical Society in Towanda.

1858, near the start of the trek to Utah.[18] This list contained the names of all of "Utah's" companions and must, of course, include his own. Here were the names of First Sergeant Frederick H. Smith, Francis W. Clinton, John S. Gould, and others mentioned in the letters. There was also the name of Henry W. Fisher.

"Utah's" letters indicate that he enjoyed special privileges and, as noted earlier, he probably held a temporary noncommissioned officer's rank while on the march. The muster roll contained the names of two sergeants in addition to Smith and four corporals. A check of the service records of these men indicated that none could be "Utah." There was always the possibility that "Utah" served as a noncommissioned officer later on in the march, perhaps after Smith and some others were detached at Fort Bridger. Or it may be that he held no temporary rank and enjoyed special privileges by virtue of being a friend of the first sergeant. The fact that both Smith and Fisher were German born probably contributed to the friendship, and especially in the light of "Utah's" rather critical comments about the Irish members of the company. It was hoped that the final report on the company's march and arrival at Camp Floyd would shed light on the matter of temporary ranks. Similar reports are in the letters to the Adjutant General, but none relating to this group of dragoon recruits has been found. The possibility of identifying "Utah" on the basis of a temporary rank had to be abandoned.

According to "Utah's" account, he was given his final pay in the form of a check on a St. Louis bank. This he had to have cashed by a Mormon at a fifty percent discount. Surely the record of this final payment would lead to the identification of "Utah." Among the records of the United States General Accounting Office is a volume kept by the Second Auditor that bears the title: "Register of Payments, U.S. Army Discharged Soldiers, 1846–1860." [19] It contained an entry for Henry W. Fisher, Company A, Second Dragoons, as well as the name of a payroll officer and a voucher number. The last two items proved to be key bits of information. Armed with them a search was made for the original voucher. After some difficulty it was found. It revealed that Fisher was born in Allsted, Germany. His civilian

[18] "Muster Roll, Company A Dragoon Recruits."
[19] Records of the U.S. General Accounting Office, R.G. 217, National Archives.

occupation was a printer. He was five feet seven inches tall, had brown hair, gray eyes, and a fair complexion. His final pay was based on nine months and twenty-seven days service since the time of his last pay, July 1, 1858, at a rate of $11 a month for a total of $108.90. Added to this was $12.50 of retained pay; $50.40 for pay while traveling back to Carlisle, Pennsylvania; and $73.25 for subsistence while traveling for a total of $245.05. From this sum $2.48 was deducted for the "Army Asylum" better known as Soldiers' Home; $3.81 for clothing withdrawn; $5.82 for ordnance, presumably for the accessories; and $.76 for Camp and Garrison Equipage for a total of $12.87.[20] The amount for clothing may be for the trousers torn or the boot lost in his slide down a rock. The $.76 might be the cost of the lost goggles. In any event, "Utah" says that he received only half the face value of his check for his final pay and was soon robbed of most of the remainder.

How does this final payment to April 28, 1859, correspond to "Utah's" account that he was discharged in December 1858 and by late April was working at the Gila mines? The explanation seems to be that when he was given pay "for travelling from Camp Floyd, Utah Terr., the place of my discharge, to Carlisle, Pa. the place of my residence," the distance was estimated at 2,523 miles and the rate of travel at 20 miles a day. One hundred and twenty-six days were allotted to get back to Pennsylvania and twelve dollars a month. If we count 126 days back from April 28, it brings us to December 24, 1858. Company A, Second Dragoons, was ordered to prepare for a month's scout on December 1. According to its muster role, the company was on detached service from December 12, 1858, to January 4, 1859. "Utah" says that he was two days out of camp when he was wounded. This would place it about December 14 or 15. He was taken to a camp where he refused to permit the amputation of his right forearm. We do not know how long it took him to reach camp, but presumably another two or three days, or about December 17 or 18. He says that three days after reaching camp he was discharged. This would place it about December 20 or 21. While we still have

[20] "Settled Accounts of Army Paymasters, 1815–1861," accounts of Henry Prince, paymaster, #9402, January 1860, voucher no. 172, R.G. 217, National Archives.

three days unaccounted for, the chronology seems close enough. It is also possible that a man in pain lost track of exactly how much time passed between events.

If Fisher or Fischer was "Utah" one event that may have had a relationship to his return to the East was the death on August 17, 1859, of John D. Fisher of 1205 Mount Vernon Street, Philadelphia, as a result of a fall while painting a house. The *Bulletin* gave his age on successive days as sixty-five and fifty-seven years. He was survived by a wife and children who were not named. On the second day the death announcement carried the notation, "Western papers please copy." [21]

Another possibly related event took place in Mexico, where "Utah" said that he had a friend, an American, who was living there amid that country's civil war. After Miramon's forces defeated the liberals before Mexico City on April 11, 1859, military officers and some civilians were executed. One of those executed was S. Fischer.[22]

Still another intriguing question concerns Frederick H. Smith, of whom "Utah" wrote that "he stuck to me as a brother and a guiding star," and who was "all in all to me, and worthy of the highest praise and honor." After presumably honorable service in Florida, he rejoined the army as a private in April 1858 and rose quickly to the rank of acting first sergeant of the dragoon recruits in the Sixth Column. "Utah" and Smith were tent mates until Smith was assigned to Fort Bridger. Later, on September 29, 1859, Smith suddenly deserted from Fort Bridger. This was 129 days after the date of "Utah's" last published letter. Did "Utah" persuade Smith to join him in a venture in the goldfields? It seems unlikely that he would induce his friend to desert. Or, in the light of "Utah's" physical disability, did he call upon his old friend for help? Possibly "Utah" stopped at Fort Bridger on his way back to the East and Smith decided to join him. Of the seven men who can be positively identified as regular or temporary noncommissioned officers of the dragoon recruits early in their march to Utah, only Smith and one corporal failed to complete their terms of service. This hardly matches the image we have of him from

[21] *Bulletin*, August 18 and 19, 1859.
[22] Bancroft, *History of Mexico*, 5: 763n.

"Utah's" letters. We shall probably never know what circumstances prompted him to desert, but going to the aid of a crippled friend far from home might well have been a compelling reason.

There is also the possibility that "Utah's" wound did get better, that he went off to the San Gabriel mines and died in that region. Or, if he returned East, he went to Carlisle or some other city for a period of time. No trace of him can be found in the 1860 census returns from Los Angeles or Carlisle. The Philadelphia city directories issued between 1859 and 1871 show various Henry Fishers or Fischers in different occupations. There is also a Henry W. Fisher who appears in the 1864 directory as a carpenter. By 1869 he is a part of the firm of Fisher & Hall. There is no reason to believe that an ex-printer and editor with an arm injury would take up carpentry as a new profession. Marriage records preserved in the Philadelphia City Archives show several Henry Fishers or Fischers who entered into matrimony between 1860 and 1880, but none of the groom's ages qualifies him to be the Henry W. Fisher of the Second Dragoons. There is also no death or naturalization record in Philadelphia that sheds any light on the missing Henry W. Fisher. If he did return to Philadelphia, perhaps it was only for a short period of time and is not reflected in the city directories.[23]

The case for considering Henry W. Fisher or Fischer as "Utah" rests on the assumption that the occupation "painter" on his enlistment record was a mistake for the term "printer" on his final pay voucher, and not the other way around. Of course, if he had the intention of writing letters to a newspaper he may have deliberately disguised his civilian connection with the press to further hide his identity. Henry Fisher's age and maturity make it more likely that he could have been an editor than some of the other men discussed earlier. His date of enlistment corresponds to "Utah's" and he was given a disability discharge from Camp Floyd at a time that closely approximates the sequence of events in "Utah's" narrative. He was German born, which probably explains in part his close friendship

[23] Census of 1860, Los Angeles, microcopy 653, roll 59; Census of 1860, Carlisle, Pennsylvania, microcopy 653, rolls 1101, 1102; *McElroy's Philadelphia Directory for 1864*, p. 230; *Gospill's Philadelphia Business Directory for 1869*, p. 181; Marriage Index, 1860–1883, Naturalization Index, 1854–1877, and Death Records, 1860–1869, Philadelphia City Archives.

with First Sergeant Frederick H. Smith, another German-born soldier, and the privileges he enjoyed on the march to Utah. Fisher may have come to the United States as a young boy and grown to maturity in a small Pennsylvania town. His schooling would then presumably be somewhat the same as other American boys, which might account for his firm grounding in English literature. His own recollections of American elections went back to 1848 when he was eighteen years of age. A large number of Germans came to the United States in 1848 as a result of the outcome of the revolution of that year. Perhaps Fisher and his family were among them. Where they settled is not known. There is no Fisher or Fischer family in the 1850 Census of Carlisle, Pennsylvania, that qualifies.[24] Fisher's comments on what went on in Company G, Second Dragoons, rather than Company A, his own company, may have been a device to protect his identity. But a close reading of "Utah's" seventeenth letter also shows that in the beginning he says that Company A is going to Salt Creek in a few days, and near the end he notes that that morning *his* company had received orders for a month's scout. Company G left Camp Floyd on December 7 and Company A on December 12. But the returns for Company G show that while its headquarters were listed as "Camp Porter in the San Pete [?] Valley, U.T.," Clinton and some other men were on detached service in Salt Creek Valley, U.T., as of December 22, 1858. Company A's returns show it as being on detached service without a fixed headquarters. Special order number 126, issued at Camp Floyd on December 26, 1858, ordered an infantry detachment to relieve Company A, Second Dragoons, in the Rush Valley.[25] This chronology suggests that Fisher might have been discharged in Rush Valley just before the company returned to Camp Floyd where amputation of his arm awaited him.

The case against Henry W. Fisher rests mainly on his age and its relationship to his assertion that he was not yet eligible to vote, on his

24 Census of 1850, Carlisle, Pennsylvania, microcopy 432, roll 773.

25 "Regular Army Muster Rolls, Inspection Returns, 1821–1860, Second Dragoons," for Company A, October 31 to December 31, 1858, and December 31 to February 28, 1859, and for Company G, October 31 to December 31, 1858, and December 31 to February 28, 1859, box 112, R.G. 94; "Post Returns, Fort Crittenden [Camp Floyd]," microcopy 617, roll 268, R.G. 393, all in the National Archives.

German birth, on the confusion about his occupation, and on the lack of a positive Philadelphia editorial connection. Comments about Pennsylvania newspapers with *Herald* in their titles, discussed in connection with Francis W. Clinton, apply as well to Henry W. Fisher. Possible explanations for all of these things have been noted.

The final answers to these questions may never be known. Although the conclusion now offered involves a great deal of speculation, the editor is inclined to identify "Utah" as Henry W. Fischer or Fisher.

No.	NAMES. PRESENT AND ABSENT. (Privates in alphabetical order.)	RANK.	ENLISTED.			
			WHEN.	WHERE.	BY WHOM.	PERIOD.
		Captain.				
		1st Lieut.				
		do.				
		2d Lieut.				
1	Thomas I. Berry	Bvt. 2d Lt.				
1	Frederick H Smith	1st Sergeant	april 10.58	Boston. Mass	Lt. McArthur	5 yea
2	John I. Blakemore	Sergeant	" 7. 58	Albany N.Y.	Lt. Johnson	"
3	Charles King	do.	" 3. 58	New York N.Y.	Capt. Granger	"
		do.				
1	John McCarthy	Corporal	march 30.58	New York N.Y.	Capt. Granger	5 yea
2	Thomas B. Willis	do.	april 8. 58	Washington D.C.	Lieut. Jones	"
3	Thomas L. Marshall	do.	" 10. 58	Baltimore Md.	Capt. Adams	"
4	Henry Wilkins	do.	march 22. 58	Albany N.Y.	Lt. Johnson	
1	Crompton John T.	Bugler	Nov 27. 57	Boston Mass	Lt. McArthur	5 y
2	Tague Francis	"	Oct 28. 57	New York. N.Y.	Capt. Granger	"
1	Byrn Richard. C.	Private	april 22. 58	Albany N.Y.	Lt. Johnson	5 yea
2	Calahan Patrick	"	mar 5. 58	Washington D.C.	Lt. Jones	"
3	Caswell George. N.	"	Feb 4. 58	Boston Mass	Lt. McArthur	"
4	Clinton Francis. G.	"	april 9. 58	Phil. Pa.	Lt. Royall	"
5	Daily Carroll	"	" 16. 58	New York N.Y.	Capt. Granger	"
6	Dennis John	"	" 16. 58	Carlisle Pa	Lt. Maury	"
7	Dippel John	"	" 10. 58	Boston Mass	Lt. McArthur	"
8	Donaldson Joseph	"	Feb 16. 58	Baltimore Md.	Capt. Adams	"
9	Driscoll John	"	april 7. 58	Boston Mass	Lt. McArthur	"
10	Fisher Henry. W.	"	" 15. 58	Carlisle Pa	Lt. Maury	"
11	Frisch August	"	" 5. 58	New York N.Y.	Capt. Granger	"
12	Goerner William	"	" 3. 58	New York	Capt. Granger	"
13	Gordon Joseph	"	" 8. 58	Buffalo N.Y.	Lt. Eagle	"
14	Gould John S.	"	" 6. 58			"
15	Hogarty Michael	"	" 14. 58	Boston Mass	Lt. Arthur	"
16	Howard Charles N.	"	" 6. 58	Albany N.Y.	Lt. Johnson	"
17	Howard Dexter	"	" 8. 58			
18	Ingalls George. I.	"	mar 29. 58	Buffalo N.Y.	Lt. Eagle	"
19	Halliday Patrick	"	april 19. 58	Boston Mass	Lt. McArthur	"
20	Law Nimrod. H.	"	" 7. 58	Phil. Pa	Lt. Royall	"
21	Martin David. I.	"	" 6. 58	New York N.Y.	Capt. Granger	"
22	McCarthy Daniel	"	" 19. 58	Boston Mass	Lt. McArthur	"
23	McCarthy James	"	" 13. 58	Phil. Pa	Lt. Royall	"

A copy of the original "Muster and Pay Roll" of Lieutenant Berry's Company A. The list contains the names of those men who served with "Utah" and must, as well, include his real name.

TAINED PAT.	BOUNTY		TOTAL AMOUNT DUE.		AMOUNT OF STOPPAGES.		BALANCE PAID.		RECEIVED PAYMENT OF—	WITNESS.
	PAID.	DUE.							*Maj. R. W. Shower*	
Cts.	Dolls	Dolls	Dolls	Cts	Dolls.	Cts.	Dolls.	Cts.		
	68		13	47	16	23			*Ph. Smith*	*Wm N Berry*
	70		5	58	25	22			*W. Blakemore*	*J N Berry*
	74		5	91	26	35			*Charles King*	*J N Berry*
	77		5	94	27	97			*John McCauley*	*J N Berry*
	69		6	87	29	56			*Thos B Willis*	*J N Berry*
	68		19	64	11	01			*Thomas Sr Marshall*	*J N Berry*
	84		12	37	24	29			*Henry Wilkens*	*J N Berry*
			22	45	21	68			*John H. Crompton*	*J N Berry*
	74		22	46	11	61			*Richard C. Byrns*	*J N Berry*
	98		16	06	26	84			*Patt Callahan*	*property*
	1 21		26	71	26	45			*George N Cawill*	*J N Berry*
	60		3	40	22	70			*Francis J Clinton*	*J N Berry*
	65		14	83	12	67			*James Feely*	*J N Berry*
	63		24	43	3	07			*John Dennis*	*J N Berry*
	68		24	73	14	97			*John Dippel*	*J N Berry*
	1 11			11		69			*Joseph Donaldson*	*J N Berry*
	70			52	10	28			*John Driscoll*	*J N Berry*
	64		5	81	22	05			*Levy W. Fisher*	*J N Berry*
	42		21	38	11	15			*Aaron Frish*	*J N Berry*
	74		10	10	22	16			*William Governor*	*property*
	69		22	47	7	96			*Joseph Jordon*	*J N Berry*
	71		19	81	11	35			*Chs S Gould*	*J N Berry*
	64		7	11	27	12			*M A Lafferty*	*J N Berry*
	77		19	67	11	49			*Charles W. Howard*	*J N Berry*
	69		14	94	10	49			*Geo Howard*	*J N Berry*
	78		21	11	13	03			*George S Ingalls*	*J N Berry*
	60		12	24	11	11			*Jeffrey*	*J N Berry*
	72		14	68	11	12			*Nimrod Law*	*J N Berry*
	71		22	43	8	72			*Daniel S Martin*	*J N Berry*
	65		14							

No.	NAMES. PRESENT AND ABSENT. (Privates in alphabetical order.)	RANK.	ENLISTED. WHEN.	WHERE.	BY WHOM.	PERIOD

Discharged

| 1 | Tailor Charles H | Pv.t | April 12.57 | Phil. Pa | Lt Royall | |

Died

| | John. T. Magruder Bv.t Fst Lt | | | | | |

Deserted

1	Alexander Joseph	Pv.t	April 1.58	Boston Mass	Lt McArthur	5 yea
2	Fitzhenry Myles	"	" 20.58	New York NY	Capt Grange	"
3	Flaus Henry	"	" 2.58	Washington DC	Lt Jones	"
4	Hall Anson	"	" 2.58	Albany NY	" Johnson	"
5	Hefferan Thomas	"	" 10.58	Boston Mass	" McArthur	"
6	Hoyle James P	"	" 2.58	Washington DC	" Jones	"
7	Kennedy Patrick	"	" 9.58	Boston Mass	" McArthur	"
8	Lindsey John H	"	" 5.58	Washington DC	" Jones	"
9	Maher Patrick	"	" 7.58	Boston Mass	" McArthur	"
10	McLennon John	"	" 5.58	New York NY	Capt Grange	"
11	Monmorencie Henry	"	Mar 21.58			"
12	Regan Andrew	"	April 10.58	Boston Mass	Lt McArthur	"
13	Smith Albion	"	April 6.58			"
14	Smith James	"	" 3.58	Buffalo NY	Lt Eagle	"
15	Staats Herman	"	" 12.58	New York	Capt Grange	"
16	Wager Wilber	"	Mar 11.58	Albany NY	Lt Johnson	"
17	Welsh Harrison	"	April 28.58	Harrisburg Pa	" Maury	"
18	Jackwith William H	"	" 26.58	"	"	"

On the "Muster and Pay Roll" Lieutenant Berry listed soldiers who died, were discharged, or deserted from Company A with specific comments about each.

NOTES.

4. Additions at pay, &c. under Sec. 2, act of ... 4, 1854, will be thus noted, viz: "For of discharged grass, ms." &c., "2d of such rations, $4 pr. ms." &c., "For id recruited $4 pr. ms." &c., &c. That due under Sec. 3 of the same act, thus: "For pay at month, $ pr. ms." That due under Sec. 4 of the same act, thus: "In lieu of ration, $2 pr. ms."

5. The instalments of Bounty due, under Sec. 7, act of June 17, 1850, are paid as follows, ½, ½, ½, ½, at the end of the 1st, 2d, 3d, and 4th years, respectively, the remainder at the expiration of enlistment; and will, under head of REMARKS, be noted thus: "Rat'd Bounty due, 1st for of 2d, 3d," for of $ ——" See G, O, 21, 2d of 1854. Besides which, in the columns headed "BOUNTY Paid" and "Bounty Due," must be entered, to ensure, the whole amount &the, &c. paid, and the share received for that, on account of said bounty.

6. The "three months' extra pay," for re-enlistment, under Sec 29 Act of July 5, 1858, being paid by the recruiting officer, should not be noted on the muster rolls.

7. The roll of those belonging to the company, will be invariably followed by that of the officers and soldiers, who, since last muster, &c. should belong to it. These will be classed in the following order, viz: Died, Transferred, Diet, ... &c. and the absolute pattern finally will be observed, in the remarks concerning them—It be said place will, in every case, be given; and No., date, &c. of orders, or description of authority, be always carefully specified. Soldiers discharged and re-enlisted, or who have deserted and been retaken, since last muster, have their place in both of the above rolls.

REMARKS.

Due to U.S ... Harness ... C ... y 243 ... Discharged to Civil
Authorities by virtue ... write of Habeas Corpus at Harrisburg Pa. May 4, 1858

Died at Big Blue June 29th 1858

Due to U.S for Clothing 61.74 1 &C. & Wipg Staves. 1 C Box & plate
Enrolled at Fort Leavenworth ... 1 CC pouch 1 pist. H, 1 H, Blan 1 C C Brush 1 Nosebag
Deserted at Portee's Landing Mo. May 5, 1858 due U.S for clothing 2452 1 Haversack 2 Pist. balls
Deserted at F.T Leavenworth K.S. May 19, 58 due U.S for clothing 19.62 1, 1 Carb
SC. 1 Wipg. 1 C pouch 1 Sling Belt 1 Swiv 1 C Box 1 CC prok 1 Mal Brid 1 Sad Blan 1 Nosebag
Deserted at F.T Leavenworth K.S May 25, 1858 due U.S for Clothing 2014 1 Har Lock
Deserted at Camp on ... June 26, 1858 due U.S for clothing 3169 1 H.S. & Wiper
1 C pouch 1 Sling Belt 1 ... 1 Saber Prok 1 Set H 1 Wat Brid 1 Sad Blan 1 CC Brush 1 Nosebag
Deserted at ... June 26, 1858 due U.S for clothing 19.64 1 S.C. 1 Wiper 1 ...
SC 1 C pouch ... 1 C Brid 1 Mat Brid 1 Sad Blan 1 ... Nosebag
Died at Battle ... due U.S for clothing 3.14 1 Har Jacket 1 Nosebag
Deserted at F.T Leavenworth K.S July 26, 1858 due U.S for clothing 20.09
1 SC & Wip 1 C Box 1 CC prok 1 Mat Brid 1 Sad Blan 1 CC Brush 1 Nosebag
Deserted at Camp Smith K.S June 2, 1858 due U.S for clothing 36.14 1 S.C & Wiper, 1 C Box & plate
1 CC prok 1 C Brush 1 Wat Brid 1 Sad Blan 1 Nosebag 1 Nap Jack 1 Hav Jacket
Deserted at F.T Leavenworth K.S May 27, 1858 due U.S for clothing 20.32 1 S.C. 1 Wiper 1 C Box
& plate 1 CC prok 1 S Knot 1 Sat H, 1 C Great Brid 1 Sad Blan 1 CC brush 1 Nosebag
Deserted at Benton's Landing Mo. May 6, 58 due U.S for Clothing 20.77 Nap Jack 1 H Lock
Deserted at Camp on Jonahaw K.S June 22, 58 due U.S for Clothing 34.14 1 Schiff N... 1 C ... 1 C pouch
1 S. Belt 1 Swiv 1 C Box & plate 1 C prok 1 Saddle Blan 1 Nosebag
Deserted at F.T Leavenworth K.S May 19, 58 due U.S for Clothing 21.64 1 H Lock 1 Nap Jack 1 Canteen
Deserted at Camp Smith June 1, 1858 due U.S for clothing 61.68 1 S.C. Wiper Tongue & Rod 1 C Box
& plate 1 C C prok 1 S Knot 1 pist 1 Sad Blan 1 CC Brush 1 ... Nosebag
Deserted at F.T Leavenworth K.S May 27, 58 due U.S for clothing 21.71 1 Carb Comp 1 Sab Belt & plate
1 ... & plate 1 ... 1 ... 1 Sling Belt & Swiv 1 C prok 1 CC Carb Brid 1 C Bay 1 C Knot 1 Nosebag
Deserted at F.T Leavenworth K.S ... due U.S for clothing 31.64 1 S.C Carb Comp 1 C pouch 1
Sling Belt & p... ... 1 ... & straps 1 Sad Blan 1 CC Brush 1 ... 1 Nosebag
Deserted at Camp Smith K.S June 1, 1858 due U.S for clothing 33.80 1 S.C & Wiper Tongue & Rod
1 S Knot 1 Wat Brid 1 Sad Blan 1 CC ... 1 Nosebag 1 Nap Sack 1 H Jack 1 Canteen
Deserted at Camp June 27, 1858 due U.S for Clothing 37.47 1 S Carb Comp
1 C pouch 1 Sling Belt 1 Swiv 1 C Box & plate 1 C C prok 1 Saber Knot 1 S.C & Wat Brid 1 Sad Blan
1 CC Brush 1 Nosebag 1 H Sad 1 Canteen

Bibliographical Essay

The major source for this book was the Philadelphia *Daily Evening Bulletin* where the series of letters signed "Utah" was published during 1858–59. This same paper contained other information that was useful for an appreciation of aspects of life in Philadelphia in the late 1850's and the interest of the editors in the developments in Europe and the American West. A number of "Utah's" allusions to people and events were clarified by items in the Washington, D.C., *Evening Star*, the St. Louis *Daily Missouri Republican*, the *New York Herald*, the Fillmore City and Salt Lake City *Deseret News*, the Salt Lake City *Valley Tan*, and the San Francisco *Herald*. Efforts to identify the newspaper on which "Utah" served as an editor involved searches in various Pennsylvania papers: the Carlisle *Volunteer Herald*, the *Greensburg Herald*, the *Catasauqua Herald*, the *Bradford Herald*, the *Norristown Weekly Herald*, the Harrisburg *Daily Herald*, the *Scranton Herald of the Union*, and the West Chester *Independent Herald* and the *Jeffersonian & Democratic Herald*.

Valuable information on the men and the record of the Second Dragoons came from Record Group 94, "Regular Army Muster Rolls, Inspection Returns, 1821–1860, Second Dragoons," boxes 108–13; "Letters Received by the Office of the Adjutant General" (Main Series), 1822–1860, M-567; "Register of Enlistments in the U.S. Army, 1798–1914," M-233, rolls 24–26: Record Group 153, "Judge Advocate General's Office, Court Martial Records," HH-976, box 166; "Indices to Pension Records for the Old Wars, Indian Wars, and Civil War": Record Group 393, Camp Floyd and Fort Crittenden, Utah, "Guard Reports, December 1860–March 1861"; "Post Returns, Fort Crittenden [Camp Floyd]," M-617, roll 268: Record Group 217, Records of the United States General Accounting Office, "Muster and Pay Roll of Lieut. Thomas J. Berry's Company A, Recruits of the Second Regiment of Dragoons, Army of the United

States, Sixth Column, Utah Forces, from the thirtieth day of April 1858, when first mustered, to the thirtieth day of June 1858"; "Register of Payments, United States Army Discharged Soldiers, 1846–1860"; "Settled Accounts of Army Paymasters, 1815–1861," accounts of Henry Prince, paymaster, #9402, January 1860, voucher no. 172, all in the custody of the National Archives and Records Service, Washington, D.C.

Additional material on the dragoons and on the United States Army came from "Reminiscences of Some Incidents in the Career of an United States Dragoon Between the Years 1839 and 1844," *The Texas Quarterly* 9 (1966): 7–20; Theo. F. Rodenbough, comp., *From Everglade to Cañon with the Second Dragoons* (New York: D. Van Nostrand, 1875); Percival G. Lowe, *Five Years a Dragoon* (Norman: University of Oklahoma Press, 1965); W. B. Ruggles, "The Story of a Regiment, the Second Dragoons," *Magazine of History* 14 (1911): 31–42, 66–72, 122–36, 172–76; Charles P. Roland, *Albert Sidney Johnston, Soldier of Three Republics* (Austin: University of Texas Press, 1964); William H. Goetzmann, *Army Exploration in the American West, 1803–1863* (New Haven: Yale University Press, 1959); Francis P. Prucha, *The Sword of the Republic: The United States Army on the Frontier, 1783–1846* (New York: The Macmillan Company, 1969); Robert M. Utley, *Frontiersmen in Blue: The United States Army and the Indian, 1848–1865* (New York: The Macmillan Company, 1967); Francis B. Heitman, *Historical Register and Dictionary of the United States Army* (1789–1903), vol. 1 (Washington, D.C.: U.S. Government Printing Office, 1903), reprint (Urbana: University of Illinois Press, 1965); Augustus Meyers, *Ten Years in the Ranks, U.S. Army* (New York: The Stirling Press, 1914); Lieutenant Joseph C. Ives, *Report Upon the Colorado River of the West* (Washington, D.C.: U.S. Government Printing Office, 1861); Thomas G. Alexander and Leonard J. Arrington, "Camp in the Sagebrush: Camp Floyd, Utah, 1858–1861," *Utah Historical Quarterly* 34 (1966): 3–21; and "Letter Describing a March to Utah in 1859," *Annals of Iowa*, 3rd series, 13 (1923): 611–18; Logan U. Reavis, *The Life and Military Services of General William Selby Harney* (St. Louis: Bryan, Brand & Company, 1878).

212

For an understanding of the Mormons, their history, and their relationships with the people and the government of the United States, I have used several books of both a general and specific nature. On the origins of Mormonism I have relied upon Fawn McKay Brodie, *No Man Knows My History: The Life of Joseph Smith, The Mormon Prophet* (New York: Alfred A. Knopf, Inc., 1945); Nels Anderson, *Desert Saints: The Mormon Frontier in Utah* (Chicago: University of Chicago Press, 1942); Thomas F. O'Dea, *The Mormons* (Chicago: University of Chicago Press, 1957); William Mulder and A. Russell Mortensen, eds., *Among the Mormons* (New York: Alfred A. Knopf, Inc., 1958); Whitney R. Cross, *The Burned-Over District*, paperback ed. (New York: Harper & Row, Publishers, 1965); Alice F. Tyler, *Freedom's Ferment* (Minneapolis: University of Minnesota Press, 1944); and Bernard De Voto, *The Year of Decision, 1846* (Boston: Little, Brown and Company, 1943). Many of these books were also of use for the period of the Mormon War. The best and most recent work on that time of tension is Norman Furniss, *The Mormon Conflict, 1850–1859* (New Haven: Yale University Press, 1960). A great deal of useful narrative history on events in Utah Territory was gleaned from Hubert H. Bancroft, *History of Utah, 1540–1886* (San Francisco: The History Company, Publishers, 1889). Also helpful for specific aspects were LeRoy R. and Ann W. Hafen, eds., *The Utah Expedition, 1857–1858* (Glendale: Arthur H. Clark Company, 1958); and Juanita Brooks, *The Mountain Meadows Massacre* (Stanford: Stanford University Press, 1950). Richard F. Burton's *The City of the Saints* (London: Longman, Green, Longman, and Roberts, 1861) was important not only for what it conveyed concerning the Mormons and their major city, but also because Burton followed much the same route as did "Utah" to Salt Lake City. Burton's descriptions helped to clarify and to reinforce some of "Utah's" comments on the natural wonders. An enlightening, useful, and recent study of a Mormon statesman is Gwynn W. Barrett's "Dr. John M. Bernhisel: Mormon Elder in Congress," *Utah Historical Quarterly* 36 (1968): 143–67. For a clarification of the role of the Sons of Dan or Danites, I have relied on Harold Schindler's *Orrin Porter Rockwell: Man of God, Son of Thunder* (Salt Lake City: University of Utah Press, 1966).

Any serious investigation into travel in the American West must begin with Henry R. Wagner's *The Plains and the Rockies: A Bibliography of Original Narratives of Travel and Adventure, 1800–1865*, 3rd ed., revised by Charles L. Camp (Columbus: Long's College Book Company, 1953). More recent and more particular in terms of a portion of "Utah's" journey is Merrill J. Mattes' comprehensive volume on *The Great Platte River Road: The Covered Wagon Mainline via Fort Kearny to Fort Laramie* (Lincoln: Nebraska Historical Society, 1969). For the clarification of other references to happenings or locales in the pre-Civil War West I have relied on Hubert H. Bancroft's *History of Arizona and New Mexico, 1530–1888* (San Francisco: The History Company, Publishers, 1889); *History of Texas and the North Mexican States, 1801–1889*, vol. 2 (San Francisco: The History Company, Publishers, 1890); *History of California, 1848–1859*, vol. 6 (San Francisco: The History Company, Publishers, 1888); and his *History of Mexico, 1824–1861*, vol. 5 (San Francisco: A. L. Bancroft & Company, Publishers, 1885), as well as on Robert G. Cleland's *A History of California: The American Period* (New York: The Macmillan Company, 1922); *This Reckless Breed of Men* (New York: Alfred A. Knopf, Inc., 1950); Theodore H. Hittell, *History of California*, vol. 4 (San Francisco: N. J. Stone & Company, 1897); Rodman W. Paul, *Mining Frontiers of the Far West, 1848–1880*, paperback ed. (New York: Holt, Rinehart and Winston, 1963; Roscoe P. and Margaret B. Conkling, *The Butterfield Overland Mail, 1857–1869* (Glendale: Arthur H. Clark Company, 1947); LeRoy R. Hafen, ed., *The Mountain Men and the Fur Trade of the Far West*, vol. 4 (Glendale: Arthur H. Clark Company, 1966); Sylvester Mowry, *Arizona and Sonora*, 3rd ed. rev. (New York: Harper and Brothers, 1864) and *Memoir of the Proposed Territory of Arizona* (Washington, 1857), reprint (Tucson: Tucson Territorial Press, 1964); Howard R. Lamar, *The Far Southwest, 1846–1912: A Territorial History* (New Haven: Yale University Press, 1966); B. Sacks, *Be It Enacted: The Creation of the Territory of Arizona* (Phoenix: Arizona Historical Foundation, 1964); Robert L. Munkres, "Ash Hollow: Gateway to the High Plains," *Annals of Wyoming* 42 (1970): 5–43; and J. Cecil Alter, *Early Utah Journalism* (Salt Lake City: Utah State Historical Society, 1938). The identification of Indian tribes was greatly assisted by the work of Frederick W. Hodge, ed., *Handbook of American Indians North of Mexico*, Smithsonian Institution, Bureau of American Ethnology Bulletin no. 30 (Washington, D.C.: U.S. Government Printing Office, 1912), reprint (Grosse Point, Mich.: Scholarly Press, 1968). For the most useful study of the Pawnee Indians I consulted George E. Hyde, *Pawnee Indians* (Denver: University of Colorado Press, 1951). A marvelous book on the early Californians is Leonard Pitt, *The Decline of the Californios* (Berkeley: University of California Press, 1966).

Aspects of national policy were set forth in the messages of President Buchanan to the Congress in 1857, 1858, and 1859, and in the annual reports of the secretary of war for the same years. These were published in the *Senate* and *House Executive Documents*, 35th Congress, 1st and 2nd sessions, and in the 36th Congress, 1st session; the *Senate Journal*, 35th Congress, 2nd session; and in James D. Richardson, ed., *A Compilation of the Messages and Papers of the Presidents, 1789–1897*, vol. 7 (Washington, D.C.: U.S. Government Printing Office, 1897).

The influence of prominent persons is treated in Allan Nevins, *The Emergence of Lincoln*, 2 vols. (New York: Charles Scribners Sons, 1950); in Philip S. Klein, *President James Buchanan: A Biography* (University Park, Pa.: The Pennsylvania State University Press, 1962); Charles H. Jones, *The Life and Public Services of J. Glancy Jones*, 2 vols. (Philadelphia and London: J. B. Lippincott Company, 1910); Edward Magdol, *Owen Lovejoy: Abolitionist in Congress* (New Brunswick: Rutgers University Press, 1967); David A. Williams, *David C. Broderick: A Political Portrait* (San Marino: The Huntington Library, 1969); William O. Scroggs, *Filibusters and Financiers* (New York: The Macmillan Company, 1916), reprint (New York: Russell and Russell, 1969); Laurence Greene, *The Filibuster: The Career of William Walker* (Indianapolis: Bobbs-Merrill Company, 1937); Roy F. Nichols, *The Disruption of American Democracy* (New York: The Macmillan Company, 1948); James M. Callahan, *American Foreign Policy in Mexican Relations* (New York: The Macmillan Company, 1932); and in H. L. Wilson's, "President Buchanan's Proposed Intervention in Mexico," *American*

Historical Review 5 (1888): 687–701. More general biographical information can be found in the pertinent volumes of the *Dictionary of American Biography* (New York: Charles Scribners Sons, 1928–58); and in the huge volume of James L. Harrison, comp., *Biographical Directory of the American Congress, 1774–1949* (Washington, D.C.: U.S. Government Printing Office, 1950).

For help in identifying other miscellaneous references, I have relied on Eric Partridge, *A Dictionary of Slang and Unconventional English*, 5th ed., vol. 1 (London: Routledge & Paul, Ltd., 1961), and the 6th ed. (New York: The Macmillan Company, 1967); Harold Wentworth and Stuart B. Flexner, eds., *Dictionary of American Slang* (New York: Thomas Y. Crowell Company, 1967); Hans Nathan, *Dan Emmett and the Rise of Early Negro Ministrelsy* (Norman: University of Oklahoma Press, 1962); and Sigmund Spaeth, *Weep Some More, My Lady* (Garden City, N.Y.: Doubleday, Page & Company, 1927).

Bibliography

Articles

Alexander, Thomas G., and Arrington, Leonard J. "Camp in the Sagebrush: Camp Floyd, Utah, 1858–1861." *Utah Historical Quarterly* 34 (1966): 3–21.

Anonymous. "Reminiscences of Some Incidents in the Career of an United States Dragoon Between the Years 1839 and 1844." *The Texas Quarterly* 9 (1966): 7–20.

Barrett, Gwynn W. "Dr. John M. Bernhisel: Mormon Elder in Congress." *Utah Historical Quarterly* 36 (1968): 143–67.

Munkres, Robert L. "Ash Hollow: Gateway to the High Plains." *Annals of Wyoming* 42 (1970): 5–43.

Ruggles, W. B. "The Story of a Regiment, the Second Dragoons." *Magazine of History* 14 (1911): 31–42, 66–72, 122–36, 172–76.

Studley, Hiram W. "Letter Describing a March to Utah in 1859." *Annals of Iowa*, 3rd series, 13 (1923): 611–18.

Wilson, Howard L. "President Buchanan's Proposed Intervention in Mexico." *American Historical Review* 5 (1899): 687–701.

Books

Alter, Cecil J. *Early Utah Journalism: A Half Century of Forensic Warfare Waged by the West's Most Militant Press.* Salt Lake City: Utah State Historical Society, 1938.

Anderson, Nels. *Desert Saints: The Mormon Frontier in Utah.* Chicago: University of Chicago Press, 1942.

Bancroft, Hubert Howe. *History of Arizona and New Mexico, 1530–1888.* San Francisco: The History Company, Publishers, 1889.

————. *History of California, 1848–1859.* Vol. 6. San Francisco: The History Company, Publishers, 1888.

————. *History of Mexico, 1824–1861.* Vol. 5. San Francisco: A. L. Bancroft & Company, Publishers, 1885.

————. *History of Texas and the North Mexican States, 1801–1889.* Vol. 2. San Francisco: The History Company, Publishers, 1890.

————. *History of Utah, 1540–1886.* San Francisco: The History Company, Publishers, 1889.

Brodie, Fawn McKay. *No Man Knows My History: The Life of Joseph Smith, The Mormon Prophet.* New York: Alfred A. Knopf, Inc., 1945.

Brooks, Juanita. *The Mountain Meadows Massacre*. Stanford: Stanford University Press, 1950.

Burton, Sir Richard F. *The City of the Saints and Across the Rocky Mountains to California*. London: Longman, Green, Longman, and Roberts, 1861.

Callahan, James M. *American Foreign Policy in Mexican Relations*. New York: The Macmillan Company, 1932.

Cleland, Robert G. *A History of California: The American Period*. New York: The Macmillan Company, 1922.

————. *This Reckless Breed of Men: Trappers and Fur Traders of the Southwest*. New York: Alfred A. Knopf, Inc., 1950.

Conkling, Roscoe P., and Margaret B. *The Butterfield Overland Mail, 1857–1869*. Glendale, Calif.: Arthur H. Clark Company, 1947.

Cross, Whitney R. *The Burned-Over District: The Social and Intellectual History of Enthusiastic Religion in Western New York, 1800–1850*. Paperback ed. New York: Harper & Row, Publishers, 1965.

De Voto, Bernard. *The Year of Decision, 1846*. Boston: Little, Brown and Company, 1943.

Dictionary of American Biography, under the auspices of the American Council for Learned Societies. 22 vols. New York: Charles Scribners Sons, 1928–58.

Furniss, Norman. *The Mormon Conflict, 1850–1859*. New Haven: Yale University Press, 1960.

Goetzmann, William H. *Army Exploration in the American West, 1803–1863*. New Haven: Yale University Press, 1959.

Gospill's Philadelphia Business Directory for 1869. Philadelphia: James Gospill, 1869.

Greene, Laurence. *The Filibuster: The Career of William Walker*. Indianapolis and New York: Bobbs-Merrill Company, 1937.

Gregory, Winifred, ed. *American Newspapers, 1821–1936*. New York: The H. W. Wilson Company, 1937.

Hafen, LeRoy R., ed. *The Mountain Men and the Fur Trade of the Far West*. Vol. 4. Glendale, Calif.: Arthur H. Clark Company, 1966.

————, and Ann W., eds. *The Utah Expedition, 1857–1858*. Vol. 8 of The Far West and The Rockies Historical Series, 1820–1875. Glendale, Calif.: Arthur H. Clark Company, 1958.

Harrison, James L., comp. *Biographical Directory of the American Congress, 1774–1949*. Washington, D.C.: U.S. Government Printing Office, 1950.

Heitman, Francis B. *Historical Register and Dictionary of the United States Army from Its Organization, September 29, 1789, to March 2, 1903*. Vol. 1. Washington, D.C.: U.S. Government Printing Office, 1903. Reprint. Urbana, Ill.: University of Illinois Press, 1965.

Hittell, Theodore H. *History of California*. Vol. 4. San Francisco: N. J. Stone & Company, 1897.

Hodge, Frederick W., ed. *Handbook of American Indians North of Mexico*. Smithsonian Institution, Bureau of American Ethnology Bulletin no. 30. 2 vols. Washington, D.C.: U.S. Government Printing Office, 1912. Reprint. Grosse Point, Mich.: Scholarly Press, 1968.

218

Hyde, George E. *Pawnee Indians*. Denver: University of Colorado Press, 1951.

Ives, Joseph C. *Report Upon the Colorado River of the West*. Washington, D.C.: U.S. Government Printing Office, 1861.

Jones, Charles H. *The Life and Public Services of J. Glancy Jones*. 2 vols. Philadelphia and London: J. B. Lippincott Company, 1910.

Klein, Philip S. *President James Buchanan: A Biography*. University Park, Pa.: The Pennsylvania State University Press, 1962.

Lamar, Howard R. *The Far Southwest, 1846–1912: A Territorial History*. New Haven: Yale University Press, 1966.

Lowe, Percival G. *Five Years a Dragoon ('49 to '54), and Other Adventures on the Great Plains*. Norman: University of Oklahoma Press, 1965.

Magdol, Edward. *Owen Lovejoy: Abolitionist in Congress*. New Brunswick, N.J.: Rutgers University Press, 1967.

Marcy, Colonel Randolph B. *Border Reminiscences*. New York: Harper & Brothers, 1872.

―――――. *The Prairie Traveler: A Handbook for Overland Expeditions*. New York: Harper & Brothers, 1859.

―――――. *Thirty Years of Army Life on the Border*. New York: Harper & Brothers, 1866.

Mattes, Merrill J. *The Great Platte River Road: The Covered Wagon Mainline via Fort Kearny to Fort Laramie*. Lincoln, Neb.: Nebraska State Historical Society, 1969.

McElroy's Philadelphia Directory for 1855, 1856, 1858, 1859, 1860, and *1864*. Philadelphia: Edward C. and John Biddle, 1855–64.

Meyers, Augustus. *Ten Years in the Ranks, U.S. Army*. New York: The Stirling Press, 1914.

Mowry, Sylvester. *Arizona and Sonora: The Geography, History, and Resources of the Silver Region of North America*. 3rd ed. rev. New York: Harper & Brothers, 1864.

―――――. *Memoir of the Proposed Territory of Arizona*. Washington, D.C.: H. Polkinhorn, Printer, 1857. Reprint. Tucson: Tucson Territorial Press, 1964.

Mulder, William, and Mortensen, A. Russell, eds. *Among the Mormons: Historic Accounts by Contemporary Observers*. New York: Alfred A. Knopf, Inc., 1958.

Nathan, Hans. *Dan Emmett and the Rise of Early Negro Minstrelsy*. Norman: University of Oklahoma Press, 1962.

Nevins, Allan. *The Emergence of Lincoln*. 2 vols. New York: Charles Scribners Sons, 1950.

Nichols, Roy F. *The Disruption of American Democracy*. New York: The Macmillan Company, 1948.

O'Dea, Thomas F. *The Mormons*. Chicago: University of Chicago Press, 1957.

Partridge, Eric. *A Dictionary of Slang and Unconventional English*. 5th ed., vol. 1. London: Routledge & Paul, Ltd., 1961. 6th ed. New York: The Macmillan Company, 1967.

Paul, Rodman W. *Mining Frontiers of the Far West, 1848–1880.* Paperback ed. Histories of the American Frontier. New York: Holt, Rinehart and Winston, 1963.

Pitt, Leonard. *The Decline of the Californios: A Social History of the Spanish-Speaking Californians, 1846–1890.* Berkeley: University of California Press, 1966.

Prucha, Francis P. *The Sword of the Republic: The United States Army on the Frontier, 1783–1846.* New York: The Macmillan Company, 1969.

Reavis, Logan U. *The Life and Military Services of General William Selby Harney.* St. Louis: Bryan, Brand & Company, 1878.

Richardson, James D., ed. *A Compilation of the Messages and Papers of the Presidents, 1789–1897.* Vol. 7. Washington, D.C.: 1897.

Rodenbough, Theophilus F., comp. *From Everglade to Cañon with the Second Dragoons.* New York: D. Van Nostrand, 1875.

Roland, Charles P. *Albert Sidney Johnston, Soldier of Three Republics.* Austin: University of Texas Press, 1964.

Sacks, B. *Be It Enacted: The Creation of the Territory of Arizona.* Phoenix: Arizona Historical Foundation, 1964.

Schindler, Harold. *Orrin Porter Rockwell: Man of God, Son of Thunder.* Salt Lake City: University of Utah Press, 1966.

Scroggs, William O. *Filibusters and Financiers: The Story of William Walker and His Associates.* New York: Russell and Russell, 1969.

Spaeth, Sigmund G. *Weep Some More, My Lady.* Garden City, N.Y.: Doubleday, Page & Company, 1927.

Tyler, Alice F. *Freedom's Ferment: Phases of American Social History from the Colonial Period to the Outbreak of the Civil War.* Minneapolis: University of Minnesota Press, 1944.

Udell, John. *Journal of John Udell Kept During a Trip Across the Plains, Containing an Account of the Massacre of a Portion of His Party by the Mohave Indians, in 1859.* Jefferson, Ohio: Ashtabula Sentinel Steam Press Print, 1868.

Utley, Robert M. *Frontiersmen in Blue: The United States Army and the Indian, 1848–1865.* New York: The Macmillan Company, 1967.

Wagner, Henry Raup. *The Plains and the Rockies: A Bibliography of Original Narratives of Travel and Adventure, 1800–1865.* 3d ed., rev. by Charles L. Camp. Columbus, Ohio: Long's College Book Company, 1953.

Wentworth, Harold, and Flexner, Stuart B., eds. *Dictionary of American Slang.* New York: Thomas Y. Crowell Company, 1967.

Williams, David A. *David C. Broderick: A Political Portrait.* San Marino, Calif.: The Huntington Library, 1969.

Congressional Documents

Senate Executive Documents, 35th Congress, 1st session, vol. 3, doc. 11.

House Documents, 35th Congress, 1st session, vol. 10, doc. 71.

220

House Executive Documents, 35th Congress, 1st session, vol. 9, doc. 33.
Senate Executive Documents, 35th Congress, 2nd session, vol. 1, doc. 1.
Senate Executive Documents, 35th Congress, 2nd session, vol. 2, doc. 1.
Senate Executive Documents, 36th Congress, 1st session, vol. 2, doc. 2.
Senate Documents, 36th Congress, 2nd session, vol. 3, doc. 2.
Senate Journal, 35th Congress, 2nd session.

National Archives

Census of 1840, Carlisle, Pa., T-5, roll 773, R.G. 29.
Census of 1850, Carlisle, Pa., M-432, roll 773, R.G. 29.
Census of 1860, Carlisle, Pa., M-653, rolls 1101, 1102, R.G. 29.
Census of 1860, Los Angeles, Cal., M-653, roll 59, R.G. 29.
"Guard Reports, December 1860–March 1861," Camp Floyd and Fort Crittenden, Utah, R.G. 393.
"Indices to Pension Records for the Old Wars, Indian Wars, and Civil War," R.G. 153.
"Judge Advocate General's Office, Court Martial Records," HH-976, box 166, R.G. 153.
"Letters Received by the Office of the Adjutant General" (Main Series), 1822–1860, M-567, R.G. 94.
"Muster and Pay Roll of Lieut. Thomas J. Berry's Company A, Recruits of the Second Regiment of Dragoons, Army of the United States, Sixth Column, Utah Forces, from the thirtieth day of April 1858, when first mustered, to the thirtieth day of June 1858," Records of the United States General Accounting Office, R.G. 217.
"Post Returns, Fort Crittenden [Camp Floyd]," M-617, roll 268, R.G. 393.
"Register of Enlistments in the U.S. Army, 1798–1914," M-233, rolls 24–26, R.G. 94.
"Register of Payments, United States Army Discharged Soldiers, 1846–1860," Records of the United States General Accounting Office, R.G. 217.
"Regular Army Muster Rolls, Inspection Returns, 1821–1860, Second Dragoons," boxes 108–13, R.G. 94.
"Settled Accounts of Army Paymasters, 1815–1861." Accounts of Henry Prince, paymaster, #9402, January 1860, voucher no. 172, Records of the United States General Accounting Office, R.G. 217.

Philadelphia City Archives

Death Records, 1860–1869
Marriage Index, 1860–1883
Naturalization Index, 1854–1877

Newspapers

Carlisle Herald, Carlisle, Pa., scattered issues 1854–1858.

Daily Evening Bulletin, Philadelphia, Pa., March 1858–December 1860.

Daily Missouri Republican, St. Louis, Mo., June 1858–May 1859.

Deseret News, Fillmore City and Salt Lake City, U.T., 1856–1859.

Evening Star, Washington, D.C., July 14, 1858.

Herald, San Francisco, Cal., January–June 1859.

New York Herald, New York, N.Y., June 1858–March 1859.

New York Times, New York, N.Y., June 1858–March 1859.

Index

A

Abolitionism: in Kansas, 22–23, 30, 30n. *See also* Free state men; Mormons, attitude of, toward slavery; Slavery

Adobe, 87, 87n, 90, 97

Alabama Bear. *See* Grattan Massacre

Anderson, Kirk, 119n, 133

Anderson, Capt. Richard H., 82, 82n, 107, 127

Anti-Mormon sentiment, 8, 9; among soldiers, 8, 26–27, 101. *See also* Mormons

Apache Indians. *See* Indian tribes, Apache

Armistead, Brev. Maj. Lewis A., 170, 170n

Arms. *See* United States Army, weapons in

Arizona: territorial petition of, 175–77

Army. *See* United States Army

Army of Utah. *See* Utah Campaign

Articles of War, 50, 83

Artillery, 11, 13, 20, 45, 87, 125, 129; Fourth, 12; Second, 12; Third, 12–13, 87n, 170, 171, 172. *See also* United States Army

Ash Hollow, Neb. Terr.: description of, 41–42; Gen. Harney attacks Indians at, 42n

Aspinwall, William H., 168n

Aubrey's Crossing, 162

B

Bands, regimental. *See* United States Army, regimental bands in

Battle of Four Lakes, 94n, 95n

Battle of Spokane Plain, 95n

Beale, Lt. Edward F., 140, 140n, 175

Beale's Crossing: reconnoitered by Lt. Col. Hoffman, 140n; Lt. Col. Hoffman establishes Camp Colorado at, 170; steamboat *Jessup* reaches, 171; soldiers under Lt. Col. Hoffman at, 172

Beecher, Rev. Henry W., 102, 102n

Bernhisel, Dr. John M., 67, 67n

Berry, Lt. Thomas J., 64n, 123–24

Big Blue River, Neb. Terr.: description of camp on, 28

Bishop, Samuel A.: fights Indians on Colorado River, 152–54; associated with Lt. Beale, 152n; crosses Colorado River at Aubrey's Crossing, 162; and his party on the Colorado River, 175

Blackfeet Indians. *See* Indian tribes, Blackfeet

Blair, Samuel S., 131, 131n

Boardman, Rev. Henry A., 141, 141n, 142, 177, 177n

Bootes, 1st Lt. Levi C., 34–35, 35n, 152, 170

Border ruffians, 22–23. *See also* Abolitionism; Slavery

Brant, Joseph, 95n

Broderick, Sen. David C., 162–63, 162–63n, 180–82. *See also* California, politics in

Broderickites, 162–63, 181. *See also* California, politics in

Bryant, 2nd Lt. Montgomery, 171, 171n

Buchanan, Pres. James: appoints officials for Utah, 6; possible intervention of, in Mexico, 21; settles Mormon War, 49; causes bankruptcy of United States, 168

Buffalo chips: use of, 40–41

Buffalo robes, 39, 44, 49; destroyed by soldiers at Spanish Fork, 104

Burch, Rep. John C., 173n

Burns, Robert: lines from, 108, 170, 170n

Burton, Capt. Henry S., 172n

Butterfield Overland Mail Company, 150n, 167–68. *See also* Central Overland Mail Route; Southern Overland Mail Route

Byron, Lord: lines from, 52

222

C

California: gold in, 50 (*see also* Gold mines, San Gabriel); Lt. Fremont helps in conquest of, 63n; deserters leave for gold mines in, 129; "Utah" leaves for, 136–37; climate of, 141, 149; gambling in, 141, 149, 177; attitude toward slavery in, 146; division of, 146, 163–64; Free Soil ticket in, 146; politics in, 146–48, 162–64, 172–73, 180–82; Chinese in, 148, 186; crops in, 148–49; William Walker in, 160–61; pardoning of convicts in, 186–87. *See also* Los Angeles, Cal.

Callaghan, Pvt. Patrick: confined for drunkenness, 83; court-martial of, 83n, 105–6; suspension of sentence of 105n

Camels: use of, 140, 140n, 152

Camp Colorado, 170

Campbell, Capt. Reuben P., 107n, 123, 127

Camp Floyd, Ut. Terr., 93, 110, 127; established by Col. Johnston, 15, 36n; description of, 86–87, 86n, 90; theatre at, 121, 121n; first flag raising at, 124–25; "Utah" leaves, 136

Camp Scott, Wyo. Terr.: description of, 72

Canby, Bvt. Lt. Col. Edward R. S., 68

Carlisle Barracks, Pa., 10

Carrington, Albert, 115n, 117

Carson, Christopher (Kit), 75, 75n

Cavalry, 10, 20, 24, 29, 34; First, 12, 13; Second, 12. *See also* United States Army

Central Overland Mail Route, 152, 175. *See also* Butterfield Overland Mail Company; Pacific Mail Steamship Company; Southern Overland Mail Route

Chapin, Rev. Edwin H., 101, 101n

Cheyenne Indians. *See* Indian tribes, Cheyenne

Chimney Rock: description of, 46–47n, 47; "Utah" climbs, 47

Chinese. *See* California, Chinese in; Los Angeles, Cal., Chinese in

Chiricahua Indians. *See* Indian tribes, Apache, Chiricahua

Chiricahua Valley, 166

Chucuana Indians. *See* Indian tribes, Apache, Chiricahua

Church of Jesus Christ of Latter-day Saints: history of, 3–5. *See also* Mormons

Clark, 1st Lt. Darius D., 172n

Clarke, Bvt. Brig. Gen. Newman S., 143, 143n, 152, 166

Clinton, Pvt. Francis G., 27; possibility of, being "Utah," 194–99, 204

Cobb, Sec. of Treas. Howell, 120, 120n

Cole, Charles P.: possibility of, being "Utah," 190–91

Colorado Indians. *See* Indian tribes, of the Colorado

Colorado River: "Utah" meets dragoons en route for, 140; Indian uprising on, 143–46; description of climate at, 157; troops under Lt. Col. Hoffman at, 160; Samuel Bishop's party crosses, 162; Lt. Col. Hoffman navigates, 171; emigrants attacked by Indians on, 184. *See also* Bishop, Samuel A.; Hoffman, Lt. Col. William H.; Indian tribes, of the Colorado

Colorado, Territory of the, 163–64

Column, Fifth, 12, 20, 28, 30, 32

Column, Sixth; leaves Fort Leavenworth, 13, 24; ordered to start for Utah, 20; military units with, 24, 34, 54; arrives at Camp Floyd, 86. *See also* United States Army, marching rate to Utah of

Columns of the Utah Forces, 12–13. *See also* Utah Campaign

Comonfort, Ignacio. *See* Mexico, civil war in

Conquering Bear. *See* Grattan Massacre

Cooke, Col. Philip St. George, 87, 87n, 97

Corley, 1st Lt. James L., 171n

Cottonwood Springs, 138

Crandebaugh, Judge John, 166n

Crosman, Lt. Col. George Hampton, 125, 125n

Cumming, Gov. Alfred: appointed governor of Utah, 6; addresses Mormons, 14; opposition to, 118–19; possible removal of, 126–27, 166; accused of antislaveryism, 127

Cumming, Rev. John, 80n

Curry, Capt. Douglass, 179

Cuyler, Asst. Surgeon John M., 128, 128n, 129

Fremont, Lt. John C., 59, 59n, 63, 63n, 148

Fremont Peak, 59, 59n, 63

French Bell tent, 76, 76n. *See also* United States Army, equipment in

G

Gadsden Treaty, 20n

Garnett, Capt. Richard B., 172n

Gay, 2nd Lt. Ebenezer: court-martial of, 111–13, 111–13n; supposedly killed, 114

Genther, Pvt. Joseph: possibility of, being "Utah," 190

Gentiles: anti-Mormon feelings of, 4; protection of, by federal government, 6; opposed to Judge Drummond, 91; elected to territorial legislature, 117; newspaper of, 119, 119n; predominantly Democrats, 130–31

Gila mines. *See* Gold mines, Gila

Gila River: gold discovered on, 142; description of, 157–59

Gold mines: in Australia, 50; in California, 50; Pikes Peak, 50–51, 50n, 142, 142n, 187; in Canada, 142, 142n; Fraser River, 142, 142n; Gila River, 142–43, 152, 155, 156–57; San Gabriel River, 143, 174–75, 174n, 187, 202; drywashing at, 152, 152n

Goldsmith, Oliver: lines from, 55

Gough, John B., 140, 140n

Gould, Pvt. John S., 27, 27n; possibility of, being "Utah," 190–91

Grass and pasturage, 40, 54, 56, 62, 64, 68, 76, 79, 81

Grattan Massacre, 48n

Green, Rep. and Sen. James S., 168, 168n

Green River, Ut. Terr.: described, 76

Greytown: bombardment of, 128, 128n, 161

Guaymas, Mex. *See* Mexico, civil war in

Gwin, Dr. and Sen. William M., 162–63, 162n, 182. *See also* California, politics in

Gwinnites, 162. *See also* California, politics in

H

Harney, Bvt. Brig. Gen. William S., 12n; ordered to command Utah Forces, 12; orders start of Sixth Column, 20; approves of free whiskey for soldiers, 22; passes Sixth Column, 27; arrives at Fort Kearney, 37, 37n; attacks Indians at Ash Hollow, 42n; leaves command of Utah Forces, 107

Harris, George, 139

Hartnett, Sec. John, 133, 133n

Hawes, 1st Lt. James M., 105, 105n

Henningsen, Charles F.: associated with William Walker, 160, 160n. *See also* Walker, William

Higgins, 1st Lt. Silas P., 172n

Hoffman, Lt. Col. William H., 143n; fights Mojaves on the Colorado River, 140n, 143, 152, 162; Bishop requests soldiers from, 154; possibility of, marching on Mexico, 160–61; makes treaty with Mojaves, 164–66, 175, 182–84; establishes Camp Colorado, 170; described by "Utah," 171; navigates Colorado River, 171

Howe, Capt., 107

Howe, Lt. Col. Marshall S., 87, 97, 111–13, 112n, 125

Humboldt Indians. *See* Indian tribes, Humboldt

I

Independence Rock: "Utah" climbs, 57–60; description of, 60, 60n

Indians: Mormon missionary activity with, 3; Mormons at Mountain Meadows Massacre with, 7; trouble with, in Oregon, 15, 38–39, 94–95, 124; attitudes of soldiers toward, 26, 39–40, 48, 49, 94–95, 99–101, 104; at Fort Kearney, 32; treaties with, 32n, 37n, 164, 183; condition of, 33, 138, 159–60; near Fort Riley, 34; attitudes of, toward United States government, 39; "Utah" buys bufflalo meat from, 76; depredations by, 77, 81–82, 94–95, 98–99, 114–15, 140, 155, 159–60, 165–66, 184, 185–86, 186n; "Utah" fights, 81–82, 136; Utah towns fortified against, 90; attacked by dragoons at Spanish Fork, 15, 99–101, 104

226

Indian tribes: of Oregon, 15, 38–39,
94–95, 94n, 95n, 124; Ute, 15, 127n;
Cheyenne, 32, 36–37, 37n, 138;
Snake, 38–39, 94; Pawnee, 32–33,
36–37, 37n, 39, 49, 138; Sioux,
39–40, 48, 48n, 49, 138; Blackfeet,
49, 94–95; Crow, 49; of Utah, 54,
94, 99–100, 99–100n, 104, 114–15,
114n, 123–24, 127–28, 130, 136;
Spokane, 94; Humboldt, 105n;
Paiute, 138–39, 138n, 140, 143–46,
154, 166; Mojave, 140, 140n,
143–44, 145, 152–55, 156–57,
159–60, 164–66, 167, 171, 175,
182–86, 185n, 186n; of the Colorado, 143, 145, 154–55, 162; Yuma,
145, 154–55, 159–60; Korekins, 149,
149n; Navajo, 154; Apache,
159–60, 186n; Apache, Chiricahua,
166–67, 167n; Pima, 185
Infantry, 29, 98; Seventh, 12, 13, 34,
69, 87; Sixth, 12, 172; with the Fifth
Column, 20; with the Sixth Column,
24, 34, 54, 69; marching difficulties
for, 34–35, 52, 55, 62, 75–76, 78–79;
crosses Platte River, 46; vs. dragoons,
57, 113, 130; at Fort Bridger, 68, 69;
Fifth, 87; Tenth, 87; at Spanish
Fork, 98; Eighth, 105. *See also*
United States Army
Ives, Lt. Joseph C., 157, 157n, 183–84

J

Jacques, John (pseud.?), 116
Johnston, Col. and Bvt. Brig. Gen.
Albert S., 7n; Utah Campaign of,
7–8; at Camp Floyd, 15, 36n; at
Camp Scott, 72; commands Depart-
ment of Utah, 87; comments on
officer's court-martial, 112–13,
112–13n; asked for help against
Indians, 114. *See also* Utah Cam-
paign
Johnston's Army. *See* Utah Campaign
Jones, Rep. Jehu Glancy, 130, 130n
Jordan River, Ut. Terr.: description of,
90
Juarez, Benito. *See* Mexico, civil war in

K

Kane, Thomas L., 13–14
Kansas Territory: abolitionism in,
22–23, 30, 30n; description of,
24–25, 28; whiskey sellers in, 25
Ketchum, Capt. William S., 172n

Kimball, Heber C., 115, 115n, 126,
137n
Korekin Indians. *See* Indian tribes,
Korekin
Kowee Indians. *See* Indian tribes,
Korekin

L

Las Vegas, 138
Latter-day Saints. *See* Mormons
Latham, Gov. Milton S., 173, 181, 181n
Longworth, Nicholas, 149, 149n
Los Angeles, Cal.: description of, 141,
148; gambling in, 141, 177; effect of
gold discoveries in, 142; Chinese in,
148, 186; mail arrival in, 167; First
Protestant Association of, 177
Lovejoy, Rev. and Rep. Owen, 165,
165n

M

Magruder, Bvt. 2nd Lt. John T., 28–29,
28–29n
Mail. *See* Butterfield Overland Mail
Company; Central Overland Mail
Route; Pacific Mail Steamship Com-
pany; Southern Overland Mail
Route
March to Utah, rate of. *See* United
States Army, marching rate to
Utah of
Marcy, Capt. Randolph, 8, 8n, 56
Marshall, 1st Lt. Elisha G., 171n
Massacres. *See* Ash Hollow, Neb.
Terr.; Grattan Massacre; Indians,
depredations by; Mountain
Meadows Massacre
May, Col. Charles A., 20, 20n, 21, 107
Mexico: civil war in, 15, 15–16n, 161,
161n, 162, 173–74, 173n, 174n;
United States intervention in, 15,
20–21, 160–61; politics in, 173–74,
174n, 178–80; recognition of, by
United States, 174n; naval forces of,
178–80
Milhau, Asst. Surgeon John J., 170,
170n
Military punishment. *See* United
States Army, military punishment in
Mines. *See* Gold mines
Miramon, Lt. Col. Miguel.
See Mexico, civil war in

Typography for *To Utah with the Dragoons* by Donald M. Henriksen;
design by Nancy Schleede. The text type is
Intertype Baskerville with handset Baskerville foundry display type.
The text paper and dust jacket are
Howard Offset Felt Finish Ivory, the endsheets are Buff Elephant Hide Paper,
and the cover material is Brown Efalin. This book was printed by
the University of Utah Printing Service and was bound at
Mountain States Bindery.